The Qur'an

A SHORT INTRODUCTION

The Qur'an

A SHORT INTRODUCTION

Farid Esack

ONEWORLD
OXFORD

THE QUR'AN: A SHORT INTRODUCTION

Oneworld Publications
(Sales and Editorial)
185 Banbury Road
Oxford OX2 7AR
England
www.oneworld-publications.com

© Farid Esack 2002

ISBN 1–85168–231–7

Cover design by Design Deluxe
Typeset by LaserScript Limited, Mitcham, UK
Printed and bound in Britain by Bell & Bain Ltd, Glasgow

For

Brother Norman Wray

who introduced me to Rahman
and whose life is a reflection of the
rahmah *of* Al-Rahman.

CONTENTS

ACKNOWLEDGMENTS

To Professors Tamara Sonn, Kambiz GhaneaBassiri, Ebrahim Moosa, and Richard Martin for their careful reading of the manuscript and ongoing support in this project as well as my other academic endeavors. Their feedback helped to improve this work considerably. As for any of its persistent inadequacies I alone bear the burden.

To Muhammad Desai for the meticulous checking of my Qur'anic citations.

To Stefan Fix, Abdul Kader Riyadi and David Schweichler for assistance in locating sources and the bibliographical details of various scholars.

To the Sondernforschungsbereich at the University of Hamburg, the Auburn Theological Seminary in New York, and the College of William and Mary in Williamsburg, Virginia for the wonderful administrative and research support provided while engaged in much of the writing of this book.

To Adli Jacobs, Sa'diyya Fakier, and Patrice Brodeur for their critique of my introductory chapter.

To my publishers Novin and Juliet Doostdar and their fellow hassler-badgerers, Helen Coward, Victoria Warner and Rebecca Clare for their boundless patience and confidence.

INTRODUCTION

M uslims have often expressed their experience of the Qur'an in an array of metaphors. It has, for example, been compared to Damascus brocade: "The patterned beauty of its true design bears an underside which the unwary may mistake, seeing what is there but not its real fullness. Or the Book is like a veiled bride whose hidden face is only known in the intimacy of truth's consummation. It is like the pearl for which the diver must plunge to break the shell which both ensures and conceals treasure" (Cragg, 1988, 14). The late Fazlur Rahman (d. 1988) has also used the analogy of a country, using the categories of "citizens", "foreigners" and "invaders", to describe approaches of scholars towards the Qur'an (1984, 81). I want to latch on to the theme of beauty to provide an overview of approaches to the Qur'an and Qur'anic scholarship. Without in any way wanting to pre-empt the discussion on the worldly nature of the Qur'an, in reflecting on the diverse scholarly approaches to the Qur'an, I draw an analogy with the personality and body of a beloved and the ways in which she is approached. The body that comes to mind immediately is a female one and this itself is remarkable for what it reveals as much as what it conceals. The female body is usually presented and viewed as passive, and more often objectified as "something" to be approached even when it is alive, and "ornamentalized" as a substitute for enabling it to exercise real power in a patriarchal world. Yet this body or person also does something to the one that approaches it. The fact that it is approached essentially by men also reflects the world of Qur'anic scholarship, one wherein males are, by and large, the only significant players. When the female body is approached by other women then it is a matter to be passed over in silence. Like the world of religion in general, in which women play such a key part and yet, when it comes to authority and public representation, they are on the periphery, Qur'anic scholarship is really the domain of men; the contribution of women, when it does occur, is usually ignored. I understand and acknowledge that my analogy fits into many patriarchal stereotypes. Questions such as: "Why does the Qur'an not lend itself to being made analogous with a male body?" "What if a gender sensitive scholar insists on doing this, and how would my analogy then pan out?" "What about multiple partners in a post-modernist age where one finds Buddhist Catholics or Christian Pagans?" etc., are interesting ones which shall be left unexplored. Like all analogies, mine can also be taken too far and can be misleading in more than one respect.

THE UNCRITICAL LOVER

The first level of interaction[1] with the Qur'an can be compared to that between an uncritical lover and his beloved. The presence and beauty of the beloved can transport the lover to another plane of being that enables him to experience sublime ecstasy, to forget his woes, or to respond to them. It can console his aching heart and can represent stability and certainty in a rather stormy world: she is everything. The lover is often astounded at a question that others may ask: "What do you see in her?" "What do you mean? I see everything in her; she is the answer to all my needs. Is she not "a clarification of all things" (16.89), "a cure for all [the aches] that may be in the hearts (10.57)? To be with her is to be in the presence of the Divine." For most lovers it is perfectly adequate to enjoy the relationship without asking any questions about it. When coming from the outside, questions about the nature of the beloved's body, whether she really comes from a distinguished lineage – begotten beyond the world of flesh and blood and born in the "Mother of Cities" (42.7) – as common wisdom has it, or whether her jewelery is genuine, will in all likelihood be viewed as churlishness or jealousy. For the unsophisticated yet ardent lover such questions are at best seen as a distraction from getting on with a relationship that is to be enjoyed rather than interrogated or agonized over. At worst, they are viewed as a reflection of willful perversity and intransigence. This lover reflects the position of the ordinary Muslim towards the Qur'an, a relationship discussed in greater detail in the first chapter.

1 In general, my description of these positions should be regarded as descriptive rather than evaluative. I am thus not suggesting that the first level is the "highest" or "lowest" level.

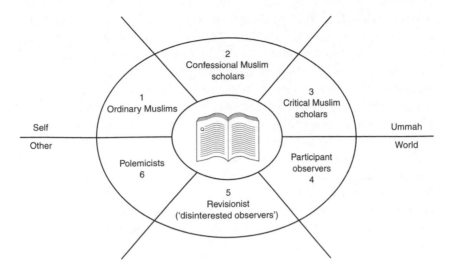

Approaching the Qur'an

THE SCHOLARLY LOVER

The second level of interaction is that of a lover who wants to explain to the world why his beloved is the most sublime, a true gift from God that cries out for universal acclaim and acceptance. He goes into considerable detail about the virtues of his beloved, her unblemished origins and her delectable nature. This pious yet scholarly lover literally weeps at the inability of others to recognize the utter beyondness of his beloved's beauty, the coherence of her form and the awe-inspiring nature of her wisdom. "She is unique in her perfection, surely it is sheer blindness, jealousy and (or) ignorance that prevents others from recognizing this!" This is the path of confessional Muslim scholarship based on prior faith that the Qur'an is the absolute word of God. Some of the major contemporary works[2] that have emerged from these scholars include the exegeses of Abu'l 'Ala Mawdudi (d. 1977),[3] Amin

2 Any literature scan or bibliographical selection on a subject as vast as the Qur'an is invariably arbitrary. In general, I have confined my references in this section to sources that I have frequently consulted. My sample range is also confined to English and Arabic with a few others in Urdu and German.

3 Mawdudi, originally from India, is one of the most influential activist-scholars of the twentieth century whose work inspired two generations of Islamic activists. His six volume exegetical work is in Urdu, entitled *"Tafhimul Qur'an"* (Understanding the Qur'an) (Lahore, 1949–1972).

Ahsan Islahi (d. 1997),[4] Husayn Tabataba'i (d. 1981),[5] and Muhammad Asad (1937–),[6] 'Aishah 'Abd al-Rahman (Bint al-Shati),[7] and the work on Qur'anic studies by Muhammad Husayn al-Dhahabi,[8] Muhammad 'Abd al-'Azim al-Zarqani,[9] (both contemporary Egyptian scholars), and Abu'l Qasim al-Khu'i (d. 1992).[10] Others have written about specific aspects of the beloved's beauty, the finery of her speech or the depth of her wisdom. In addition to the world of books, the other relatively new domain of some of the lovers in this category is the internet, where a large number of Muslim researchers, often autodidacts, engage in vigorous combat with all those who challenge the divine nature of the Qur'an.[11] (In depicting the positions of the scholars in this category, I have, in the main, utilized the works of earlier Cairene scholars such as Badr al-Din Zarkashi (d. 794/1391) and Jalal al-Din al-Suyuti (d. 911/1505), and among the contemporary ones, Zarqani and Al-Khu'i.

4 Islahi was an Indian scholar who wrote *Tadabbur-i-Qur'an* (Reflections on the Qur'an) an exegetical work in Urdu based on the ideas of Hamid al-Din Farahi (d. 1930) which strongly emphasizes the Qur'an's structural cohesion and harmony. Various parts of *Tadabbur-i Qur'an* were published in Lahore by three publishers over the period 1967–80. It is currently being reprinted in nine volumes (Lahore).

5 Muhammad Husayn Tabataba'i, one of the great contemporary Shi'i theologians, is the author of a twenty-volume work, *Al-Mizan fi Tafsir al-Qur'an* (Beirut, 1995) which is a comprehensive philosophical, mystical, linguistic, and theological exposition of the Qur'an.

6 Muhammad Asad, a Polish scholar translated the Qur'an in 1980 (Gibraltar: Dar al-Andalus). Entitled, *The Message of the Qur'an*, and dedicated to "people who think", his translation, which has extensive comments, is widely used by modernist and progressive English-speaking Muslims.

7 Among the few women Qur'an scholars is the Egyptian 'Aishah 'Abd al-Rahman who has distinguished herself by her literary and exegetical studies of the Qur'an, of which the most important are *Al-Tafsir al-Bayan li'l-Qur'an al-Karim*, 2 vols. (Cairo: Dar al-Ma'arif, 1962–69), *Al-Qur'an wa'l-Tafsir al-'Asri* (Cairo: Dar al-Ma'arif, 1970). Another noteworthy Egyptian woman Qur'an scholar is Zaynab al-Ghazali al-Hubayli who authored *Nazarat fi Kitab Allah* (Glimpses into the Book of Allah) (Cairo: Dar al-Shuruq, 1994).

8 Al-Dhahabi, a professor in Qur'anic Sciences at the University of Al-Azhar in Cairo, has produced an exhaustive four volume account of the development of exegesis (*Tafsir*) and commentators from the earliest period until today. His *Tafsir wa'l-Mufassirun* (Exegesis and Exegetes) was first completed in 1976 and has since seen four subsequent editions (Cairo: Maktabah al-Wahbah, 1989).

9 Muhammad 'Abd al-'Azim al-Zarqani's four volume *Manahil al-'Irfan fi al-'Ulum al-Qur'an* (Springs of Knowledge in the Sciences of the Qur'an) (Cairo: Maktabah al-Wahbah, 1996) follows the traditional format of most works on Qur'anic Sciences.

10 Abu'l Qasim al-Khu'i's *Al-Bayan fi Tafsir al-Qur'an* (The Elucidation of the Exegesis of the Qur'an) is a brilliant contribution to the area of Sunni-Shi'i polemics around the Qur'an and its beginnings as a canon. I have made use of the translation of part of this work into English by Abdulaziz Sachedina appearing as *The Prolegomena to the Qur'an* (Oxford, 1998).

11 Rudiger Lohker has published an extensive overview of a number of English and German articles on the Qur'an. This appears on the internet at http://www.sub.uni-goettingen.de/ebene1/orient/koran1.htm

THE CRITICAL LOVER

The third kind of lover may also be enamored with his beloved but will view questions about her nature and origins, her language, or if her hair has been dyed or nails varnished, etc., as reflecting a deeper love and more profound commitment, a love and commitment that will not only withstand all these questions and the uncomfortable answers that rigorous enquiry may yield, but that will actually be deepened by them. Alternatively, this relationship may be the product of an arranged marriage where he may simply never have known any other beloved besides this one and his scholarly interest moves him to ask these questions. As for the Qur'an being the word of God, his response would probably be "Yes, but it depends on what one means by 'the word of God'. She may be divine, but the only way in which I can relate to her is as a human being. She has become flesh and I cannot interrogate her divine origins; I can therefore only approach her as if she is a worldly creature." ("The study of the text", says Nasr Hamid Abu Zayd, "must proceed from reality and culture as empirical givens. From these givens we arrive at a scientific understanding of the phenomenon of the text" (1993, 27). This is the path of critical Muslim scholarship, a category that may be in conversation with the preceding two categories – as well as the subsequent two categories – but does not usually sit too well with them. What cannot be disputed is the devotion of this lover to his beloved. The anger with the objectification of the beloved by the first two categories, in fact, stems from an outrage that the "real" worth of the beloved is unrecognized. "My world is in mess," says this lover. "I cannot possibly hold on to you just for your ornamental or aesthetic value; I know that you are capable of much more than this!" As Abu Zayd asks, "How much is not concealed by confining the Qur'an to prayers and laws? ... We transform the Qur'an into a text which evokes erotic desire or intimidates. With root and branch do I want to remove the Qur'an from this prison so that it can once again be productive for the essence of culture and the arts in our society" (1994, 27). Some of the major works by these scholars include the exegetical work of Fazlur Rahman (d. 1988),[12] the linguistic-philosophical studies by Mohammed Arkoun,[13] the literary enquiry into the Qur'an and

---

12 Rahman was a Pakistani scholar and remains the doyen of contemporary modernist Muslim scholarship. His views on the Qur'an are represented in numerous articles and books. His *Major Themes of the Qur'an* (Minneapolis, 1989) is a significant contribution to thematic Qur'anic exegesis.

13 Arkoun is a Sorbonne educated Algerian scholar who has done pioneering work on the Qur'an, revelation and semiotics. He does, however, distance himself from the more reformist orientation of other scholars that I have placed in this category (Arkoun, 1987b, 2).

critique of religious discourse by Abu Zayd,[14] and the related literary studies done by Fuat Sezgin.[15]

THE FRIEND OF THE LOVER

The line between the last of the categories above, the critical lover, and the first below, the participant observer, is often a thin one. In the same way that one is sometimes moved to wonder about couples: "Are they still in love or are they just sticking to each other for old time's sake?", one can also ask about one's intimate friends who display an unusual amount of affection to one's own beloved: "What's up here?" In other words, is the critical lover really still a lover, and is the ardent friend of both the lover and the beloved not perhaps also a lover? Similarly, questions have been raised about the extent to which the participant observer has internalized Muslim sensitivities and written about the Qur'an in a manner that sometimes makes one wonder if they are not also actually in love with the Muslim's beloved. Thus what these two categories have in common is that those at the other ends of the continuum really accuse them of being closet non-Muslims or closet Muslims.

The participant observer, the first in the category of those who do not claim to be lovers or who deny it, feels an enormous sense of responsibility to the sensitivities of the lover, who is often also a close friend of lover and beloved. "Beauty is in the eye of the beholder," he reasons, "and if this is what the Qur'an means for Muslims and if they have received it as the word of God, then so be it. We don't know if Gabriel really communicated to Muhammad and we will never know. What we do know is that the Qur'an has been and continues to be received by the Muslims as such. Can we keep open the question of "whatever else it may be" and study it as received scripture which is also an historical phenomenon?" Wilfred Cantwell Smith (1980) who places more emphasis on the spiritual dimensions of this reception – in contrast to Montgomery Watt who emphasizes its sociological dimensions – is arguably the most prominent scholar who adopts this position.[16] "Given that it was first transmitted in

14 Abu Zayd was condemned as an apostate by conservative Muslims scholars in his native Cairo for his views on the Qur'an expressed in *Mafhum al-Nass – Dirasa fi 'Ulum al-Qur'an* (Interpreting the Text – Studies in Qur'anic Sciences) (Cairo, 1993) and is currently (2002) based in the Netherlands.
15 Cf. Fuat Sezgin, *Geschichte des Arabischen Schriftums*, 6 vols. (Leiden, 1967). Sezgin's work is a compilation of mostly manuscripts from the first four centuries of Islam which is used to validate Hadith (the traditions of Muhammad) transmission.
16 Smith's views on the Qur'an as scripture are covered in a series of articles entitled "The True Meaning of Scripture: An Empirical Historian's non-Reductionist Interpretation of the Qur'an" in *The International Journal of Middle Eastern Studies*, 1980.

an oral form," asks William Graham further, "can we focus on the Qur'an as an oral scripture rather than written text?"[17] Others in this category may have their own objects of adoration and love but acknowledge the beauty of the Muslim's beloved. They can possibly also love her, although in a different sense, but would be hesitant to declare this love for fear of being misunderstood. ("I have always taken the view that Muhammad genuinely believed that the messages he received – which constitute the Qur'an – came from God. I hesitated for a time to speak of Muhammad as a Prophet because this would have been misunderstood by Muslims ..."; Watt, 1994, 3.)[18] Another scholar in the genre whose work I have found inspiring is Kenneth Cragg, the Oxford based Anglican clergyman whom Rahman has described as "a man who may not be a full citizen of the world of the Qur'an, but is certainly no foreigner either – let alone an invader!" (1984, 81).[19] This irenic approach to the study of the Qur'an seemingly seeks to compensate for past "scholarly injuries" inflicted upon Muslims and is often aimed at a "greater appreciation of Islamic religiousness and the fostering of a new attitude towards it" (Adams, 1976, 40). This category of scholar accepts the broad outlines of Muslim historiography and of claims about the development of the Qur'an. While the first two categories – the "ordinary Muslim" and confessional scholar, the latter being increasingly aware of their presence – find them annoying or even reprehensible, they are often in vigorous and mutually enriching conversation with the third category, the critical Muslim scholar.

---

17 Graham's views on the Qur'an must seen within the context of his notion of "humane scholarship" which recognizes that to reduce another person's faith to purely psychic, social, or genetic determinants, alone, to consider it eccentric, is to pass judgment on matters to which the historian at least has no ability to penetrate with any kind of final assurance' (1983, 25). His views are dealt with in, among others, a book titled "*Divine Word and Prophetic Word in Early Islam*" (The Hague and Paris, 1977) and several articles, the most relevant here being "The Earliest Meaning of 'Qur'an'" published in *Die Welt des Islams*, 23–24:361–377 (1984). See also Wilfred Cantwell Smith's critique of analytical mode[s] of thinking "[... that are] inherently oriented away from human wholeness, creativity, and synthesizing vision" (1980, 497).

18 Cf. Montgomery Watt, "Early Discussions About the Qur'an." *Muslim World*, XL 50:27 (1950); *Companion to the Qur'an* (Oxford, 1994); and *Islamic Revelation in the Modern World* (Edinburgh, 1969).

19 Kenneth Cragg has written a large number of books on the Qur'an and responses to it as well as numerous articles. His most important works are *The Event of the Qur'an – Islam and its Scripture* (Oxford, 1994); *Readings in the Qur'an* (London, 1988); and *The Pen and Faith – Eight Modern Muslim Writers and the Qur'an* (London, 1985). For an overview of contemporary Christian perspectives of the Qur'an as sacred scripture, see Ford, 1993.

THE VOYEUR

The second observer in this category feels no such responsibility and claims that he is merely pursuing the cold facts surrounding the body of the beloved, regardless of what she may mean to her lover or anyone else. He claims, in fact, to be a "disinterested" observer (Rippin, 2001, 154). Willing to challenge all the parameters of the received "wisdom", he may even suggest that the idea of a homogenous community called "Muslims" which emerged over a period of 23 years in Arabia is a dubious one – to put it mildly. The beloved, according to him, has no unblemished Arab pedigree, less still is she "begotten-not-created". Instead, she is either "the illegitimate off-spring of Jewish parents" ("The core of the Prophet's message ... appears as Judaic messianism" [Crone and Cook, 1977, 4]); or of Jewish and Christian parents ("The content of the Qur'an ... consists almost exclusively of elements adapted from the Judeo-Christian tradition" [Wansbrough, 1977, 74]). These scholars view the whole body of Muslim literature on Islamic history as part of its Salvation History which "is not an historical account of saving events open to the study of the historian; salvation history did not happen; it is a literary form which has its own historical context ... and must be approached by means appropriate to such; literary analysis" (Rippin, 2001, 155). Based on this kind of analysis, the work of John Wansbrough (1977),[20] Andrew Rippin (who has done a good bit to make Wansbrough's terse, technical, and even obtuse writing accessible) and the more recent work by a scholar writing under the name of "Christoph Luxenborg" (2000),[21] seek to prove that the early period of Islam shows "a great deal of flexibility in Muslim attitudes towards the text and a slow evolution towards uniformity ... which did not reach its climax until the fourth Islamic century" (ER, see "Qur'an"). While some of these scholars, often referred to as "revisionists", have insisted on a literary approach to the Qur'an, their views are closely connected to the idea of Muslim history as essentially a product of a Judeo-Christian milieu, argued by Patricia Crone (1977) and Michael Cook (Crone and Cook, 1977 and Cook,

20 Wansbrough's *Quranic Studies: Sources and Methods of Scriptural Interpretation* is still the leading work on the Qur'an for all subsequent revisionist scholars, although nearly all of them arrive at different and even conflicting conclusions, which is probably due to their emphasis on method. Wansbrough argues that all of Islamic scripture was generated in the midst of sectarian controversy over a period of two centuries and then fictitiously projected back to an Arabian point of origin.

21 While I am unfamiliar with Syraic or Aramaic and can therefore not comment authoritatively on Luxenborg's work, from a superficial perusal, it does seem set to become at least as significant as Wansbrough's *Qur'anic Studies* and Crone and Cook's *Hagarism* for revisionist scholarship.

1981), two other scholars whose contribution to revisionist thinking is immeasurable.[22] The basic premise of this group of scholars is the indispensability of a source critical approach to both the Qur'an and Muslim accounts of its beginning, the need to compare these accounts with others external to Muslim sources, and utilizing contemporary material evidence including those deriving from epigraphy, archaeology, and numismatics.

Needless to say, this approach, a kind of voyeurism, and its putative disinterestedness, has not been welcomed by those who openly acknowledge a relationship between themselves and the lover and/or the beloved. Like the voyeur who may delude himself into thinking that he is a mere observer without any baggage, these "objective" scholars claim to have no confessional or ulterior motive in approaching the Qur'an other than that of examining the body in the interest of scholarship. Alas, there is no innocent scholarship.

THE POLEMICIST

Attached to this last category is a polemicist, who really has little in common with the methodology of his sustainers, the revisionists, although the uncritical lover – and occasionally the critical lover as well (cf. Rahman, 1984, 88) – perhaps unfairly – lumps them all together.[23] This man is, in fact, besotted with another woman, either the Bible or Secularism. Having seen his own beloved exposed as purely human – although with a divine spirit in the case of the former, i.e., the Bible as beloved – and terrified of the prospect that his Muslim enemy's beloved may be attracting a growing number of devotees, he is desperate to argue that "Your beloved is as human as mine." Having tried in vain for

---

22 Crone and Cook combine early Muslim accounts with that of Greek and Syriac sources in their enquiry into the early history of Islam. They conclude that the whole of Islamic history up to period of 'Abd al-Malik ibn Marwan (d. 86/705) is fabrication and, in reality, the product of identity struggles among peoples united only by their common status as conquered communities. In a footnote to *Hagarism*, Crone and Cook, acknowledge their mutual admiration and scholarly collaboration with Wansbrough (1977, viii). This is a significant point given the argument by those who favour a literary approach to the Qur'an. Fazlur Rahman attacks them saying, "having unanchored the Qur'an from its historical moorings in the Prophet's life, one basic task of Wansbrough and Rippin is to anchor it historically elsewhere" (2001, 200). I, however, think that it is a mistaken view to suggest that Wansbrough and company hold that the only useful approach to the Qur'an is that of literary criticism.

23 Muslims have often viewed much of non-Muslim Qur'anic scholarship as part of an onslaught against Islam, and the origins of critical Qur'an scholarship dating back to Peter the Venerable (d. 1156) certainly bear this out. Contemporary Qur'an criticism, regardless of whose anti-Islam polemics it may serve, is, however, essentially a combination of the post-Enlightenment critique of all religious thinking and of the colonialist project rather than an "anti-Islam" or "anti-Qur'an" undertaking. In the words of David Tracy, "We are in the midst of a deconstructive drive designed to expose the radical instability of all text and the inevitable intertextuality of all seemingly autonomous text" (1987, 12).

centuries to convince the Muslim of the beauty of his own beloved (the Bible), he now resorts to telling the Muslim how ugly his (i.e., the Muslim's) beloved is. Another species in this category is one that is alarmed by the supposed rise and political influence of the lover and assumes that his doings are the result of the whisperings of the beloved. The blame-it-on-the-woman character asks rhetorically "Doesn't the Qur'an tell Muslims to kill?" "And, so", he reasons, "the beloved should be unmasked and cut down to size so that she would no longer be able to exercise such a pernicious hold over her lover." The methodologies of the revisionists are never seriously discussed by this polemicist – of this he is incapable – for if he were to seriously consider the methodology of the revisionists then his own fundamentalist mindset would probably collapse. All that matters to the polemicist are the conclusions of the revisionists – however disparate and tentative (Wansbrough refers to his own work as "conjectural", "provisional", and "tentative and emphatically provisional") – of the utterly human and fallible nature of these Muslims' beloved. Pamphlets, tracts and the internet are where these polemicists hang out.

WHERE DOES THIS WORK FIT IN?

The reader may be justified in asking where this work fits in. While it is essentially a descriptive work, I will not make any unsustainable claims of "disinterestedness". I am a critical and progressive Muslim, a student of the Qur'an with a respect for all serious scholarly endeavor. I have thus calmly described and critiqued various positions without impugning the motives of any particular group of scholars. The simplicity of the work aside, this is arguably the first attempt to present various views and trends in Qur'anic scholarship in a critical manner without forcing a particular position. I acknowledge that some may argue that a particular view does not deserve further airing; this is left for the reader to judge. I believe that it is essential for any person trying to understand the Qur'an and approaches to it, to also be introduced to the array of opinions surrounding it in a non-polemical manner. While this work thus follows the broad contours of critical Muslim scholarship in most of its assumptions about early prophetic history,[24] other opinions are presented for consideration.

24 I use the term "prophetic" throughout this work entirely in the Muslim sense of a person designated by God to convey God's messages to the world. Furthermore, unless the context clearly states otherwise, I use it as referring to Muhammad, whom Muslims recognize as the last of a large number of Prophets.

In the years of my own journeying into the world of the Qur'an I have been struck by the adversarial nature of the relationship between Muslims and others. With some noteworthy exceptions, it often appears as if we are simply incapable of hearing what critical outsiders have to say about our text. This ability to listen – even if only as a prelude to subsequent rejection – is a condition for surviving in the world of scholarship today. This is arguably the first introductory book on the Qur'an by a Muslim that reflects that attempt to listen.

Not only am I a critical Muslim student but also a South African one. One of the notions that the world of confessional scholarship shares with modernist scientist thinking is the putative ahistoricity of the scholar. Referring to commentators of the Qur'an, Jane McAuliffe notes that "the reader searches in vain for such reference [to their current political, social, and economic environment] … It is frequently difficult to determine from internal evidence alone whether a commentary was written in Anatolia or Andalusia, whether its commentator had ever seen a Mongol or a Crusader or had ever conversed with a Christian or conducted business with one" (1991, 35). Both confessional Muslim scholars as well as those who claim scholarly "disinteredness" are loath to acknowledge their own histories for fear of suggesting that the truths that they write about may be relative to those histories. Like other progressive scholars such as liberation and feminist theologians, I insist that scholars do have inescapable histories of class, gender, race, and period. I freely acknowledge mine, particularly in the first chapter where I draw upon my South African Muslim heritage in explaining what the Qur'an means to Muslims.

CLARIFYING TERMS

Doctrine in Islam, like in any other religion, has developed over a long period and one of the words that one should use with caution in any critical scholarly work to describe the opinion of the majority of Muslim scholars on a particular subject is "orthodoxy". This description implies that there is a fixed belief determined by a universally recognized body of scholars, those who disagree with it or its finer points are "heretics" and that this is the opinion held by the majority or all of the Muslims. This word itself is alien to Islamic scholarly tradition and words used for a similar effect are "*qawl al-salaf al-salih*" (the opinion of the righteous predecessors) or "*jamhur*" (the people). The fact that Islam does not have an *ecclesiae* to irrevocably determine that opinion and measure the degree of righteousness of its proponents, or that the majority of people in the world today who would describe themselves as "Muslims" are probably adherents of what has variously been described as "low", "folk", "rural", "non-scriptural", or esoteric (*batini*) Islam, suggests that even fairly innocuous terms such as "majoritarian" or "mainstream" would not be entirely accurate. Yet there are notions about the Qur'an that are stabilized and accepted by the vast majority of scholars in the last millennium or longer. For lack of an alternative, I have described this as "the majority opinion". Other terms such as traditional, progressive, *Shi'ah*, etc., are all explained in a footnote when they are used for the first time.

USING THE QUR'AN

Wherever possible, I have tried to use Qur'anic texts when illustrating a point or asserting a statement. Thus, the reader, besides being drawn into a conversation about the Qur'an, also constantly hears the Qur'an, albeit in a context that I have chosen. I have used the translation of Muhammad Asad, dispensing with the more dated English rendition of the second form of the personal pronoun (thee, thou, thine, etc.). The system of referencing followed is chapter, followed by the verse or verses separated from it by a period, e.g., 2.28.

1 THE QUR'AN IN THE LIVES OF MUSLIMS

It is always wrapped in a specially stitched bag; not only "it", but also anything leading to "it". Thus during my childhood my basic Arabic reader was always treated with enormous reverence. If our Arabic primers, perchance, fell to the ground they had to be hastily picked up, kissed, placed against our foreheads to renew our commitment to their sanctity, as if to say "please forgive me" in the same way that one would treat a dearly beloved baby. The speed with which we retrieved it was also necessitated by the need to avert any possible immediate divine retribution that could befall the careless culprit. Back home from madrasah – or Qur'an schools – where we had to go daily for about two hours after school, mostly to learn how to recite the Qur'an, the primer was placed underneath the Qur'an on the highest shelf in the house that was built specifically for that purpose. As kids we looked forward to the day when any fellow learner completed his or her primer to commence with the Qur'an itself; the learners' family had to provide small sweet packages to all his or her fellow learners. Completing the recitation of the Qur'an was an even grander celebratory occasion, possibly a whole day affair. Until the emergence of kindergartens in the seventies, the madrasah was the first place of learning for South African Muslims. Indeed, for numerous other Muslims in many poorer parts of the world, it remains the only place of learning. We were connecting with a universal and centuries-old Muslim tradition of learning to read the Qur'an. In England I came across an Egyptian Copt who memorized half of the Qur'an because this was the only kind of learning that took place in his village and his parents felt that some learning was better than none.

Our experience of the Qur'an commences with the alphabet, moving on to stringing words together and from there to the Opening Chapter (*Al-Fatihah*) and then skipping the entire book to get to the short chapters right at the end of the Qur'an's last thirtieth part, working our way "backwards". As we learn these short chapters we are "not simply learning something by rote, but rather interiorizing the inner rhythms, sound patterns, and textual dynamics – taking it to the heart in the deepest manner. Gradually [we move] on to other sections of the Qur'an. Yet the pattern set by this early, oral encounter with the text is maintained throughout life" (Sells, 1999, xx).

My late mother, as any good Muslim housewife – we do not have an abundance of househusbands – commenced cooking by reciting a specific verse from the Qur'an in order to ensure that more people were able to enjoy the meal. On spotting an approaching dog, we hastily recite any memorized verse to deflect its possible ill-intentions. The Malayu-Afrikaans phrase *"toe batcha ek alles wat ek ken"* ("and then I recited everything that I knew") is often an intrinsic part of a local Muslim's recounting of a threatening or dangerous incident. The die-hard Marxists of the Baluchistan Communist Party in Pakistan, I found some years ago, commenced their annual conference with a recitation from it. Back in Cape Town, the local rugby club will organize a cover-to-cover recitation of the Qur'an to celebrate its fiftieth jubilee. In California, the international Muslim homosexual organization takes its name, *Al-Fatihah*, from the name of its first chapter ("The Opening"). It is memorized in small parts by virtually all Muslims, recited in the daily prayers, or rehearsed at funerals and memorial rituals, chanted at the side of the newly born, the sick or the dying. Anyone who memorizes it entirely can get complete remission from his or her prison sentence in Dubai and a memorization of each thirtieth part is rewarded by an equivalent amount off one's sentence. An immediate end can be brought to many an argument by resorting to it: "But God says ...!" Virtually every Muslim home is adorned with some verse from it in various forms of calligraphy as a means of both beautifying one's home and protecting it; with the inhabitants seldom knowing the meaning of the framed piece of calligraphy. I remember seeing a love couplet in Urdu on the wall of a Cape Town house and, upon enquiring from the inhabitants as to its meaning, was told that "it's a verse from the Qur'an". To this family the script appeared to be Arabic and, it must have therefore been an excerpt from the Qur'an. Just being from the Qur'an is adequate to warrant being framed and hung on the wall ['I just want to have you around me; knowing that you are here with me is good enough']; notwithstanding the lamentation of the critical lover who cries out for its use beyond ornamentation. "In the manner we have dealt with the written text as an object that is supposedly valuable – the attention has gradually detracted from the possibilities of reading it with the intention of understanding it. Thus the text has been transformed into an object that is valuable in itself … an ornament for women, an amulet for children and a display piece hanging on the wall and exhibited alongside silver and gold valuables" (Abu Zayd, 1993a, 337).

Its language, Arabic, is a sacred one for Muslims and a part of our identity. Visiting pilgrims to Mecca from the non-Arab world tell how they often have to resist the temptation to pick up every scrap of paper with some Arabic printed on it from the streets; any torn or worn out pages from our primers would be burnt or buried. Arabic as part of a Muslim's identity – wherever he or she may be – is reflected in the following anecdote narrated by two Connecticut College students observing a group of madrasah learners:

> A couple of boys started joking in a language that I could not quite place. After a few minutes of play, Tim stops and asks the boy what language he speaks. He responded, "I speak Bengali, English and Muslim." Tim and I exchange glances and he says laughingly, "I didn't know 'Muslim' was a language." The boys protested and argue and one says, "Come on, what do you think we have been doing here?!" And then another boy comes up and pushes him and says "Hey! No wait – we're not learning Muslim, we're learning Arabic, remember?" They all smile and agree and then another boy of about five says "It's Arabic; that's the language the Koran is in" (Thompson and Talgar, unpublished).

For many Muslims throughout the world the boy may as well have stuck to his confusing of "Arabic" with "Muslim" – so intertwined have they become. (Not, I daresay, without resentment in many cultures from Iran to Morocco to Indonesia where people resent the Arabization of Islam and the concomitant lack of respect for their own cultural and linguistic heritages.) Mukarram ibn Manzur (d. 1312), in the introduction to his famous lexicon, *Lisan al-'Arab*, says that God made the Arabic language superior to all languages and enhanced it further by revealing the Qur'an through it and making it the language of the people of Paradise. He cites a hadith (tradition) attributed to the Prophet Muhammad:[1] "They [the

---

1 A hadith, which I render as "tradition", refers to a saying or tradition of the Prophet reported by one of his family members or a companion. It comprises of the names of the narrators –

people], love the Arabs for three reasons: I am an Arab, the Qur'an is in Arabic; and the language of Paradise is Arabic" (Ibn Manzur, 1994, 1:7). Written texts conform to or deviate from a language and its rules; in the case of this text, the development of the language is based on it and its rules are rooted primarily in the text.

This is the Qur'an. In the words of Cragg, "liturgically, it is the most rehearsed and recited of all the Scriptures. Islam takes its documentation more explicitly, more emphatically, than any other household worship ... So held in veneration and custody, it is the most decisive of the world's Scriptures in the regulation of law and life" (1988, 15). No, it is not the "Bible of the Muslims". While the Qur'an fulfills many of the functions in the lives of Muslims which the Bible does in the lives of Christians, it really represents to Muslims what Jesus Christ represents for devout Christians or the pre-existent Torah, the eternal law of God, for Jews.[2] Similarly, the history of theological controversy around the nature of the Qur'an in early Islam, until "orthodoxy" finally "settled" on what is "true dogma", is not unlike the early controversies in the Christian world about the nature of Jesus Christ and his relationship to the Father, which was finally settled – not that there was anything "final" about it nor "settled" – by the Council of Nicaea in 325 CE.[3] (In the same manner that small remnants have survived of the dissident opinions on the nature of Christ, now re-awoken under the impact of critical modern and post-modern thinking in Christianity, so have they in Islam about the nature of the Qur'an.[4])

usually referred to as the chain of narrators – and the statement attributed to the Prophet or a recount of an incident where he was present. Hadith are found in a number of collections which vary in the degree of their acceptability to Muslims. Sunni Muslims generally accept six collections, that of Muhammad ibn Isma'il al-Bukhari (d. 256/870) and Abu'l-Husayn Muslim ibn al-Hajjaj (d. 261/875), being the most authoritative. The Shi'is refer to "Akhbar" (reports) instead of Hadith and hold five collections in particular regard, foremost among them being the collections of Muhammad ibn Ya'qub al-Kulini (d. 328/939) and Muhammad ibn 'Ali ibn Babuya al-Qummi (d. 381/991). Hadith as a source of authority and a form of "unrehearsed revelation" is discussed in chapter five.

2 Cragg explains that "the heart of Christian revelation is the 'event' of Jesus as Christ, acknowledged as disclosure, in human form, of the very nature of God. Hence, New Testament Scripture is derivative from the prior and primary revelation of the Living Word 'made flesh and dwelling among us'. The Gospels are thus held to be a reliable means of access to Christ, made adequate, for that role, by the Holy Spirit" (1988, 17). Muslims would argue in a similar vein about the role of Muhammad with respect to accessing the Qur'an. Although there is no direct equivalent for the Holy Spirit referred to by Cragg above, Muhammad's interpretative role is still seen as divinely inspired.

3 For a fascinating and wonderfully readable account of this debate and the political drama accompanying it, see Richard Rubenstein's When Jesus Became God – The Struggle to Define Christianity during the Last Days of Rome (New York, 2000).

4 See, for example, Defenders of Reason in Islam – Mut'tazilism from Medieval School to Modern Symbol by Richard C. Martin et al. (Oxford, 1997). The authors make the connection about the debates in early Islam around matters such as the creation of the Qur'an which were seemingly settled and strands in contemporary modernist and post-modernist approaches to Islam.

The Qur'an is the one central miracle of Islam and this miracle of the Divine Word is actualized again and again, not in visual and material form but verbally in recitation ... Its phrases are repeated in cantillations at the mosque, in teaching and memorization at the mosque school and in the prayers of the believers. The book provides the basis for the study of Muslim theology and law. At the popular level its texts may be regarded as talismans ... and in the sphere of art it has conferred something of its religious power on the Muslim art of calligraphy (Moore, 1993, 56).

THE QUR'AN IS ALIVE

For Muslims the Qur'an is alive and has a quasi-human personality. I have come across friends in India who do not change in their bedrooms in deference to and respect for the fact that "there is a copy of the Qur'an on the top shelf". The Qur'an, Muslims believe, watches over us and will intercede with God for us on the Day of Judgment.[5] Mahmoud Ayoub, the contemporary Lebanese scholar, explains this as follows:

Although the Qur'an has taken on the form of and character of human speech, it remains "in its essence a celestial archetype free from the limitations of human sounds and letters". Because the Qur'an intersects the human plane of existence and the transcendent word of God, it is imbued with this quasi-human personality, imbued with feelings and emotions, ready even to contend on the Day of Resurrection with those who abandoned it in this life and to intercede for those who have lived by its teachings (*Encyclopaedia of Religion*, see "Qur'an", 176).

The power of the Qur'an is reflected in one *ayah* (verse) which says "Had We bestowed this Qur'an from on high upon a mountain, you would indeed see it [the mountain] humbling itself, breaking asunder for awe of God" (59.21). Passages from it are used as amulets to protect from illness or "the evil eye": a few verses containing the prayer that the Qur'an suggest Noah offered when he entered the ship[6] are stuck on the windscreens of vehicles from Chicago to Jakarta to offer protection to the driver and passengers; palatial mansions in many Muslim countries have the verse "This is [an outcome] of my Sustainer's bounty" (27.40) stuck on the gates or walls to ward off any evil intention – be it robbery or envy (or to divert any suggestion that the owner's wealth is ill-begotten). As for its inhabitants, they believe that protection is offered by pasting a

5 The idea of intercession with God on the Day of Judgment against the horrors of that day is one frequently mentioned in the Qur'an, which often portrays God himself as the only intercessor (6.70, 6.51 and 32.4) or states that any other intercession will only occur with His permission (2.255 and 10.3).
6 "In the name of God, be its run and its riding at anchor! Behold, my Sustainer is indeed much-forgiving, a dispenser of Grace!" (11.41).

few verses, known as "the Verses of the Throne" (*Ayat al-Kursi*) behind the front door.[7]

Muslim tradition has it that on the Prophet Muhammad's way back from Ta'if in 619, where he had just suffered a deep personal humiliation and even physical assault, he paused to engage in the optional midnight prayers and a group of Jinns[8] came to listen to him. Deeply moved, they went off as firm believers in Muhammad and the Qur'an: "We have really heard a wonderful recital! (*qur'anan 'ajaban*) It gives guidance to the right and we have believed therein" (72.1–2). In this statement, which the Qur'an attributes to the Jinns, lies perhaps the two major functions that it plays in the lives of Muslims: recital and guidance.

THE QUR'AN AS THE RECITED WORD OF GOD

In addition to the solace that the Qur'an promises to provide to the believers in the Hereafter, Muslims find in its recitation an enormous source of comfort and healing in this world. It is recited at the bedside of the ill and when they depart from this world, to ease the passage of the departed soul into the next and to provide comfort for those left behind; as if to say "whatever, be assured God is here; just listen to His speech!" The Qur'an describes itself as a source of "healing and mercy for people of faith" (17.82). For Muslims, the Qur'an is possessed of enormous power: It – or even a few letters leading to it – can possibly stop an earthquake in its tracks. The story goes that sometime in 1967, Salie Manie, now a senior member of South Africa's Parliament, was in bed, down with the flu, when he was visited by a friend. After a while the house started shaking and various items fell to the ground. Realizing that it was either a major earth tremor or an earthquake, Salie screamed: "*Batcha! Batcha!*" (Recite! Recite!, i.e., recite from the Qur'an), to which his friend responded: "*Wat moet ek batcha*" (What shall I recite?). Salie answered: "*Batcha alles wat jy ken*" (Recite whatever you know!). And the friend let

---

7 "God – there is no deity save Him, the Ever-Living, the Self-Subsistent Fount of All Being. Neither slumber overtakes Him, nor sleep. His is all that is in the heavens and all that is on earth. Who is there that could intercede with Him, unless it be by His leave? He knows all that lies open before people and all that is hidden from them, whereas they cannot attain to aught of His knowledge, save that which he wills [them to attain]. His eternal power overspreads the heavens and the earth, and their upholding wearies Him not. And he alone is truly exalted, tremendous" (2.255).

8 The Jinn are mentioned a number of times in the Qur'an and would seem to have little or nothing to do with the genie familiar in folklore. Muhammad Asad suggests that they are concealed "spiritual forces beyond perceptions because they have no corporeal existence (Asad, 1980, 995)." Jinns are "not invisible in and by themselves but rather hitherto unseen beings ..." References to the Jinn are sometimes meant to recall certain legends deeply imbedded in the consciousness of the people whom the Qur'an addressed in the first instance, the purpose being ... not the legend itself but the illustration of a moral truth (ibid.).

go: "*alif, ba, ta, tha, jim* ..." (the equivalent of "a, b, c, d, e ..."). What effect the Arabic alphabet had on the course of events is rather unsure; the following day's newspapers did report, however, that we were saved from a full-blown earthquake and experienced only a tremor.

Michael Sells, the author of *Approaching the Qur'an*, writes about an afternoon in Cairo when he found himself in an "unusual situation":

> The streets of the noisy bustling city were strangely quiet, yet the cafes were crowded with people clustered around televisions. For special events – the death of a great figure, an important soccer game, one might expect to find people on cafes following the event on television. What had drawn people from the streets into the cafes today was the appearance of one of Egypt's popular Qur'an reciters. When I returned to my hotel, the lobby was filled with men, some of them Egyptian Christians, watching and listening to the televised recitation with intense interest (1999, ix).

God, a hadith ascribed to the Prophet tells us, read the Chapters *Taha* and *Yasin* a thousand years before He created the universe and when the angels heard the Qur'an being recited, they said: "Blessed is the community to which it will be sent down, blessed are the minds which will bear it, and blessed are the tongues that will utter it." For many a believer there cannot conceivably be a greater activity than that which God Himself engages in. "Read the Qur'an," the Prophet is reported to have said, "for you will be rewarded at the rate of ten good deeds for reading every letter of the Qur'an; Note, I do not say that *alif lam mim* is one word, but rather, *alif* is one letter, *lam* is another and *mim* is still another." Numerous other sayings attributed to the Prophet speaks of the mere recitation of the Qur'an, or parts thereof, as an act of virtue by itself independent of approaching it as a book of moral or legal guidance.

> On the Day of Judgment it will be said to the person devoted to the Qur'an: "Go on reciting the Qur'an and continue ascending levels of paradise and recite in the slow manner you had been reading in your worldly life; your final abode will be where you reach at the time of the last verse of your recitation" (Maliki, 1980, 6:36)

> Never do a people collect in one of the houses of God reciting the Qur'an and reading it to one another, but tranquillity descends upon them and mercy enshrouds them, the Angels surround them and God mentions them in the assembly of Angels (ibid.).

Abu Hamid al-Ghazali (505/1111) gives an account of a "conversation" that Ahmad ibn Hanbal (d. 241/800) a great Muslim jurist and theologian, is reported to have had with God in a dream. Ibn Hanbal asked God how have those who have drawn near to Him achieved this nearness. When God replied, "By my speech [i.e., the Qur'an] O Ahmad," Ibn Hanbal asked [God]: "By understanding the meaning of your speech or without understanding it?" To this God reportedly responded: "By understanding as well as without understanding" (Ghazali, cited in Quasem, 1979, 26). The oral dimension to the Qur'an was obviously very important in a society where poetry and the spoken or recited word were so highly valued. It is also evident that the activity of committing the Qur'an, or sections thereof, to memory and reciting it were important parts of the religious life of the earliest Muslims and regarded as acts of great spiritual merit. The Prophet himself would often recite from the Qur'an and, at other times, ask others to read for him. 'Abd Allah ibn Mas'ud (d. 652), a Companion[9] of the Prophet, reports that the Prophet told him: "Read [from] the Qur'an for me." I [Ibn Mas'ud] said: "Shall I read it for you when it was revealed unto you?" He said: "I love listening to it from someone else". Ibn Mas'ud goes on to say: "I then read from the The Women (4) until I came to the verse 'How then [will the sinners fare on Judgment Day] when we shall bring forward witnesses from within every community and bring you [O Prophet] as witnesses against them?" He then said: 'That's enough for now.' Tears were running from his eyes."

This overwhelming preponderance of the Qur'an as recited speech in contrast with it as written or read speech, as William Graham (1984) and Fazlur Rahman (1966) have shown, is found in the meaning of the word Qur'an itself, in the way the earliest Muslims viewed the text, and in several verses of the Qur'an. In the following chapter I deal with the meaning of the word "Qur'an" and how it initially denoted oral speech and not a fixed and completed scripture.[10] "The 'proper noun' sense of qur'an[11] in the Qur'an is that of a fundamentally oral and certainly an active ongoing reality, rather than that of a 'written and closed' codex such as it later represented by the masahif [written copies]" (Graham,

9 A Companion (sahabi) is a follower of Muhammad who embraced Islam during Muhammad's lifetime and who physically encountered Muhammad. As a group they are referred to as the "Sahabah" and enjoy a pre-eminent position in Islamic tradition. The Shi'is accord a greater pre-eminence to the family of the Prophet rather than a general respect for all Sahabah.

10 Graham reminds us that "'books' as such were until relatively recent times basically texts to be read aloud from or learned by heart and recited [and that] ... this was a fortoiri true of sacred books ... The explosion of the book culture fixed the notion of text inextricably to the printed rather than the spoken word". (1984, 367).

11 The first form without the initial capital letter is intended to underline its rebulous nature and to highlight the fluidity of the meaning at this stage. The revelations can only properly be described as "the Qur'an" – i.e., a proper man describing something – during or after the process of canonization.

1984, 373). In the Qur'an itself, the imperative *"qul"* ("say!"), which introduces more than three hundred passages, "is itself a striking reminder that these texts are intended to be recited aloud" (ibid., 367). The oral nature of the Qur'an, seen in the response of the Jinn mentioned above, is also borne out by a number of *ayat* (verses) in the Qur'an:

> Move not your tongue in haste [repeating the words of revelation] for behold, It is for for Us to gather it [in your heart] and to cause it to be read as it ought to be read (*qur'anah*); Thus when we recite, follow its wording (75.15–18).

> And do not approach the Qur'an in haste (20.114).

> Hence, indeed, We made this Qur'an easy to recall (54.17).

> And recite the Qur'an calmly and distinctly, with your mind attuned to its meaning (73.4).

Meaning, for the vast majority of Muslims today, is still located primarily in the act of recitation or listening to it. A recognition of the beauty and extraordinary power of the recited Qur'an is nearly instinctual to Muslims:[12]

> Generations of Qur'anic commentators have tried to account for the compelling nature of the composition, articulation, or voice of the Qur'an in Arabic. But the fact that there was something special about it for the commentators and their contemporaries was assumed: It was apparent from the love of people for the Qur'anic voice; from the intertwining of the Qur'anic allusions and rhythms in the fabric of art, literature, and music; from the way the Qur'an is recited at great occasions and in the most humble circumstances of daily life; and from the devotion people put into learning to recite it correctly in Arabic. The sound of Qur'anic recitation can move people to tears, from 'Umar, the powerful second Caliph of Islam, to the average farmer, villager, or townsman of today, including those who may not be particularly observant or religious in temperament (Sells, 1999, x).

THE QUR'AN AS CONTESTED SCRIPTURE

When one has a text that wields such phenomenal power and influence over a people it is reasonable to expect that it would become a rather

---

12 While some linguists would draw comparisons with other societies, such as Slavic, Latin, and African, and point to a similar impact where the classics, broadly defined, also have an enormous evocative power over those audiences, most Muslims would say that this response, rather than being rooted in the oral nature of their societies – or its residue – is due to the Qur'an itself.

powerful weapon in the hands of those who have access to it and that various interest groups would compete for the right to own, access, and interpret it. Here I want use one such contemporary situation, the South African one, as the backdrop to elucidating the main diverse approaches that Muslims seeking to understand the Qur'an have adopted. In South Africa, as in most of the world of Islam, this battle has for long essentially been between traditionalism[13] and modernism.[14] Later, Islamists – those seeking to find a contemporary socio-political expression of Islam – built on the foundations of the "direct to the Qur'an" approach of the modernists. Some of these Islamists who often described themselves as "progressive Muslims",[15] and who regarded Islam as opposed to all forms of oppression, took this further to see how the Qur'an could be used as an ideological tool in the struggle against racial and class oppression (cf. Esack, 1997).

Among the Muslims of South Africa, as in most parts of the Sunni Muslim world, contemporary religious thought is largely being shaped by the traditionalist scholars who are schooled on the Indo-Pak Sub-continent, and the Middle East, most notably Saudi Arabia and Egypt. (For the Shi'i Muslims, Qum in Iran and Najaf in Iraq are the primary centres of religious learning. All other Muslim countries also have locally based institutions of higher religious learning that provide their countries with formal religious leadership.[16]) Schooled in the traditional materials as they are purported to have developed from the Prophet Muhammad through the medieval centuries, these scholars are 'ulama ("scholars", sing. 'alim) only in the sense that they are the carriers of this tradition.[17]

13 Traditionalism can be defined as "the will to freeze society according to the memory of a past one, where religion and custom are fused, and society's historicity is obliterated in favour of an imaginary timeless society under attack by a pernicious modernity" (Oliver, 1985, 122).

14 I define modernism as the post-enlightenment willingness to re-think tradition and traditional material in the light of contemporary scientific data and sociological findings; and to fuse these without necessarily specifiying a commitment to do so for any social or political objectives.

15 This term has since the mid-eighties been in vogue amongst a number of Islamists in South Africa and elsewhere (cf. Irfani, 1983). It has subsequently been defined "that understanding of Islam and its sources which comes from and is shaped within a commitment to transform society from an unjust one where people are mere objects of exploitation by governments, socio-economic institutions and unequal relationships." See: www.freespeech.org/pmn/

16 From the word "shi'ah" which literally means "followers", "party", "group" or "partisan" the word appears several times in the Qur'an. (19.69, 28.15, and 37.83) It now refers to those Muslims whose essential religious inspiration – after Muhammad – is his family. They regard his cousin, Ali as his rightful heir. The Twelver Shi'is believe that after Muhammad religious authority devolved upon twelve guided and sinless Imam starting with 'Ali and ending with Muhammad ibn Askari, who disappeared in 872. According to the Shi'is he is in occultation and is the Messiah who will appear before the resurrection. These infallible imams are regarded by the Shi'is as possessing the right to rule and having the final authority in all matters of jurisprudence and exegesis.

17 To the extent that the syllabi in which they are schooled at madrasahs are overwhelmingly fiqh (jurisprudence) oriented, a more correct appellation would be "fuqaha" (jurists).

With varying degrees of intensity the *'ulama* regard the pursuit of understanding the Qur'an to be their function exclusively. Yet, few, if any, among them, however, would claim for themselves any kind of thorough understanding of the Qur'an, nor would they be engaged in a systematic and ongoing study of it. Classes in *Tafsir* (exegesis) are conducted by a few *'ulama* and lectures are frequently held on various Qur'anic themes during the month of Ramadan.[18] In awe of the Qur'an itself and terrified of making errors in interpreting it, these lectures are usually based on a classic orthodox *mufassir* (commentator)'s work such as that of Isma'il ibn Kathir (d. 1373), the Basra scholar of law and teacher of Hadith, or a compilation of orthodox *Tafsir* works such as *Ma'arifah al-Qur'an* by Muhammad Shafi' (d. 1976), a Pakistani theologian and jurist, rather than on the scholar's own reflections or research involving a range of interpretations. Some of the *'ulama* have even suggested that the orthodox classical commentators "were specifically created" for the task of explaining the Qur'an (*The Majlis*, Astray, 7:8, 10). Ignoring these early *mufassirun*, [commentators], they argue, is "the path to *dalal* [confusion] and *batil* [falsehood], leading to ultimate destruction of *iman* [faith]" (ibid.). This system of teaching runs true to the traditionalist scholars' own culture and didactic methods that rotate around exegetical commentaries, super-commentaries, and supra-commentaries. As Rahman points out, in this tradition, the Qur'an *qua* Qur'an had gradually been eroded as a serious subject of studies at institutions of higher religious learning. The Qur'an has consequently acquired a reverential distance which has made it cognitively unapproachable even to graduates from these institutions.[19]

In those parts of the Muslim world, and in some Muslim minority countries where madrasahs function in parallel to a secular education system, madrasah education is generally viewed as an inferior alternative to secular education or as the choice of the underprivileged. Consequentially, sons who display the least visible scholarly potential are sent off at an early age to pursue full time religious learning with the choice of *hifz*

18 Ramadan is the ninth month of the Muslim calendar and the only one mentioned in the Qur'an. It is the month wherein the Qur'an is believed to have been revealed. It is a month of fasting and one wherein religious activity in general is escalated. See chapter seven.
19 Rahman contextualizes and describes madrasah learning in the following manner: "With the decline in intellectual creativity and the onset of ever-deepening conservatism, the curricula of education ... shrank and the intellectual and scientific disciplines were expurgated, yielding the entire space to purely religious disciplines in the narrowest sense of the word. Mechanical learning largely took the place of original thought. With the thirteenth century, the age of commentaries begins and it is not rare to find an author who wrote a highly terse text in a certain field, in order to be memorized by students and, then, in order to explain the enigmatic text, himself authored both a commentary and a super commentary!" (1980, 239–240).

(memorization of the Qur'an) or Islamic studies, and more often than not, the former as a precursor to the latter. From the *pesantren* in Indonesia to the *mektab* in Iran, the style is the same; learners are seated in a semi-circle before a teacher who calls on each student in turn to recite; learners at all levels of competence sit together; and the more accomplished assist the less learned with their readings. The quality of the raw material notwithstanding, many of these institutions have succeeded in producing some of the most outstanding scholars of Muslim traditional learning.

Often, when the student is able to go abroad for studies, he will spend anything from three to twelve years in the Middle East or on the Indo-Pak Sub-continent immersed in memorization or studying the classical sciences of Islamic Studies.[20] Divorced from their environment and ignorant of contemporary issues, they are hardly able to interpret Islam in a manner that would make sense to those who remained behind to pursue "secular learning".[21] While the ones who confined their pursuit to the memorization of the Qur'an do not really have any claim to religious leadership, they are nevertheless embraced as part of the "*'ulama* fraternity" – the scholarly managers of the sacred. In societies that place a high value on learning and intellectual competence while ignoring the power of aurality, it is hard to imagine that three years spent memorizing a book without any understanding of its contents can catapult one into socio-religious leadership.

In South Africa, as in other parts of the world, many Western-educated Muslims who sought religiously based contemporary answers to the issues facing an unjust society felt that the traditionalist *'ulama* failed to be of any relevance to their quest. This inability to interpret the Qur'anic message creatively in "contemporary terms" blended well with the centrality of the Qur'anic oral tradition in Muslim society. This combination resulted in the neglect of the Qur'an as the active Speech of God addressing itself to every age. For most Muslims, the message of the Qur'an is comprehended by listening to the perceived authentic messengers of His Messenger – the *'ulama*. While the symbolic or spiritual value of such interaction may be considerable, it is not difficult to appreciate the frustration of non-*'ulama* Muslims who desire a more

20 This movement of knowledge from the Indo-Pak Subcontinent and the Arab world to the rest of the World of Islam has contributed immensely to the development of more formal, scriptural, law-oriented, and "orthodox" Islam.

21 See Roy Mottahedeh's *Mantle of the Prophet* (Oxford, 2001) for a brilliant introduction into traditional learning and its tensions with the larger socio-political world. Although his work is set in Iran, in many ways is a mirror into the larger world of traditional Islamic scholarship.

intellectual or socially relevant appreciation of the Qur'an. Their contempt for confining the Qur'an to the realm of the sacred and mysterious, something that Abu Zayd referred to as a prison, is summed up in a somewhat mocking question posed in *Inqilaab*, a student magazine: "What would you say if someone got a doctor's prescription and hung it around his neck after wrapping it in a piece of cloth or washed it in water and drank it?" (*Inqilaab*, 1987, 15). (The student, of course, works from all the unchallenged assumptions of allopathic medicine and had little awareness of how traditional medicine works, or if it did at all.) Throughout the Muslim world, the emotional and spiritual ties to Islam of many young professionals and intellectuals cause them to turn elsewhere for answers to sustain their religious commitment and to nurture their spiritual lives. They usually resolve to discover the message of the Qur'an directly. These professionals and intellectuals challenge the centuries-old oral tradition whereby Muslims read and listen to the Qur'an without necessarily attempting to understand its contents. The struggle to "come to grips with the Qur'an" by non-*'ulama* was – and continues to be – waged in the face of immense opposition from the traditional *'ulama*. (Like the student mentioned above, these intellectuals make unchallenged assumptions about the "truth" of modernity.)

In South Africa, the earliest group to grapple with the Qur'an in a socially relevant and intellectually creative manner was the Durban-based Arabic Study Circle (est. 1950). "We were", said Daud Mall, founder of this group, "disillusioned by the relegation of Arabic as a minor subject in *madrasah* syllabi, the absence of dedication to understanding the Qur'an as a message and prescription" (Interview with Mall on 12 January 1990). "As for the clerics, they were bogged down by tradition and were producing an encapsulated form of a Muslim" (ibid.). The group studied the Qur'an within the "framework of the Arabic language and a commitment to an enlightened Islam". (ibid.) They sought to promote the study of Islam, "to make Arabic the *lingua franca* of the Muslims of Southern Africa and to make the Holy Qur'an a living, meaningful and dynamic message in every Muslim home in the Republic of South Africa" (ibid). Their commitment to understanding the Qur'an provoked the ire of the *'ulama* who, fearful of the loss of power entailed once their own position as gatekeepers to the text were forfeited, warned that the lay students of the Qur'an, would "get lost" and argued that "it is not possible for a layman to study the *Quran*

Majeed [Holy Qur'an] without the guidance of a qualified *Ustaaz* [(teacher) and that] ... such study ... paves the path to *jahannam* [hell]" (*The Majlis*, 7:8). The Arabic Study Circle responded that it was precisely because they were already lost that they wanted to gain access to the Qur'an! Instead of "getting lost and confused", as the clerics warned, the participants in the weekly Qur'an classes claim that they found themselves being exposed "to new horizons and fresh vistas". They "were ashamed", says Mall, "that for years they had also regarded the Qur'an as a closed stricture" and now found themselves "fortified" in their "intellectual perceptions and spiritual lives" (Interview with Mall).

Virtually all members of the group were educated businessmen or professionals who were schooled in Western institutions – if not in the West itself. Being emotionally committed to Islam, they experienced what Rahman describes as "the ferment that resulted from the impact of certain important modern Western ideas on the Islamic tradition" (1981, 28). They connected to the world of Islam through its primary source, the Qur'an, and did so in intellectual fellowship with the classical Muslim modernist reformers such as Sayyid Ahmad Khan (d. 1898), Jamal al-Din al-Afghani (d. 1897), and Muhammad 'Abduh (d. 1905). The Arabic Study Circle represented Islamic liberalism and focused on individual thought and action. Their liberalism precluded them from paying any serious attention to social transformation; nor were they inclined towards becoming a popular movement. There is little to suggest that the Qur'an was viewed by the Circle as a vehicle for comprehensive socio-political transformation, nor did their political concerns transcend vague moralizations about social equality. However, their commitment to the understanding of the Qur'an in the light of prevailing socio-religious conditions and the open hostility of the *'ulama*, was trailblazing and their work paved the way for those with the broader objective of utilizing the Qur'an as a text for social transformation and political liberation.

The Muslim Youth Movement (M.Y.M.) (est. 1970) continued and enhanced the Islamic modernism of the Study Circle from where a number of its founding members came. Considerable interaction with Islamic movements such as the *Jamati Islami* (Pakistan), the Muslim Brotherhood (Egypt), and the then Muslim Students Association (U.S.A.) at international gatherings led to the M.Y.M. adopting the program of what is commonly referred to as "the Islamic movement". Their own modernism consequently fused with what is widely described as Islamic fundamentalism (cf. Tayob, 1995). "The M.Y.M.", says a Call of Islam internal unpublished document, "is solely responsible for the flood of Islamic literature during the last ten years and for the access that lay Muslims have to (understanding) the Qur'an." Like their counterparts in the broader Islamic movement throughout the world, they propagated the idea of *halaqat* (study-cum-formation circles) where Muslims meet on a weekly basis to study translations of the Qur'an and engage in what Sugirtharaja calls "communitarian exegesis" (1990, 1.13). These *halaqat* were part of the *tarbiyyah* (formation) programme inherited from the Islamic movement, an important stream of contemporary Islamic revivalism. Their reflections on the Qur'an were complemented by group readings from the works of other luminaries of the contemporary Islamic Movement such as Hassan al-Banna (d. 1949), Sayyid Qutub (d. 1966), both Egyptians, and Abu al-'Ala Mawdudi, the Indo-Pak born scholar.

The seventies was a period of considerable anguish for socially and politically aware South Africans. This period saw the 1976 anti-apartheid uprisings in Soweto and elsewhere accelerating the demise of racial oppression in South Africa. The Muslim community had earlier also suffered the murder of a prominent *'alim*, Abdullah Haron, in detention. The resulting heightened awareness of the injustices of apartheid society led numerous young Muslims to search for new responses to the challenges of living in a divided society. The M.Y.M. spearheaded this search. The tentative and essentially intellectual nature of their engagement against apartheid ensured that their ideological horizons were not shaped by active involvement in concrete socio-political struggles. Rather, the M.Y.M. approach to the Qur'an was informed by the ideological orientation of the Islamic movement. The M.Y.M. had a large number of *halaqat* operating in various parts of the country. Most – if not all – of the Muslims who later employed the Qur'an as the basis of their commitment to the struggle against apartheid belonged to one of these M.Y.M. *halaqat* at some point or other. The individual remained the primary object in this stream of resurgent Islam although the M.Y.M. did represent a significant progression of the narrow-based liberalism of the Arabic Study Circle. Society, the M.Y.M. believed, was going to be transformed by a core group of key individuals. Three key ideas enabled this *tarbiyyah* programme – albeit belatedly – to be connected to the South African socio-political reality: (1) the idea of Islam being a religion and a state (*din wa dawlah*), (2) the continuity of jihad; and (3) the Qur'an as *the* comprehensive basis for everyday personal and socio-economic guidance. The first two ideas, applied in an apartheid society, meant the linking of one's Islam with a religio-political struggle to eliminate oppression (even if, for some, only as a prelude to establishing an Islamic state). The third meant bypassing the traditional *'ulama* for interpretative guidance and a reassertion of the right to search for direct Qur'anic guidance.

South African Muslims experienced the impact of these ideas in the form of what is referred to as "progressive Islam". The period immediately following the June uprisings against apartheid education in 1976 saw a definite pattern emerging whereby the Qur'anic exhortations regarding sacred struggle (*jihad*) and justice were interpreted by the progressive Muslims in a politically meaningful manner. This interpretation supported fundamental socio-political change and justified anti-state insurrection to achieve the same. A number of verses from the Qur'an were "summoned" so frequently that, to casual observers, they were often reduced to the slogans peculiar to a particular political tendency. Interpretations of these Qur'anic texts ranged from the calculatingly vague to the very transparently elastic to suit *a priori* socio-political assumptions – the sincerity of the Islamist/activist never being in dispute.

If the M.Y.M. in its initial stages represented liberalism in resurgent Islam, then the Call of Islam shifted its focus onto those whom Chopp describes as "the non-subjects of history, those who have been denied any voice or identity by their fellow humans". (1989, 3) The Call of Islam spoke about "a search for a South African Islam" (Esack, 1988, 67). By this they meant "an Islam which grows from and inspires the South African crucible of oppression and liberation", "an Islam which flows from and relates to direct involvement" (ibid.) in the liberation struggle. This theology would be "the synthesis of action (for justice) and the theological reflection on that action" (ibid.). They furthermore, argued that it is "unethical and strategically unwise" to work out models of Islamization in "the comfort of drawing rooms because people are dying for hunger *now* and others are engaged in a struggle for liberation *now*"; "a new order (in South Africa) can only accommodate elements that had grown alongside it" (ibid.).[22] The Call of Islam had largely retained the commitment to search for answers in the Qur'an, bypassing the clergy,

---

22 Their "action – theological reflection – action" paradigm bears a close resemblance to that of Christian liberation theology, a resemblance that they have openly acknowledged (Esack, 1997).

which was an intrinsic part of their M.Y.M. heritage, but shifted the discourse to one dealing with various approaches to its interpretation.

ISLAM – A QUR'AN BELT

The Qur'an is at the heart of Islamic religious life, even when Muslims come to be as "heterodox" as the Isma'ilis, who may believe that Prince Karim al-Husayni, the Agha Khan, is a living reflection of the Qur'an, "better than the written guidance" (cited in Rippin and Knappert, 1990, 146). From the scholar to the Sufi; from the housewife desiring to stretch a meal to feed an extra mouth to the terrified child confronting an approaching dog, from the liberal modernist to the radical revolutionary; from the laid back traditionalist cleric to the Kalashnikov toting Afghan tribalist – the Qur'an provides meaning. In the words of Ernest Geller, "Christianity has its Bible belt; Islam *is* a Qur'an belt" (1994, xi).

2 THE WORD ENTERS THE WORLD

From the Arabic root "*qara'a*" (to read), or "*qarana*", (to gather or collect), the word "*qur'an*" is used in the Qur'an in the sense of "reading" (17.93), "recital" (75.18), and "a collection" (75.17). The Qur'an also describes itself as "a guide for humankind" and "a clear exposition of guidance", "a distinguisher" (25.1), "a reminder" (15.9), "ordinance in the Arabic tongue" (13.37), "a healer" (10.57), "the admonition" (10.57), "the light" (7.157), "the truth" (17.81) and "the rope of God" (3.102). From this literal meaning, especially the idea of a "collection", it is clear that the word "*qur'an*" is not always used by the Qur'an in the concrete sense of a scripture as it is commonly understood. It refers to a revealed oral discourse which unfolded as seemingly a part of God's response to the requirements of society over a period of twenty-three years. Only towards the end of this process is the Qur'an presented as "scripture" rather than a recitation or discourse. The closest the Qur'an comes to employing the word "*al-qur'an*", in the sense which Muslims currently use it, is where it is mentioned with the *Tawrat* and *Injil* (the revelations to Moses and Jesus respectively)[1] as the name of the scripture of Muslims (9.111). The word "*qur'an*" is thus used in two distinct senses: first, as the designation of a portion or portions of revelation and, second, as the name of the entire collection of revelations to Muhammad. This twin meaning of "*qur'an*" as both a "collection" and as a "book", we shall later see, makes for fascinating differences on the nature of

---

1 Sometimes the Qur'an refers to the *Tawrat* and *Injil* as scriptures revealed to Moses and Jesus respectively and, at other times, to the actual scripture that these communities had in their possession. Contemporary Muslims normally use these terms to refer to the entire New Testament and the Torah.

revelation: is it a collection of divine responses to earthly events or is it a pre-existing canon according to which events must play out in order that its narratives, injunctions, exhortations, etc., can acquire flesh and blood?

For Muslims, the Qur'an as the compilation of the "Speech of God" does not refer to a book inspired or influenced by God or written under the guidance of His Spirit: rather it is viewed as God's direct speech. Zarqani reflects the view of the vast majority of Muslims when he defines the Qur'an as "That miraculously revealed to the Prophet, written in the canon (*al-maktub fi'l-musahif*), narrated uninterruptedly and enthralled by its recitation (1996, 1:21). Ibn Manzur, defines it as "the unique revelation, the Speech of God revealed to the Prophet Muhammad through the Angel Gabriel (always existing) literally and orally in the exact wording of the purest Arabic" (Ibn Manzur, 1994, s.v. "*qur'an*"). It is therefore not surprising that, for Muslims, the Qur'an stands at the heart of Islam as a worldview and is the only valid contemporary revelation; to invoke the Qur'an is to invoke God. The Qur'an is God speaking, not merely to Muhammad in seventh-century Arabia, but from all eternity to all humankind. It represents, as Wilfred Cantwell Smith says, "the eternal breaking through time; the knowable disclosed; the transcendent entering history and remaining here, available to mortals to handle and to appropriate; the divine become apparent" (1980, 490).

THE STAGES (HISTORY?) OF QUR'ANIC REVELATION

In the same way that believers in general do not speak of the history of God, Muslims do not really speak of the "history of the Qur'an". This reflects a deep belief in its other-worldliness, the idea that it is an extension of the divine. It is easier to speak of the history of its revelation or the history of the written text, although even here we run into difficulties if we insist on understanding history as something that happens in the world of people and physical matter. Most classical scholars of the Qur'an such as Muhammad ibn 'Abd Allah al-Zarkashi (d. 1392) and Jalal al-Din al-Suyuti (d. 1440), on the basis of various traditions ascribed to the Prophet, believe that that the "descent" of the Qur'an took place in three stages (Suyuti, 1973, 1.40–44). First, from God to the "protected tablet" (*al-lawh-al mahfuz*).[2] The Qur'an says that

2 The "protected tablet" is also regarded as the repository of destiny upon which "the pen" writes. In this sense the *qur'an* was sent to the tablet as an event which was to occur in the future. Both these notions of the Tablet as containing the laws of God as well as the knowledge of destiny are also found in the Torah where the Book of Jubilees 3:10 speaks of

it is "a sacred *qur'an* in the protected tablet" (85.21–22). This tablet or *lawh*, a term for metaphysical substance, is often regarded as the original copy of the *qur'an* and identical to what the Qur'an describes as the "*umm al-kitab*" (mother of the book): "God annuls or confirms whatever He wills and with Him is the Mother of the Book" (13.39). The nature of this metaphysical existence is seldom discussed in Muslim writings and there are no hadith references to the subject. In the words of Zarqani, "This existence in the tablet was in a manner and time which only God knows" (1996, 1.39). There is, however, another opinion which believes that the "Mother of the Book", rendered by Asad as "the source of all revelation", (1980, 368) really refers to the source of all revelation and that the revealed Qur'an was only a part of this more encompassing "Mother of the Book". The second stage of the *qur'an's* putative descent is as a completed entity in the "protected tablet" above the seventh heaven to the "Abode of Honour" (*bayt al-'izzah*) in the lowest heaven (ibid., 41).[3] The idea of this second stage is based on traditions ascribed to the Companions of the Prophet and on the statements that it was revealed on a night described in the Qur'an as "the Night of Majesty" (*laylah al-qadr*).

> Behold from on high have We bestowed this [divine writ] on the Night of
> Majesty
> And what could make thee conceive what it is, that Night of Destiny?
> The Night of Majesty is better than a thousand months.
> In hosts descend in it the Angels, bearing divine inspiration, by their
> Sustainer's leave;
> From all [evil] that may happen does it make secure, until the rise of the
> dawn (97.1–5).

Given that revelation to Muhammad was a gradual process covering twenty-three years, it became general belief that an intermediate revelation whereby the entire Qur'an was descended must have occurred. 'Abd Allah ibn 'Abbas, (d. 68/687) one of the Companions, reports that "the Qur'an was revealed as an entirety to the worldly heaven on the Night of Majesty after which it descended in twenty years" (Suyuti, 1993, 1:40). The third and final stage of revelation is believed to have been from the Abode of Honour to the earth in stages to the Prophet

the laws relating to the "purification of women after childbirth being written on tablets in heaven". Jubilees 5:13 speaks of the judgment on all that exists on earth being written on the tablets from heaven.

3 The figure seven features quite extensively in Islamic cosmogony and is used to indicate "several" or "a number". The notion of seven heavens appears often in the Qur'an and is not to be taken literally.

Muhammad. This, according to the Hadith material, occurred through the medium of the Angel Gabriel.[4] The first of these revelations, beginning with Chapter 96, *The Pen*,[5] is widely believed to have commenced on the Night of Majesty during the month of Ramadan in 610 and revelation continued for a period of twenty to twenty-three years.

Here we need to pause. What kind of social environment did this revelation speak to? While Muslims, of course, believe that this revelation came from God and was addressed to the entire humankind; it nevertheless also entered a specific place and time and spoke to a people who lived within history. Who was its immediate recipient, Muhammad? What was he doing in the cave on that fateful night in the month of Ramadan?

THE SOCIAL WORLD OF THE REVELATION OF THE QUR'AN

Most of the inhabitants of the Arabian Peninsula during this period were nomads although some tribes settled in small towns or villages such as Mecca, the birth place of Muhammad, and Yathrib, later to be renamed Medina after becoming the home of Muhammad. These towns were usually the centres of interaction between the settled communities and the Bedouins, where both mixed freely for trade, pilgrimage,[6] and the great fairs which attracted poets from all over Arabia. Arab life was largely determined by the harsh geographic conditions. Group action conformed to ancestral customs of assisting members of the tribe without any reference to the objective morality of the tribe or group's action. Social ethics revolved around the tribe, which was not a permanent entity, and co-operation took place around tribal solidarity pacts or asylum for an individual. Loyalty was a keystone of morality and betrayal was met with ostracism. In such a society the individual

---

4   Watt and Bell, on the basis of the fact that Gabriel is only mentioned twice in the Qur'an, both in revelations said to have occurred in Medina, suggests that his association with the original call "appears to be a later interpretation of something that Muhammad had at first understood otherwise" (1970, 19).

5   This is the most widely accepted notion, based on a hadith narrated by 'Aishah bint Abi Bakr (d. 58/678) and found in Bukhari and Muslim. Suyuti cites other views including the beginnings of Surah *al-Mudatthir* (Chapter 74, *The Enfolded One*) and the *Al-Fatihah* (Chapter 1, *The Opening*) as the first revelation (1973, 1:24).

6   The pilgrimage was an old Semitic custom, as is evident from Ex. 34.22: "Three times a year you shall celebrate for me a *hag*." Pre-Islamic Arabia had several places of pilgrimage in Arabia where festivals were also celebrated. The three months designated for the performance of pilgrimage were Dhi'l-Hijjah, Dhi'l-Qa'da, and Muharram and during this period tribal feuds were outlawed and all weapons were left outside the sanctuary of pilgrimage.

had no value of his or her own; only the tribe's honor and bravery upheld the mores of the group.

In the sixth century, the Hijaz, a strip of arid land running parallel to the Red Sea, was a place of great social ferment with Mecca emerging as a cosmopolitan centre in the middle of a growing significant trade route between the south (Yemen) and the north (areas such as Greater Syria and Iraq). Time-honored values such as tribal loyalty, honour, hospitality, valor and patriarchy were exposed to a lot of stress and by the time of Muhammad individualism was on the rise. The major factor responsible for this was the trading economy in Mecca with its growing urban environment which made private financial resources possible. However, the growing individualism gradually took its toll on the sense of community and the notion of group immortality, giving way to immortality of wealth – usually by hoarding. Alternately, individuals wasted wealth in the hope that extravagance could buy them an immortal reputation.

While the nomadic Arabs paid homage to numerous deities, they nevertheless believed in a single Deity, called "Allah", above these. "And if you ask them, 'Who created the heavens and the earth and made the sun and the moon subservient?' they will surely answer 'Allah'" (29.61). Mecca, the city of Muhammad's birth, was home to "the Ancient House", a cube-like construction believed to have been built by the Prophet Abraham and his son, Ishmael. "And when Abraham and Ishmael were raising the foundations of the House, [they prayed:] 'Our Lord, accept [it] from us; surely you are the hearing, the knowing'" (2.127). Known as the "ka'bah", Muslims believe that this is the House of God (Bayt Allah) and, in the words of the Qur'an, "the first house to be established for humankind" (3.96). In Pre-Islamic Arabia, the Ka'bah housed a large number of idols and was the site of regular pilgrimage while its immediate surroundings were also regarded as sacred. "Whoever enters it will be secure" (3.97). More significant for the inhabitants of Hijaz than belief in these gods or the single Deity, though, was the deeply entrenched notion that a person's life was determined by Time or Fate (dahr). Life was a purely this-worldly matter governed by an unfeeling Time which eventually destroys everything. Time had pre-arranged the four fundamentals of existence: food, the sex of children, happiness or misery, and one's life span. "They say: 'There is nothing but this present life; we die and we live, and only Time destroys us'" (54.24).

Some forms of Christianity and Judaism were practised in various pockets throughout the peninsula. In Mecca itself there were a number of individual Christians, most of them slaves, while a settled Christian community lived in the southern part of the peninsula, in an area called Najran. In Yathrib, later to become the home of Muhammad, there was a large settled community of Jews comprising two major tribes. Another religious group at this time was the *Hunafa*, which *The Concise Encyclopaedia of Islam* describes as "generally hermitic adherents of a primordial – or perennial – monotheism that went back to Isma'il and Abraham".[7] The presence of Christians, Jews and the *Hunafa* led to considerable speculation by non-Muslim scholars about their impact on Muhammad's ideas and the shaping of the Qur'an – with not a few direct "allegations" that Muhammad had "borrowed" his ideas from one or more of these communities.[8] I place the word "allegations" in inverted commas because the Qur'an itself is quite explicit about Muhammad's message being both a continuation and a purification of the earlier revealed religions. Quite clearly, there was a growing trend towards monotheism in Arabia at the time of Muhammad and Muslims argue that this was part of preparing Muhammad and his environment for his mission.[9]

The oral tradition in general, and more specifically poetry, played a very significant role in Arab cultural life. Poetry was the principal art form of the Bedouins and during the Pre-Islamic days at great events such as the fairs held at Ukaz, an important attraction was the declaiming of poetry. "The poet", says Anwar Chejne, "was the spokesman, leader and oracle of the tribe; a master of satire and praise, a guide in peace and a champion in war. His words 'flew across the desert faster than arrows'" (1968, 6). Eloquence was regarded as a symbol of a perfect human being and an indication of wisdom. Arab poets competed with each other by composing eloquent poetry. Their linguistic skills and eloquence were sources of immense pride and the subject of ongoing inter-tribal rivalry and boasting. Arab lexicographers explain the word "'arab" as meaning "eloquent expression" or "effective oral communication" and non-Arabs were called "al-'ajam", i.e. "those who cannot express themselves eloquently".

---

7 The Qur'an uses the word "*hanif*" (pl. "*hunafa*") for the patriarch Abraham (3.67 and 2.135) and postulates the *hanif* against both corrupt monotheism as well as polytheism. Later in Medina it came to used synonomously with the term "Muslim".

8 See particularly C.C. Torrey, *The Jewish Foundations of Islam* (1967) and Abraham Geiger, *What did Muhammad Borrow from Judaism?* (1989).

9 Watt asserts that although the Qur'an does not mention these matters [the tendency towards a vague monotheism], and ostensibly makes a completely fresh start, the nascent Islam did, in fact, act as a centre for these values and nebulous tendencies (1953, 96).

MUHAMMAD, THE RECIPIENT OF THE QUR'AN

Most Muslims hold that Muhammad was born and lived out his mission in the broad daylight of history and that details of his life are encapsulated in the body of knowledge known as the *Sirah*, which has also acquired the status of sacred history. Scholars such as Ibn 'Adi ibn Hisham (d. 218/834), who based his work on that of Abu 'Abd Allah ibn Is'haq (d. 150/767), and Abu Ja'far ibn Jarir al-Tabari (d. 310/923), the famous Baghdadi historian and traditionist, combined piety and scholarly rigor to produce accounts of the *Sirah* which became the basis for all subsequent historical enquiry into the life of the Prophet. The Qur'an itself provides a very fragmentary account of his life. Others who claim greater objectivity see his life and time in more nuanced ways and dispute many of the established "facts", including the year of his birth. Depicting the scepticism of many supposedly disinterested scholars, Maxine Rodinson says: "Nothing is certain about Muhammad's child- hood. The void has gradually become filled with legends which grow even more beautiful and edifying with the passage of time" (1974, 43).

The most commonly accepted year of Muhammad's birth, into the Hashimite clan, is 570.[10] His early childhood was quite a tragic one. His twenty-five-year-old father, 'Abd Allah, the son of 'Abd al-Muttalib, died in Yathrib on a trade journey to Syria a few months before he was born. Two years after his birth his mother, Aminah bint Wahb, passed away on a return journey from a visit to his father's grave near Yathrib. Muhammad had accompanied his mother on this journey and she had introduced him to his maternal relatives among the Khazraj tribe. "The youthful Muhammad, already an orphan, and now more than ever conscious of the memories of his dead father because of his visit to Yathrib, must have been almost crushed by the loss of his mother. The child became more and more withdrawn and sad, and of a mild and sensitive disposition" (Bashir, 1978, 48). Many years later he stopped by the site of his mother's grave and wept bitterly. Asked by his companions, about his weeping, he replied: "I was overwhelmed by my memories of her affection and I wept for her" (Ibn Sa'd, 1967, 1.129). He was cared for by his grandfather, 'Abd al-Muttalib, the leading figure of Mecca, for about six years, until the latter also passed away, aged eighty-two. By all

---

10 In an article "Abraha and Muhammad" (1987), Lawrence Conrad re-examines the evidence for a plausible date for the invasion of the Hijaz by Abraha from the Yemen, described as the Year of the Elephant, and believed to be the birth date of Muhammad, 570. Conrad concludes that the most likely date is actually 552.

accounts, 'Abd al-Muttalib showered Muhammad with affection. Umm Ayman, Muhammad's nurse, recounts the day 'Abd al-Muttalib passed away: "I saw the Apostle of God, may God bless him, weeping that day behind the bier of 'Abd al-Muttalib" (ibid., 1.132). Much later, after he became a recipient of divine revelation, God reminded him of his early days of loss, poverty and bewilderment:

> Did He not find you an orphan and gave you refuge?
> Did He not find you lost and guided you?
> Did He not find you poor and made you self-sufficient? (93.6–8)

As was common practice among the more settled Arabs, during his infancy Muhammad was entrusted to a Bedouin foster mother, Halimah al-Sa'diyyah, in the belief that the desert conditions make for healthier children.[11] Muslim tradition holds that even during this early period there were certain indications that Muhammad was going to have an extraordinary life. The son of Halimah reported that two men came dressed in white and opened his breasts and stirred their hands inside (Tabari, 1989, 6.63). Later Muhammad explained that the visitors were angels who had washed a dark spot from his heart with snow. Referring to this and other similar traditions, Watt says it is "almost certain that they are not true in the realistic sense of the secular historian for they purport to describe facts to which we might reasonably have expected some reference at later periods in Muhammad's life but there is no such reference. Yet they certainly express something of the significance of Muhammad for believing Muslims and in that sense are true for them and a fitting prologue to the life of their prophet" (Watt, 1953, 34).

When 'Abd al-Muttalib passed away, Muhammad's uncle, and later protector, Abu Talib, reared him for many years until his adulthood. At the age of twelve, Muhammad accompanied Abu Talib on the first of several trade journeys to Syria. Muslim tradition has it that during one of these journeys, a Nestorian monk, Bahirah, predicted that Muhammad would become a prophet of God and exhorted Abu Talib to take good

---

11 The narratives of Ibn Hisham contain a poignant account of Muhammad as a marginalized figure from his earliest days. Halimah narrates how she was part of a larger group of Bedouin women in search of children to nurse as a form of income. Upon hearing that Muhammad was fatherless, none of the women was willing to take him: "We were thinking of the gifts that we would get from the child's father. We kept saying: 'An orphan! What are his mother and grandfather likely to do?' So we did not want him. Every woman in our group found a baby except myself. So when we agreed to go home I said to my man, By God, I will go back to that orphan and take him; 'by God, I do not like to go home with the other women without a baby.'" (1985, 1:215–16).

care of his nephew, who was destined for greatness.[12] Muhammad ibn Sa'd (d. 230/845) one of the early Muslim historians, reflects the Muslim appreciation of Muhammad's youth when he writes:

> God protected him and kept him safe against the practices of the days of *jahiliyyah* [pre-Islamic Ignorance] and its evils … He followed the faith of his people till he attained manhood and proved to be the most excellent of them, best in disposition, most respected in society, sweet of tongue, most forbearing and trustworthy, most truthful in speech, and remote from obscenity and teasing the people; he was never noticed quarrelling or suspecting any one. Thus the nation gave him the appellation of *al-amin* [the trustworthy]. It was because God had united virtuous deeds in him and so he was mostly known as *"al-amin"* at Mecca … (1967, 1.134–135).

Largely due to the experience and reputation acquired during his trade journeys, a wealthy merchant and widow, Khadijah bint al-Khuwaylid (d. 620), engaged his services. Deeply impressed with his honesty and character, she, then aged forty,[13] proposed to the twenty-five-year-old Muhammad. They became the parents of two sons, both of whom died in infancy, and four daughters. Despite the comfort and happiness that Muhammad obviously enjoyed in his marriage to Khadijah, he was deeply disturbed by events around him. He found the idolatry and fetishism of Hijaz vulgar and the many prevalent social injustices deeply distressing. The major cities of Hijaz, Mecca, and Yathrib, were moving towards greater social strife, particularly after the collapse of Hashemite rule, precipitated by the death of his grandfather, 'Abd al-Muttalib. Muhammad increasingly began to search for a response to his own agony at the injustice and chaos around him by resorting to mountain retreats. "The quest of his soul was for explanation and truth and the longing of his heart was for communion with the true God, the nature of whom he knew not" (Bashir, 1978, 75). A particularly favourite period of the year for Muhammad was the month of Ramadan when he would spend the entire month in seclusion in a small cave, since named Hira', on one of the mountains on the outskirts of Mecca. It was one night during one of these retreats in Ramadan of 610 that Muhammad, then aged forty,

12 While this incident, real or otherwise, has passed into Muslim history as a significant indicator of Muhammad's veracity, others have suggested that this is where Muhammad first acquired his knowledge of Christianity which was later displayed in the Qur'an. Alfonso Mingana has also suggested that "Bahira" is, in fact a misnomer for "Bhira", a title given by the Arameans to every monk. According to Mingana, he was Sergius, a Nestorian monk excommunicated and exiled to Arabia in expiation of his sins (1919, 407).

13 Watt suggests that the age of Khadijah was exaggerated given that she subsequently bore seven children with Muhammad and this is not singled out in any of the early writings as "sufficiently unusual to merit comment" had she indeed been 40 years old (Watt, 1953, 38).

underwent a traumatic experience, the first of a series of revelations, the beginning of the Qur'an as we know it.[14] Such was the world into which the Qur'an came and such was the personality unto whom it was revealed. In the words of Cragg,

> The Messenger has locale, circumstance, context and a history. The language is Arabic and the local setting is that of a commercial metropolis and a pilgrim's shrine. The vocabulary reflects a range of influences and associations already current within the immediate society. Whatever enters into time must necessarily exist at a given time. Nor can an apostleship in God's name be other than into a "here and now" which in retrospect becomes a "there and then" (1988, 18–19).

The tensions between the other-worldliness of this intervention and the world wherein it intervened were to prove as vexatious among Muslims and theologically devisive as were questions in the Christian world about God becoming human. In speaking about the "world into which the Qur'an came" and "the personality unto whom it was revealed" there is a suggestion of a tangible relationship between the two. The nature of this relationship and its tension with the idea of a text which has always existed outside history has been a very controversial one in Islam and is further examined in chapter five.

THE EARLY QUR'ANIC REVELATIONS

There are a number of different versions of the tradition that recounts the first revelatory event.[15] In a fairly lengthy hadith recorded in the collection of Bukhari (1981, 5–8), 'A'ishah (d. 678) one of the wives of the Prophet, says that the first Qur'anic revelation occurred when the Angel Gabriel visited Muhammad and asked him to read. There are three different versions of Muhammad's response: *ma dha aqra'u* ("What shall I read?"), *ma ana bi qari'in* ("I am not a reader/reciter") and *ma aqra'u* ("I do not read").[16] Gabriel reportedly pressed him "until all the strength went out of me; thereupon he released me and said: 'Read!'" This was repeated thrice and when Gabriel released him the third time, Gabriel said: "Read in the name of your Sustainer who created humankind from

14 The Hira event was not really Muhammad's first revelatory experience. According to 'A'ishah, the first kind of revelation to Muhammad occurred in the form of sacred dreams (*al-ru'yah al-salihah*) which came "like the dawn of the morn" (Bukhari, 1981, 5).
15 The chronology of the Qur'anic text was a pre-occupation of much of early Orientalist Qur'anic scholarship and is discussed in chapter four.
16 Watt suggests that the earlier version ("What shall I read?") gave way to the other versions in order to find support for the dogma that Muhammad could not write, which was an important part of the proof of the miraculous nature of the Qur'an (1953, 46).

a clot! Read! And your Sustainer is the Most Bountiful." This text was later to form the first three verses of Chapter 96, al-'Alaq (The Clot).[17]

> And thus the Apostle of God returned, his heart trembling, and came unto Khadijah bint al-Khuwaylid [his wife] and said "Wrap me up! Wrap me up!" Then he told Khadijah what happened and said unto her: "I fear for myself." Thereupon Khadijah said: "Nay, By God! Never will God humiliate you! Behold, you fulfil the duties of kinship and support the weak and benefit the destitute, are bounteous towards a guest and assist all those in genuine distress. Then Khadijah went with him to Waraqah ibn Nawfal ibn As'ad ibn al-'Uzza, her cousin. He had embraced Christianity at the time of Ignorance ... and was an old man who had become blind. And Waraqah said unto him "[Muhammad] what did you see?" Thereupon the Apostle of God told him what he had seen. And Waraqah said unto him: "That was the Angel of Revelation whom God sent down upon Moses. O, If only I were a youth! If only I were alive when your people drive you away!" Then the Apostle of God said: "Why! Are they going to drive me away? He said: "Yes, never has a man come with what you have come except that he was persecuted; And if your day of need sees me [alive] then I shall support you. Thereafter Waraqah took no part in [these matters] until he died. And the revelation broke off (ibid., 7).

Muhammad was thoroughly shaken by this extraordinary experience and for a long period thereafter he doubted its genuineness. These doubts were accentuated by a prolonged absence of Gabriel. A hadith in the collection of Bukhari tells how this break in revelation came to an end.

> And while speaking of the break in the revelation [the Prophet] said in his narrative: "Once while I was walking, I heard a voice from heaven – and there was the angel who had come unto me at Hira', sitting on a throne between heaven and earth. And he inspired me with awe, and I returned home and said "Wrap me up! Wrap me up!" Then God, the Most High, sent down [the revelation]: "O you who are wrapped in a cloak! Arise and warn!" [continuing up] to his words and "shun all evil." Thereupon the revelation became intensive and continuos (1981, 9).

Thus the first section of the Chapter al-Mudaththir (The Enfolded One) (74.1–5) was the second revelation. Some scholars such as Zarkashi suggest that the first revelation – "Read in the name of your Lord who created; created humankind from a single clot. Read for your Lord is bounteous" – was to anoint to Muhammad as a Prophet in the sense that he first had to become acquainted with God as Lord, Creator and

---

17 Based on a hadith in the collection of Muslim, some scholars add the following two verses of the same chapter as part of the first revelation: "4) Who taught by the Pen. 5) He taught humankind what it did not know."

Sustainer. The second revelation – "O covered one! Arise and warn ..." – was intended to confirm Muhammad in his role as God's Messenger to humankind (Zarkashi, 1972, 1:209).

There are two other reports regarding the first revelations; the one is that al-Mudaththir (The Covered One) was the first to be revealed and the other that Al-Fatihah (The Opening) was the first. The two most authentic collections of Prophetic traditions according to the Sunnis, those of Bukhari and Muslim, contain a statement attributed to Jabir ibn 'Abd Allah when he was asked what was the first [part of the] Qur'an revealed. He responded saying The Enfolded One (Zarqani, 1996, 1:78–79). This account is generally dealt with by suggesting that Jabir either entered the conversation late and only heard the latter part of the Prophet's lengthy account of the first revelation or that he meant the first revelation subsequent to the long period of Gabriel's absence. The second account, that Al-Fatihah (The Opening) was the first revelation, occurs in Baihaqi's collection of Prophetic traditions and seems to be a conflation by the narrator, Abu Maysarah, with the early account given by 'A'ishah of the first revelation. Here the Prophet is reported to have told his wife, Khadijah, that "I was meditating alone when I heard a voice; By God! I was terrified at what this could be." Thereupon Khadijah said: "I seek refuge in God! What would God do to [harm] you? Behold, you fulfill the duties of kinship and support the weak and benefit the destitute and are bounteous towards a guest and assist all those in genuine distress." In this version Abu Bakr ('Abd Allah 'Atiq, d. 13/634), one of his companions and later the first Caliph, accompanied him to Waraqah ibn Nawfal. Muhammad narrated that he heard a voice calling "O Muhammad! O Muhammad!", whereupon he fled. Waraqah advised him against fleeing again when the angel appears, but to remain steadfast. The narration then seems to skip a few steps and concludes: When the call "O Muhammad!" ended, it said: "in the Name of God, the Gracious, the Dispenser of Grace. All praise is due to God, the Lord of the universe" until it reached "Nor those who are astray" (i.e., the entire chapter Al-Fatihah (The Opening), which, in the present arrangement of the Qur'an, is the first chapter). This version is generally rejected on the grounds that: (1) there is no companion of the Prophet in its chain of narrators; (2) the narrator seems to have confused two separate accounts; and, (3) there is no reference in this version to the cave of Hira', while there is consensus that this was the place where the first revelation occurred.

THE NATURE AND MODES OF REVELATION

The Qur'an uses the word "*wahi*" (revelation) in several different ways, each having the idea of inspiring, directing, or guiding the object receiving revelation. The way this term is usually translated also reveals other beliefs or assumptions. For example, when the Qur'an uses the word "*wahi*" in relation to women, birds, or angels ("we sent this *wahi* to the mother of Moses" (28.7) or "Your Lord sent *wahi* to the bee to build its hives in hills, on trees and in humankind's habitation" (16.68), then it is invariably translated as "we inspired" for the assumption is that women, birds or angels cannot become messengers of God in the same way that men do. When it relates to men though, it is invariably rendered as "revelation" in the sense of God's word, along with the assumption that this implies prophethood for the recipient of such revelation. In the following verse, the Qur'an outlines the modes for this revelation:

> It is not fitting for a person that God should speak to him except by inspiration, or from behind a veil, or by sending of messenger to reveal with God's permission what God wills: for He is the Most High, Most Wise (42.51).

An example of the first mode, inspiration, indicated here is Surah 37, ayah 102 where Abraham, the Patriarch, receives guidance in a vision during his sleep that he is to sacrifice his son. The second mode, behind a veil, is found in the Qur'an (27.8) where God addressed Moses from the fire. The third mode is that exemplified throughout the Qur'an, where the Angel Gabriel was the relayer of God's messages to Muhammad. In this mode, Gabriel is said to have uttered the direct words of God into Muhammad's ear and/or heart while he was in a state of ecstasy so that he would later recall the exact words. Another word that the Qur'an uses for revelation, perhaps even more frequently than "*wahi*", is "*tanzil*" ("to send or come down"). For example, "We sent it down in truth and in truth it came down" (17.105). In the Arabic language, "*tanzil*" has the general connotation of movement from a higher plane to a lower one. How does this communication from Gabriel relate to what Muslims hold to be our most sacred text? Rather than a message from God, it may be described as a letter from God, written by God and read out by the Prophet.

> It is the Qur'an in the sense of the actual miraculous words from "The Opening" [the first chapter] to "Humankind" [the last chapter]; and these

words are the speech of God only without any intervention from Gabriel or Muhammad in the construction or arrangement. Quite the contrary, it is God who first arranged them. Thus it is ascribed to Him and to none other (Zarkashi, 1972, 1:44).

The nature and modes of revelation, its authenticity and that of its recipient has long vexed critical scholars of Islam and of the Qur'an. Accusations against Muhammad have ranged from outright fraudulence to hallucinations and epileptic spasms. Muslims maintain that Muhammad always made a clear distinction between his own speech and that which he claimed to receive from God. In a reply to a question from one of his companions about the experience of revelation, the Prophet is reported to have said that, "sometimes it is revealed like the ringing of a bell. This form of inspiration is the hardest of all and then it passes off after I have grasped what is inspired. Sometimes the Angel comes in the form of a man and talks to me and I grasp whatever he says." Elsewhere the Prophet is reported to have described revelation as a painful and agonizing experience. His face was covered with sweat, seized with a violent shuddering: "Never once did I receive a revelation without thinking that my soul had been torn away from me" (Asqalani, cited in Suyuti, 1973, 1:46).

Watt presents two main alternative views about the revelations of the Prophet to the Muslim one outlined above: that the Qur'an is the product of some part of Muhammad's personality other than his conscious mind and that it is the work of the divine personality but produced through the personality of Muhammad in such a way that certain features of the Qur'an are to be ascribed primarily to the humanity of Muhammad (1953, 53). Rodinson, who reflects quite extensively on the state of Muhammad's mind and possible physio-psychological explanations for his revelation experience also ascribes the Qur'an to Muhammad's humanity but as something that emerges from some deeper part of his sub-consciousness – entirely unconnected to ambition or philanthropy" (1980, 77). "Muhammad really did experience sensory phenomena translated into words and phrases", says Rodinson, "that he interpreted as messages from the Supreme Being. He developed a habit of receiving these revelations in a particular way" (ibid, 218).

The problem of the nature of revelation and its relationship to Muhammad is perhaps best reflected in the question of what has become known as "the satanic verses".[18] In a section entitled "Satan Casts a False Revelation on the Messenger of God's Tongue", Tabari provides a glimpse into how the Prophet may have subconsciously willed revelation.

> When the Messenger of God saw how his people draw away from him, it gave him great pain to see what a distance separated them from the word of God which he brought to them. Then he longed in his heart to receive a word from God which would bring him closer to his people. Because of his care for them he would gladly have seen those things that bore too harshly on them softened a little, so much so that he kept saying it to himself, and desiring it and wishing for it; It was then that God revealed to him the *Surah* of the Star (*al-Najam*). When he came to the verse "Have you considered God and al-Uzza and Manat,[19] the third, the other?" Satan put upon his tongue what he had been saying to himself and would have liked to hand on to his people: "They are the Exalted Birds and their intercession is to be hoped for." When the Quraysh[20] heard this verse they were highly delighted and all prostrated themselves, Muslims and non-Muslims alike. Later Gabriel revealed to Muhammad that he had been deceived by Satan (Tabari, 1989, 75–6).

The additional verses were supposedly replaced by others rejecting the cult of the three birds "and after this splendid but temporary display of unanimity the Meccans were once more divided" (Rodinson, 1980, 107).[21] In attempting to explain Muhammad's seeming compliance with the request of the Quraysh, Watt argues that "his [Muhammad's] monotheism was originally, like that of his more enlightened contemporaries, somewhat vague and in particular was not so strict that the recognition of inferior divine beings was felt to be incompatible with it" (1953, 104).

18 This is the title of the famous novel by Salman Rushdi (London, 1988) wherein he latches onto this incident to highlight the porous borders or absence thereof between truth and falsehood, and light and darkness. Publication of the novel led to demonstrations in many parts of the world and the late Ayatullah Ruhullah Khomeini, then Spiritual Leader of Iran, issued a *fatwa* (legal opinion) in 1989 denouncing him as a heretic warranting a death sentence.
19 Al-Lat was a goddess worshipped at Tai'if, Al-Uzza at Nakhlah, near Mecca, and Manat at a shrine between Mecca and Medina.
20 The Quraysh was a tribe inhabiting Mecca. These descendants of Fihr – of whom Muhammad was of tenth generation – originated from the Northern Arabs. A sixth generation leader, Kusayy, had seized control of the Meccan sanctuary and established the hegemony of the Quraysh over Mecca.
21 There is a pattern in much of non-Muslim critical scholarship that whenever a text is seemingly "prejudicial" to Muslim belief then it is vouched as "authentic". This is also the case with this text from Tabari despite its controversial nature (Rodinson, 1980, 152).

MUHAMMAD'S MISSION AS A RESPONSE TO THE QUR'AN

The Qur'an, as indicated earlier, was revealed over a long period in response to immediate issues or the long-term social and religious challenges facing the community. "And [it is] a Qur'an which we have divided [into sections] in order that you may recite it to humankind at intervals. And we have revealed it in stages" (17.106). The gradual nature of the Qur'an's revelation irked Muhammad's opponents who challenged him to produce a single book in one stroke. "And the rejecters say: 'Why was the Qur'an not bestowed on him in one single revelation?' [It has been revealed] ... in this manner so that We may strengthen your heart thereby. And we have revealed it to you gradually in stages" (25.32).[22] Revelations, in slightly varying modes, continued sporadically over a period of twenty-three years until shortly before Muhammad's departure from this world in 632. These revelations at times comprised short pieces and, at other times, much longer ones and were invariably responses to the various challenges – personal or socio-political – which Muhammad and his followers faced.

MECCA – LAYING THE FOUNDATIONS OF THE FAITH COMMUNITY

The Qur'anic focus of the early stages of Muhammad's prophethood was essentially threefold; the absolute unicity of God (*tawhid*); Muhammad's own prophethood (*risalah*); and the ultimate accountability (*hisab*) of all people to God on the Day of Resurrection. It is noteworthy that even at this early stage the Qur'an insisted on relating the correct beliefs to the correct practices and makes it clear that it was both the rejection and ignorance of *tawhid* that had led to social and economic oppression in Meccan society. Muhammad's call and his vehement denunciation of Meccan idolatry were virulently opposed by the Meccan ruling class. According to Muslim accounts, Muhammad's few followers, particularly the poor among them, were subjected to unspeakable persecution. His clan, the Hashemites, refused to abandon him and were subjected to a commercial boycott and social ostracism for more than two years. In 615 Muhammad advised some of his followers to go into exile to Abbysinia,

---

22 The challenge from Muhammad's detractors seemed to be based on the belief that previous revelations occurred in a single moment. Wansbrough holds that this verse is part of a "predominant [Muslim] concern to distinguish it [Qur'anic revelation] from the manner in which the Torah was revealed" (1977, 36).

today's Ethiopia, where they found asylum under the Christian ruler, the Negus.[23] The subsequent exile is referred to as the "Hijrah". Flight from persecution in order to strengthen oneself and to continue the struggle to establish Islam, what Kenneth Cragg refers to as "purposive exile" (1971, 133), became an act of religious merit and duty. "Those who believe and those who fled their homes and strove hard in God's way – these surely hope for the mercy of God. God is forgiving, merciful" (2.218). When Muhammad's uncle and protector, Abu Talib died in 619, the leadership of the Hashemites passed on to another uncle, Abu Lahab, a bitter enemy of the new religion, who rapidly withdrew the clan's protection from Muhammad.

At about the same time, Muhammad initiated contacts with some pilgrims to Mecca from the Khazraj tribe in Yathrib and they embraced Islam. The following year they returned with seven others of another important tribe, the 'Aws. The entire group, besides entering the faith of Islam, also took an oath of allegiance, known as the First Pledge of 'Aqabah, to the Prophet. This was followed a year thereafter by the Second Pledge of 'Aqabah where seventy-three men and two women pledged to protect the Prophet with their own lives. Subsequent to this Second Pledge, it became common for Muslims to flee to Yathrib to escape the persecution of the Meccan opponents of Islam.

And those who rejected said to their messengers: We will certainly drive you out of the land, unless you come back to our religion. So their Lord revealed to them: "We shall certainly destroy the wrongdoers and We shall certainly settle you in the land after them. This is for him who fears standing in My presence and fears My threat" (14.13–14).

As the danger to Muhammad's life accelerated and after most of the Muslims had already gone into exile in Medina, he fled to Mecca under the cover of darkness, accompanied by Abu Bakr, his father-in-law in September 622.[24] Escorted out of the city by Amir ibn Fuhayra, a young

23 Watt believes that persecution was limited to economic measures, verbal and other minor insults that affected only the individual and not his clan (1953, 123–135). He also suggests that nascent rivalry among the early Muslims and possible dissatisfaction with the "political direction" that Muhammad's mission was taking was partly responsible for the immigration of Muslims to Ethiopia. Most of his reasoning is rather conjectural on this score: he, for example, cites the case of a prominent Medinan Companion who returned from Ethiopia only six years after Muhammad had already been established in exile, suggesting that persecution could not have been the main reason which drove him to Ethiopia: this is akin to arguing that South Africans who were driven into exile by apartheid and who decided not to return home after its demise must have gone into exile for reasons other than political persecution.
24 It is significant that Muhammad was among the very last to flee after virtually all of his followers had already reached safety. This event also denotes the breaking of ties of kinship with the Meccans who had persecuted him.

associanist (*mushrik*)[25] freedman of Abu Bakr, they evaded search parties by hiding in a cave on the Thawr mountain near Mecca.

> If you help him not, [know that] God will do so – [just as] God helped him at the the time when those who rejected him drove him away, [and he was but] the second of the two; when they were both [hiding] in the cave, [and] the Apostle said to his companion: Grieve not, surely God is with us. So God bestowed from on high inner peace and strengthened him with hosts which you saw not (9.40).[26]

THE QUR'AN AND THE CHALLENGES OF A NEW SOCIETY IN MEDINA

On 17 September 622, the Prophet arrived at Yathrib[27] Muhammad and Islam/*islam*[28] now entered a new phase: that of spiritually based socio-political responsibility and leadership. Here in Yathrib, now renamed al-Madinah (lit. "the city", i.e., the city of the Prophet), Muhammad became the leader of a community of diverse elements while a few of his Meccan followers remained behind. The emerging community of those committed to Muhammad's message comprised the host community, known as the "*Ansar*" (lit. "helpers") and the emigrant community known as the "*Muhajirun*" (lit. "migrants"). Soon after he entered Medina, Muhammad twinned all the *Muhajirun* with the *Ansar* in a formal relationship of fraternity which personified the basis of the new society: faith rather than tribe.

> Surely those who believed and fled [their homes] and struggled hard in God's way ... and those who gave shelter and helped – these are the friends and protectors one of another. And those who believed and did not flee, you are not responsible for their protection until they flee (8.72).

This community of the righteous was one which had to proclaim the word of God to all and express it in their personal and social lives.

> And the believers, men and women are friends one of another. They enjoin good and forbid evil and keep up prayer and pay the tax for the poor, and

25 The *mushrikun*, (lit. "associanists") refer to those Meccans who revered physical objects such as sculptures or heavenly bodies as religiously sacred entities worthy of obeisance.
26 This verse is typical of the Qur'an's cryptic style. The reference to "the second of the two" is to Abu Bakr, who was subsequently often affectionately referred to by this phrase.
27 The Hijri calendar designated by the second Caliph, 'Umar ibn al-Khattab (d. 23/644) dates back to the first day of the lunar year in which this event took place, reckoned to coincide with 16 July 622. Islamic dates are thus denoted by A.H., i.e., After Hijrah/Anno Hijrah.
28 When I use the word "*islam*" I refer to its literal meaning, a personal submission to the will of God, the way it is most used in the Qur'an. A gradual process of reification led to the erosion of the more pluralist understanding of the term until it was used as a rigid and formal religious system called "Islam".

obey God and His Messenger. As for these, God will have mercy on them. Surely God is Mighty, Wise. (9.71).

In Medina, however, we encounter a group of people who publicly gave the impression of belonging to the community of Muslims but secretly identified with the enemies of the Prophet. Most prominent among them was 'Abd Allah ibn Ubayy and many of them occupied key positions in Yathrib society before Muhammad's coming. The Qur'an refers to them as "the *munafiqun*" (hypocrites), "propped up pieces of wood" (63.4), and "those in whose hearts there is a disease" (5.52). According to the Qur'an they were unreliable during times of crises (33.12–4), avoided participation – financial or physical – in *jihad* (47.20–31), and even looked forward to the time that the Prophet would be expelled from Medina (63.8). They were rarely named and the Prophet went out of his way to conceal the identity of those suspected of hypocrisy.

> And there are some people who say "we believe in God and the last day," and they are not believers. They seek to deceive God and those who believe, and they deceive only themselves and they perceive not ... And when it is said unto them, "Make not mischief in the land", they say "We are but peace makers." Now surely they are mischief makers but they perceive not. And when it said unto them, "Believe as the people believe", they say: "Shall we believe as the foolish believe?" Now surely they are the foolish but they know not. And when they meet those who believe, they say, "We believe"; and when they are alone with their evil ones, they say: "Surely we are with you, we were only mocking". God will pay them back their mockery, and He leaves them alone in their stubbornness, blindly wandering on (2.8–15).

At a socio-political level, Muhammad also exercised leadership over a large Jewish community. Along with the Christians, they are referred to in the Qur'an as the *Ahl al-Kitab* (People of the Book).The Jewish community played a significant economic, political, and cultural role in Medina. Not infrequently the power-brokers of Arabian tribes from whose regular inter-tribal wars much political gains were made, they comprised twenty odd tribes who, on the whole, denied the veracity of Muhammad's mission and his claims to prophethood. The relationship between the *Muhajirun* and the *Ansar* and between the Muslims and the Jews were formally outlined in a document referred to as the protocol of Medina, "forming all of them into a single community of believers but allowing for differences between the two religions" (Lings, 1983, 125). Despite the treaty which they had entered into with Muhammad, the

Jews, nevertheless, longed for a return to their erstwhile position of influence and authority (Rodinson, 1980, 160). Muslim accounts suggest that this resentment was sufficient to lead many Jews to, initially secretly and later openly, identify with the Quraysh in their desire to annihilate Muhammad and his followers (Lings, 1983, 160). Subsequent Jewish breaches of the treaty, usually on the eve of or during a war with the Quraysh, or alleged attempts on the life of Muhammad, led to their expulsion from Medina.[29] Another religious community who were, in the main, physically absent from Medina but, nevertheless, a significant part of the Muslim–other Qur'anic discourse were the Christians. Muhammad had encountered Christians as religious ascetics on his travels as a businessman, in Mecca as slaves and visiting tradespersons, and even as neighbors in Medina. The Qur'an accuses the local Jews and the Christians of willfully altering their scriptures (tahrif), sometimes by distorting the words themselves, other times by using them in an unjustified context.

> They distort the meaning of the [revealed] words, taking them out of their context; and they have forgotten much of what they had been told to bear in mind; and from all but a few of them will you always experience treachery. But pardon them, and forebear: verily God loves the doers of good (5.13).

In general, Muslim scholars, because of this "distortion", believe that the previous scriptures have no contemporary validity. Thus, while belief that all the previously revealed books indeed came from God is required for Muslims, in effect they hold that the only valid scripture is the Qur'an and the only path to salvation is through Islam.[30] This refusal to recognize the possibility of salvation through other religious paths after the coming of Muhammad is embodied in the doctrine of super-cessionism. According to this doctrine "any given religious dispensation remains valid until the coming of the one to succeed it; then the new dispensation abrogates the previous one" (Ayoub, 1989, 27). Those who heard of the message of Moses were thus obliged to believe in it and to

---

29 Although tensions between the Jews and the Muslims were evident for some time before the Battle of Badr (624) the first time that Muhammad acted against the Jews was immediately after this battle when the Banu Qaynuqa' tribe was expelled for allegedly plotting his assassination. Two other tribes, Banu al-Nadir and Banu Qurayzah were expelled subsequent to their alleged collaboration with the enemy at the Battles of Uhud (625) and the Trench (627) respectively. The last Jewish stronghold, Khaybar, fell to the Muslims in 628 after a long siege in response to their alleged incitement of the Meccans to re-start hostilities against the Muslims. For two very different perspectives on the fate of Banu Qurayzah subsequent to the Battle of the Trench, see al-'Umari 1991, 1:134–138 and Ahmad 1979, 67–94.

30 I have challenged this position in my book "Qur'an, Liberation and Pluralism" (Oxford: Oneworld, 1997).

follow the *Tawrat* until the coming of Jesus when his message, the *Injil*, superseded that of Moses until the coming of Muhammad when the final form of faith was irrevocably determined.[31]

Earlier I said that in the Meccan revelations, the Qur'an links correct beliefs with righteous conduct. The texts of opprobrium revealed in Medina which relate to the various Jewish and Christian communities and individuals encountered there by the Prophet and the early Muslims suggest a similar relationship between erroneous beliefs and the socio-economic exploitation of others as was the case of the Meccan idolaters. According to the Qur'an, the Jews and Christians justified their exploitation of their own people by claiming that their Scriptures permitted such practices. The Qur'an denounced this exploitation of the ignorance of ordinary illiterate people who had "no real knowledge of the Scriptures" (2.78) by the priests of the *Ahl al-Kitab*.

> And among the *Ahl al-Kitab* there is many a person who, if you entrust him with something of value, will faithfully restore it to you; and there is among them many a person who, if you entrust him with a tiny gold coin, will not restore it to you unless you keep standing over him. This is the outcome of their assertion, "No blame can attach to us [for anything that we may do] with regard to these unlettered folk": and [so] they lie about God, being well aware [that it is a lie] (3.75).

According to the Qur'an, many among the Jews and the Christians believed that they were not like any other people whom God had created, that their covenant with God had elevated their status with Him; and that they were the friends of God to the exclusion of other people (62.6). The Qur'an alleges that they claimed a privileged position with God merely by calling themselves Jewish or Christian, i.e., it was a claim based on history, birth, and tribe rather than on conduct and morality. Thus, they claimed to be "the children of God and His beloved" (5.18) and "considered themselves pure" (4.49). In response to these notions of inherent "purity", the Qur'an argues, "Nay, but it is God who causes whomsoever He wills to grow in purity; and none shall be wronged by even a hair's breadth" (4.49). During the Medinan phase of Qur'anic revelation, much of its focus was on the immediate needs of building a socio-religious community as well as the political challenges facing them.

---

31 This theory is neatly supported by a lengthy account regarding the spiritual search of Salman al-Farsi (d. 658) before he encountered the Prophet. Salman was said to have grieved at the inability of deeply pious friends of his who died before hearing about his new faith, Islam, to embrace it. The Prophet is reported to have told him: "Whoever has died in the faith of Jesus and died in *islam* before he heard of me, his lot shall be good. But whoever hears of me today and yet does not assent to me shall perish" (Tabari, 1954, 1:323).

The Qur'an's response was a combination of immediate injunctions and exhortations which had a long term impact on the community's social and spiritual foundations.

Other than the internal stresses of the new community in Medina emerging from the twinning of *Muhajirun* and *Ansar,* the presence of a large dissident Jewish community and establishing the leadership of the Prophet, the community also had to confront the Meccans and their allies. A series of campaigns and battles, the most famous being Badr (624), Uhud (625), and the Trench (627) followed. These wars were invariably portrayed as defensive:

> Permission [to fight] is given to those on against whom war is being wrongfully waged, because they are oppressed. And surely, God is able to assist them (22.39).

> And fight in God's cause against those who wage war against you, but be not commit aggression. Surely God does not love aggressors. (2.190).

The Qur'an presents the hand of God as evident in all the victories and attributes the losses suffered by the Muslims to their own mistakes or inability to carry out the Prophet's injunctions.

> And when you went forth early in the morning [of the Battle of Uhud] from your family to assign the believers their positions for battle. And God is Hearing, Knowing. When two parties from among you thought of showing cowardice and God was the Guardian of them both. And in God should the believers trust. And certainly God helped you at [the Battle of] Badr when you were weak. So keep your duty to God that you may give thanks. When you said to the believers: Does it not suffice you that your Lord should help you with three thousand angels sent down (3. 120–123).

Throughout this period Muhammad also sent emissaries to a number of rulers in southern Arabia, Byzantium, and Persia inviting them to accept the religion of Islam. Some responded by sending gifts, thus keeping their options open, while others rejected his invitations.

In March 628, Muhammad concluded a non-aggression treaty with the Meccans. This treaty, signed on the outskirts of Mecca at a place called Hudaybiyyah, allowed Muhammad to lead a group of Muslims into Mecca the following year to undertake the pilgrimage. The Meccans were to vacate the city for a few days and allow the pilgrimage to proceed. This abandoning of the city, even if by mutual agreement, sent a powerful message to many of the vacillating tribes of the new power and authority of the Muslims and in the following year numerous delegations came to Medina to embrace Islam. During this period several campaigns also resulted in the surrender of other tribes in the Arabian Peninsula. In January 630, Muhammad and a force of approximately 10,000 Muslims entered Mecca after the Quraysh allegedly breached the Treaty of Hudaybiyyah and, in the course of the following weeks, virtually every Meccan accepted Islam. Muhammad returned to Medina. In the following year he led a pilgrimage caravan from there comprising about 30,000 men and women. Afterwards he delivered a moving sermon wherein he proclaimed that "Verily God has made inviolable for you each other's blood and each other's property, until you meet your Lord even as he has made inviolable this, your day, in this your land, in this your month." At the conclusion of the sermon, he is reported to have looked up and said: "My Lord! Have I delivered aright the message I was charged with and fulfilled my calling?" The multitude responded: "By God, you have!"

The entire latter period of Muhammad's life, despite the fact that Mecca featured again after the Hijrah, is nevertheless referred to as the Medinan period. Other than the attitudes towards the other religious communities and the armed struggle dealt with above, the Medinan texts also deal with fundamental religious practices such as the daily and weekly congregational prayers and fasting during the month of Ramadan. These were formalized and a host of rules connected to them enunciated, either through Qur'anic revelations or through the practice or statements of the Prophet. Some of these revelations are dealt with in chapters seven and eight where I discuss the contents of the Qur'an.[32]

THE LAST REVELATIONS

While there is some unanimity regarding the first revelation among Muslim scholars, none exists about the final revelation: there are at least ten different accounts of the verses or verse that constitute/s the last revelation. In many ways, this variety is symptomatic of how the community had grown and of the difficulties presented by the transmission of prophetic traditions. The following three texts, dealing with divine and economic justice are offered individually or collectively by scholars such as 'Abd Allah ibn 'Abbas and Ibn Abi Hatim, both Companions, as the final revelation:

---

32 For an overview of the Qur'an's overall position on a number of social and ethical issues see Fazlur Rahman Ansari's *Qur'anic Foundations and Structure of Muslim Society* (Karachi, 1973) and Fazlur Rahman, *Major Themes of the Qur'an*, 1989.

a) "And be conscious of the day on which you shall be brought back unto God, whereupon every human being shall be repaid in full for what he [she] has earned and none shall be wronged" (2.281).[33]
b) "O you who have attained unto faith! Remain conscious of God and give up all outstanding gains from usury, if you are [truly] believers" (2.278).
c) "O you who have attained unto faith! Whenever you give or take credit for a stated term, set it down in writing ... God has full knowledge of everything" (2.282).

Umm Salamah (d. c. 60/680), one of the wives of the Prophet, offers an interesting account of the last verses to be revealed. Besides being insightful into the gender dynamic of the age and God's putative response to it, it is also an example of how the Qur'an portrays God in conversation with the believers. Umm Salamah says that she told the Prophet: "O Prophet of God, I see that God mentions men but omits women" (Zarkashi, 1972, 1:82–83). According to her, the following verses were revealed in response to her complaint:[34]

a) "Do not covet the bounties which God has bestowed more abundantly on some of you than on others" (4.32).
b) "Verily all men and women who have surrendered themselves unto God, and all believing men and believing women, and all truly devout men and truly devout women, and all men and women who are true to their word, all men and women who are patient in adversity, and all men and women who humble themselves [before God] and all men and women who give in charity, and all self-denying men and women, and all men and women who are mindful of their chastity and all men and women who remember God unceasingly: for [all of them] God has readied forgiveness of sins and a mighty reward (33.35).
c) "And thus does their Sustainer answer their prayer: 'I shall not lose sight of the labour of any of you who labours [in My way], be it man or woman: each of you is an issue of the other'" (3.195).

The following are some of the other verses suggested as the final revelation due to their poignancy and seeming appropriateness in concluding the Qur'an:

---

33 Of those who opt for this selection, the first verse is the more obvious one to have been the final revelation. The Prophet is reported to have lived for only nine days after the revelation of this verse and there are no accounts of subsequent revelation (Zarkashi, 1972, 1:82).
34 Although these verses are now interspersed throughout the Qur'an, it is one of the few occasions in early Islam where one finds reference to a cluster of verses around a common theme.

a) "Indeed there has come unto you [O humankind] an Apostle from among yourselves: heavily weighs upon him [the thought] that you might suffer [in the life to come]; full of concern for you [is he, and] full of compassion and mercy towards the believers. But if those [who are bent on denying the truth] turn away, say: 'God is enough for me! There is no deity save Him. In Him have I placed my trust, for He is the Sustainer, in awesome almightiness enthroned'" (9.128–129).

b) "Whosoever looks forward [with hope and awe] to meeting his [her] Sustainer [on Judgment Day], let him [her] do righteous deeds, let him [her] not ascribe unto anyone or anything a share in the worship due to his [her] Sustainer!" (18.110).

c) "When God's succour comes, and victory and you see people enter God's religion in hosts, extol your Sustainer's limitless glory, and praise Him, and seek His forgiveness; for behold, He is ever an accepter of repentance" (110.1–5).

It is said that a number of companions were deeply saddened by the revelation of the last mentioned verse because they viewed it as an omen of Muhammad's departure from this world. Muhammad passed on to the mercy of God on a Monday morning, the thirteenth of the month of Rabi" al-Awwal or the eighth of June in 632.

THE BEGINNING OF DIVERSE CLAIMS ABOUT THE WORD OF GOD

While the Prophet's family was in mourning, a group of *Ansar* (the Medinese host community) had gathered to elect one among them as the Prophet's successor. Upon hearing about this Abu Bakr and 'Umar ibn al-Khattab (d. 23/644) hastened there and after extolling the virtues of the *Ansar* argued that the leadership of the Muslims ought to vested in the *Muhajirun*, the Meccans, a view that the Ansar accepted. The Prophet's immediate family, the *"Ahl al-Bayt"* (lit. "people of the household") headed by his cousin, 'Ali ibn Abi Talib (d. 40/661), was not party to this dispute. While Sunni history of this period excludes the notion of *"Ahl al-Bayt"* as a coherent and concrete socio-religious entity during the Prophet's time, Shi'i history is not only replete with it but can, in some ways, be said to be founded on it. They hold that the Prophet's family occupied a privileged and leadership position in the socio-religious life of the community (*ummah*) and that 'Ali was the only legitimate claimant to the leadership of the community. (The Prophet's household, held to be free from sin, is also regarded as a source of jurisprudential and theological authority by the Shi'is.) 'Ali became very reclusive for several months after the Prophet's demise. While the Sunnis say that this was just due to the sense of desolation that he experienced, the Shi'is argue that it was to show his disapproval of Abu Bakr's leadership. Both, however, agree that during this period, he was quietly engaged in the collection and transcribing of the Qur'an. Later, the existence or otherwise of 'Ali's manuscript was to be the cause of much debate around the authenticity of the Qur'an. The Prophet had left this world and, in the absence of his cementing and guiding hand, the word had to be become a fixed canon – the essentially oral word had to become a written and collated one.

3 THE QUR'AN AS WRITTEN WORD

While for outsiders the Qur'an exists primarily as a literary text (*al-kitab*, the book), for Muslims it continues to function as both a written text (*mus-haf*) and an oral one (*al-qur'an*) with an organic relationship between these two modes. In the first chapter I spoke about the Muslim appreciation of the Qur'an as an oral discourse. Here I shall confine myself to the external characteristics of the Qur'an and, in doing so, I shall highlight the organic relationship between the Qur'an as both a written and oral text. This is an important point because most critical scholarship has focused on the written dimensions of the text – without reflecting too hard on its message – and has failed to appreciate that its centrality to Muslims transcends this. Thus questions are raised by critical scholars about, for example, the identity of Mary as the sister of Aaron[1] and the seeming discrepancy with Mary as the mother of Jesus, without appreciating that the Qur'an is essentially evocative to Muslims and that it is often informative through its being evocative. In other, words, comprehension can follow from the emotive and intuitive response that is evoked in the hearer and reciter rather than from a study of its contents.

DIVISIONS OF THE QUR'AN

Modern editions of the Qur'an include a heading that provides some basic information at the beginning of each *surah* (usually translated as "chapter") such as its name, the number of *ayat* (usually translated as

---

1 The Qur'an names one Aaron both in the context of the brother of Moses (2.248, 7.142 etc.), as well as the sister of Mary (19.28). Cf. Asad, 1980, 460, n. 22.

"verses") it contains, and whether it is regarded as revealed in Mecca or Medina. The Egyptian print versions, those most widely used in the Muslim world today, also suggest which verses are exceptions; i.e., which verses occurring in a Medinan text were actually revealed in Medina and vice versa. There are two major divisions in the Qur'an, *surah*s (chapters) and *ajza* (parts) and each *surah* contains a number of verses (*ayat*).

Ayat

From the singular *"ayah"*, the word literally means "signs", "indications", or "wonders". *Ayat* are the shortest divisions of the Qur'an and the word is usually rendered as "verses", although they may also be understood as "phrases" or "passages". The following text (69.40–43) shows how the *ayat* or verses are strung together. (Note that the words in brackets do not appear in the text itself but have been added by the translator):

40. Behold, this [Qur'an] is indeed the [inspired] word of a noble apostle,
41. And is not – however little you may [be prepared to] believe it – the word of a poet;
42. And neither is it – however little you may [be prepared to] take it to heart – the word of a soothsayer:
43. [it is] a revelation from the Sustainer of all the worlds.

A collection of *ayat*, usually separated from each other by the occurrence of rhythm, rhyme or assonance, comprise a *surah*.

However, the word *"ayah"* as it pertains to this division of the Qur'an, is not the primary meaning that the Qur'an uses the word. It occurs frequently in the Qur'an in the sense of the signs of God's presence in the universe. Muslims, however, believe that, given its miraculous and inimitable nature, the Qur'an as well as every component of it are signs of the presence of God in the world.

> Verily, in the creation of the heavens, and of the earth, and the succession of night and day; and in the ships that speed through the sea with what is useful to humankind; and in the water which God sends down from the sky, giving life thereby to the earth after it had been lifeless, and causing all manner of living creatures to multiply thereon; and in the change of the winds, and the clouds that run their appointed courses between sky and earth: [in all this] there are *ayat* indeed for people who use their reason (2.164).

The Muslim sense of the entire Qur'an being *ayat* and the notion of *ayat* as revelation itself is supported in the following *ayah* of the Qur'an (2.42). Note also how several statements are made in this single *ayah)*:

> [O Children of Israel] Believe in that which I have now bestowed from on high, confirming the truth already in your possession, and be not foremost among those who deny its truth; and do not barter away My *ayat* for a trifling gain; and of Me, of Me, be conscious.

There is considerable disagreement among scholars of the Qur'an, both confessional and otherwise, about the precise division between *ayat* and sentences or phrases within a single *ayah*. Some of the differences make for fascinating disagreement on serious theological issues. The following *ayah* is one such example:

> He it is who has bestowed upon you from on high this divine writ, containing messages that are clear in and by themselves – and these are the essence of the divine writ – as well as others that are allegorical. Now those whose hearts are given to swerving from the truth [from the straight path] go after that part of the divine writ which has been expressed in allegory, seeking out [what is bound to create] confusion, and seeking [to arrive at] its final meaning [in an arbitrary manner]; but none save God knows its final meaning. Hence those whose hearts are deeply rooted in knowledge say: "We believe in it; the whole [of the divine writ] is from our Sustainer – albeit none takes this to heart save those who are endowed with insight" (3.7).

The text basically says that some of the *ayat* in the Qur'an are explicit while others are allegorical, a subject to which we shall shortly return. The question arises as to whether the meaning of the allegorical *ayat* is knowable to humankind or not. The answer to this question depends on where the particular sentence within the *ayah* stops. If one assumes that the phrase "but none save God knows its actual meaning" stops where it does in the rendition above with a full stop – which was unknown is the Arabic script of the Prophetic period – after "meaning", then the answer is clear: no one should dabble any further into it. If, however, one ignores the full stop and proceeds, then one arrives at an entirely different meaning: "None save God *and* those whose hearts are rooted in knowledge know their actual meaning". The rest of the text can then be rendered as: "They [i.e., those rooted in knowledge] say: 'We believe in it; the whole [of the divine writ] is from our Sustainer.'" In this case, one ends up with books written on the meaning of the allegorical verses by those who believe that they are among those "rooted in knowledge", who are condemned by those who choose to pause (and insert a full stop) as having "hearts inclined to swerve from the truth" for dabbling into something which only God knows.

Surahs

The Qur'an comprises 114 *surahs*, each of which is divided into *"ayat"*. The word *"surah"*, literally means "row" or "fence" and appears nine times in the Qur'an. It seems to denote both a section or chapter and revelation itself. In the following verse we see, for example, how it is used as a unit of revelation:

> A *surah* [is this] which We have bestowed from on high, and which We have laid down in plain terms; and in it have We bestowed from on high messages which are clear [in themselves], so that you might keep [them] in mind (24.1).

In the following *ayat* we see how the word is used to denote "chapter":

> Now, this Qur'an could not possibly have been devised by anyone save God; nay indeed, it confirms the truth of whatever there still remains [of earlier revelations] and clearly spells out the revelation [which comes] – let there be no doubt about it – from the Sustainer of all the worlds. And yet, they [who are bent on denying the truth] assert, "[Muhammad] the Prophet has invented it!" [Say unto them]: "Produce, then, a *surah* of similar merit; and [to this end] call to your aid whomever you can, other than God, if what you say is true!" (10.37–38).

While most Muslim scholars hold that the reference here is to a single *surah*, the meaning of *"surah"* can easily be revelation. Surah *Qasas* (28), ayah 49 supports this view: "Say: 'Produce, then, [another] revelation discourse [*kitab*] from God which would offer better guidance than either of these two [i.e., revelations to Moses and Muhammad] – [and] I shall follow it, if you speak the truth!'" While *"surah"* may be safely rendered as "chapter", provided one is flexible in one's application of the term, there are exceptions to this. The following surah, *Al-Fatihah*, usually referred to as *The Opening Chapter*, and often considered as the Muslim equivalent of the "Lord's Prayer", is really a prayer and is always concluded by the expression *"amin"* (amen) even when it is recited in the ritual prayers.

1. In the Name of God, the Most Gracious, the Dispenser of Grace
2. All praise is due to God alone, the Sustainer of all the worlds

3. The Most Gracious, the Dispenser of Grace
4. Lord of the Day of Judgment
5. You alone do we worship; unto You alone do we turn for aid
6. Guide us unto the straight way
7. The way of those upon whom You have bestowed Your blessing, not of those who have been condemned nor of those who go astray.

Similarly, the following concluding two *surahs* of the Qur'an, known as *"Al-Mu'awwadhatayn"* (the two [*surahs*] of "seeking refuge") are really incantations:

1. Say: I seek refuge with the Sustainer of the rising dawn,
2. From the evil of aught that He has created,
3. And from the evil of the darkness whenever it descends,
4. And from the evil of all human beings bent on occult endeavours,
5. And from the evil of the envious when he envies (113).

1. Say: "I seek refuge with the Sustainer of humankind,
2. The Sovereign of humankind,
3. The God of humankind;
4. From the evil of the whispering elusive tempter,
5. Who whispers in the hearts of humankind;
6. From all [temptation to evil by] invisible forces as well as humankind (114).

As I shall discuss in some detail in the following chapter, Muslims believe that the contents of the Qur'an were arranged by the Prophet in his lifetime and that this was done annually under the guidance of the Angel Gabriel. After *Al-Fatihah* (*The Opening*) the chapters are arranged roughly in order of descending size, beginning with *Al-Baqarah, (The Cow)* and concluding with *Al-Nas. (Humankind)*. These *surahs* are all of unequal length, the shortest consisting of three *ayat* (*The Fountain*) and the longest of 286 *ayat* (*The Cow*). With one exception, *al-Tawbah* (*The Repentance*), all *surahs* commence with "In the name of God, the Gracious, the Dispenser of Grace." This formula is known as the *"basmalah"* and was initially used to denote the boundaries between two *surahs*.[2] Muslims suggest that because *Surah al-Tawbah* commences with God's disavowal of the rejecters and a declaration of war on them, the omission of God's grace and mercy as contained in the *basmalah* was intentional. Others again suggest that because this *surah* was revealed

---

2 The *basmalah*, also referred to as the *"tasmiyah"* also serves as way of invoking the presence of God with the commencement of any conscious permissible act ranging from switching on the car's engine to commencing a meal. The Prophet is reported to have said: "Every act of significance that does not commence with the name of God is cut off [i.e., removed from God's grace]."

towards the end of the Prophet's earthly life, he did not have the time to insert the *basmalah*. Some scholars have argued that this *surah* was originally a part of the preceding one, hence the absence of the *basmalah*. Although this expression was invariably used before commencing with the reading of the Qur'an, there are differences among the scholars as to whether the *basmalah* is a part of the *surahs* or not. Most, however agree that it is an integral part of the first *surah*, *The Opening*.[3]

All *surahs* have names and some are known by more than one name. These names are based on diverse criteria with no obvious pattern to their naming.[4] Most *surahs* are named after a distinguishing word that usually appears early in the text.[5] A large number of *surahs* have names related to a subject matter referred to in the *surah*. The rest are named after the first few disjointed letters that occurs right in the beginning of that *surah*. A number of hadith refer to specific *surahs* by name thus indicating that they were named by the Prophet. Given that this is a matter directly relating to the Qur'an, Muslims believe that it was a case where "He does not speak of his own whim", i.e., he was guided by God in this (Suyuti, 1973, 1:68). Some have, however, suggested that these names do not belong to the "Qur'an proper" and have been "introduced by later scholars and editors for convenience of reference" (Bell, 1970, 59).

In Muslim circles it is customary to refer to the *surah* when referring to a particular verse without mentioning the number of the verse, for example "Allah says in *Surah Baqarah* ..." or just "Allah says in the Qur'an..." It is also common to hear Muslims just saying "the Qur'an says ..." and then reciting the verse without any reference to the chapter or the number of the verse. In most cases, they would usually be unable to actually locate the verse with ease. As Muslims scholars increasingly interact with critical scholarship and adopt Western ways of citation, the method of referring to the number of the chapter and the verse is becoming common, e.g., 24.4, or *Surah 24, verse 4*.

The *surahs* of the Qur'an have also been divided into four categories based on their length. This division is based on a hadith regarded as weak (*gharib*) which is probably rooted in early Muslim apologetics. "I have

3 In the text of the Qur'an itself, the *basmalah* features only in 27.30 at the beginning of a letter from the Prophet Solomon to the Queen of Sheba, as a form of introduction. It later also appeared at the head of all the Prophet's dispatches, replacing an earlier formula, "In your name, O God!" (*bismikallahumma*).
4 Interestingly, the question of the name of a *surah* has never been of any particular significance to classical Muslim scholars.
5 In *Surah* 16, "The Bee" (*Al-Nahl*), the bee is only mentioned half way in the text while in *Surah* 26, "The Poets" (*Al-Shu'ra*), the poets are mentioned only towards the end of the text.

been give the seven long ones in place of the Torah, the *ma'un* in the place of the Gospel (*Injil*), the *mathani* in the place of the Psalms (*Zabur*); and I have been distinguished with the *mufassal*." Muslim traditional scholarship have described these as follows: the *tiwal* (long ones) are *Surah*s 2–10; the *ma'un* are those with approximately one hundred verses (10–35); the *mathani* are those with less than a hundred verses; and the *mufassal* are the shorter ones (50–114).[6]

THE DISJOINTED LETTERS

Immediately following the *basmalah* we find some disjointed letters of the Arabic alphabet in the beginning of twenty-nine *surahs*. Known as "*al-huruf al-muqatta'at*" (the disjointed letters), these letters are meaningless in the literal sense and their presence has intrigued both confessional and traditional scholars. With the exception of the second and third *surahs*, they occur in *surahs* belonging to the later Meccan period. Altogether fourteen, they occur from a single letter to five together. Some of these collections appear only once while others appear in the beginning of as many as six *surahs*. Some Muslims hold that these were simply letters of the alphabet used to draw the Prophet's attention to the impending revelation. (These letters are thus invoked as alternative names for the Prophet, since God used them to draw his attention.)[7] Others suggest that these words are abbreviations of actual words or phrases relating to God and His attributes. The endless possibilities resulting from this kind of speculation have led the vast majority of Muslims to conclude that they may have some kind of deeply spiritual meaning accessible only to those who walk the path of fellowship with God. Most conclude though that "they are meant to illustrate the inimitable, wondrous nature of the Qur'anic revelation which though originating in a realm beyond the reach of human perception (*al-ghayb*) can be conveyed to man by means of the very sounds (represented by letters) of ordinary human speech" (Asad, 1980, 992). "In every divine writ (*kitab*)", said Abu Bakr, the Prophet's successor, "there is some element of mystery, and the mystery of the Qur'an is the openings of [some of] the *surahs*" (cited in Rida, 1980 vol. 8, 303).[8]

---

6 This division is one wherein the majority of traditional scholars concur. There are, however, differences with regard to it and these have been documented in most of the works on Qur'anic sciences. See Zarkashi, 1972, 1:244–245.
7 Some Muslims are thus named "*Yasin (y-s)*"; "*Taha (t-h)*" or "*Hamim (h-m)*".
8 Maxime Rodinson suggests that they have something to do with the "confused attempt" of the Prophet "to hasten the expression of what he had heard by stammering and mumbling" (1980, 75).

Critical text scholars have also forwarded several theories about the origins of these letters, all of them suggesting that the letters are external to the text and were later additions. Some of these theories include the idea that they were initials denoting the names of the scribes or that they are abbreviations for disused names of the *surahs*. The "proofs" offered for these theories, summarized by Watt and Bell (1970, 61–65), also supply an insight to the arbitrariness of what passes as critical scholarship and the tenuousness of its theories. How something as mundane as someone's signature could have entered sacred chanting in a deeply oral society, or that one "signature" could been appended to several *surahs*, has not been explained by these scholars. In every single *surah* where these letters appear, the immediate subsequent reference is some form of revelation using words such as *"wahi"* (revelation), *"tanzil"* (descent) or *"kitab"* (the book) suggesting that they had far more to do with the act of revelation itself, drawing attention to it or evoking responses to it.

PARTS AND SECTIONS (*AJZA* AND *AHZAB*)

This division into thirty equal parts, each called a *"juz"*, is a fascinating phenomenon of the Qur'an and is probably unique in literature. This is the primary division known to millions of Muslims all over the world who learn to read or memorize the Qur'an from childhood without ever learning to understand Arabic. For years as children we plod through the reading of the Qur'an, getting a small portion every day to practice its reading or its memorization and our progress is measured by the number of *ajza* we have completed. In the same manner that we would be asked by relatives about which class at school we were currently in, we would be asked "Which *juz* are you in at the moment?" This division is intended to facilitate the recitation of the Qur'an in a month, particularly the month of Ramadan. Throughout the Muslim world, often the only book that one will find in a mosque is the Qur'an, usually all thirty *ajza* in one book and more often than not, also as separate texts. The *ajza* are further divided into four neatly divided sections that are marked along the edges of the text. These sections are called *ahzab* (sing. *"hizb"*, i.e., section), each comprising a quarter of the *juz*. To facilitate reading on a daily basis, the *juz* is divided into seven divisions, called *"manazil"* (sing. *"manzil"*, lit. "stage"), which are also marked along the margins. It is significant that none of these divisions, pivotal to Muslim usage of the

Qur'an, bear any relation to the meaning of the text or the subject. This is another window into the use of the Qur'an as a scripture that is essentially recited rather than read or studied.

THE ARRANGEMENT OF THE QUR'AN

The current arrangement of the Qur'an is neither chronological nor thematic. To those accustomed to reading in a linear or sequential fashion, this can prove tedious and frustrating.[9] The Qur'an also does not have a clear narrative pattern where stories neatly unfold. The story of Joseph is the only exception to the rule of narratives appearing in different accounts and various bits of the same account being interspersed throughout the Qur'an. The disjointed appearance of these narratives in the Qur'an have been the subject of vigorous scholarly debate, much of it losing sight of its objectives. "Even where the narrative predominates, the story is hardly ever told in a straightforward manner but tends to fall into a series of short-word pictures; the action advances incident by incident, discontinuously, and the intervening links are left to the imagination of the hearers" (Bell, 1970, 81). This seeming "disjointedness" is also characteristic of the rest of the Qur'an, comprised of exhortations, injunctions or liturgical pieces.

> After a short prayer, the Qur'an begins with the longest and one of the most complex chapters, one from Muhammad's later career, which engages the full array of legal, historical, polemical, and religious issues in a fashion bewildering for the reader not immersed in the history and law of early Islam. For those familiar with the Bible, it would be as if the second page opened with a combination of the legal discussions in Leviticus, the historical polemic of the Book of Judges and the apocalyptic allusions from Revelation, with the various topics mixed in together and beginning in mid-topic (Sells, 1999, xi).

While there is unanimity around the placement of the *ayat* within a *surah*, traditional scholars have differed as to whether the sequence of all the *surahs* have also been divinely ordained or only some of them.[10] Most Muslims have accepted this "disjointedness" although there have been a number of attempts to offer structural explanations for the way the *surahs* are set out in the Qur'an. Zarkashi says that the location of

9 When the reader unfamiliar with Islam and unversed in Arabic picks up the standard English translation of the Qur'an, that spirit can be hard to find. What the person who learns the Qur'an in Arabic experiences as a work of consummate power and beauty, most outsiders can find it difficult to grasp, confusing, and in most English translations, alienating.

10 Ghazi 'Inayah has set out the various opinions and their arguments in this regard (1996, 4:60–71).

the *surahs* reflects its origin in divine wisdom when we observe the following: (1) the location of *surahs* starting with *h-m*, all following each other; (2) the relationship between the content/meanings of the endings of *surahs* with the beginnings of subsequent ones; (3) the balance or rhyming in the words such as the endings of *Surah al-Masad* (*The Twisted Strands, Surah* 111) and that of the one following it, *Al-Ikhlas* (*Perfection, Surah* 112) – all the verses in these *surahs* end on the "*ad*" sound; (4) the resemblance between the rhyming pattern of entire chapters clustered together such as *Al-Duha* (*The Morning Hours, Surah* 93) and *As-Sharh* (*The Opening of the Heart, Surah* 94) (1972, 1:260). The overall "disjointedness" of the *surahs* though is accepted by most traditional scholars. Some, however, hold that this acceptance is a form of "concessionism" to critical scholarship. Hamid al-Din al-Farahi (d. 1930), a scholar from the Indian Sub-continent, argued that Qur'an, in fact, has a remarkable structure, with its contents arranged in a perfectly harmonious manner, and that appreciating this impeccable arrangement is the basis of understanding its meaning. His ideas have been elaborated upon by one of his students, Amin Ahsan Islahi (d. 1997), who based his entire commentary of the Qur'an "*Tadabbur-i-Qur'an*" (Reflections on the Qur'an) on the notion of its structural cohesion and harmony.[11] Mustansir Mir has provided the following summary of Islahi's theory, articulated in the introduction of his commentary (Mir, 1986).

1. Each *Qur'anic surah* has a dominant idea, called the axis of that *surah*, around which all the verses of that *surah* revolve. Thus no verse, or group of verses, stands alone but has a direct relation with the axis of the *surah* ...
2. The *surahs* of the *Qur'an* exist in pairs, the two *surahs* of any pair being complementary to each other and, together constituting a unit. There are a few exceptions, however. The first *surah, Fatihah*, does not have a complement, because it is a kind of a preface to the whole of the *Qur'an*. All the other exceptions too are not

---

11 Islahi's *Tadabbur-i Qur'an* was originally published in eight volumes (see Bibliography). It is currently being published in nine volumes by Lahore's Faran Foundation. Muhammad Ali in his English translation of the Qur'an (Lahore, 1973) also makes an attempt to provide what he considers some kind of logical sequence for the relationship between the various *surahs* in brief introductions that precede each one. His more extensive introduction to the translation also briefly attempt to link the entire Qur'an thematically beginning with *Al-Fatihah* (the Opening) and concluding with *al-Nas* (*Surah* 114). His comments though are so broad that one can easily switch *Surahs* and his comments intended to provide content or meaning coherence would still be applicable.

exceptions in the real sense of the word since each one of them is an appendix to one or the other *surah*.

3. The 114 *surahs* of the Qur'an fall into seven groups. The first group comes to an end at *surah* 5, the second at *surah* 9, the third at *surah* 24, the fourth at *surah* 33, the fifth at *surah* 49, the sixth at *surah* 66, and the seventh at *surah* 114. Each group contains one or more *Meccan surahs* followed by one or more *Medinan surahs* of the same cast. Like individual *surahs* or each pair of *surahs*, each group has a central theme which runs through all its *surahs*, knitting them into a distinct body. In each group, the themes of the other groups also occur but as subsidiary themes.

4. Each group logically leads to the next, and thus all the groups become variations on the basic theme of the *Qur'an*, which is: "Allah's call to man to adopt the right path."

The divisions proposed above, while certainly innovative, come across as arbitrary and depend rather unduly on what the reader chooses to see. It is also somewhat difficult to imagine the Prophet and the Companions working their way through an elaborate system of textual division as presented above. Because the Qur'an is the recited word in addition to being the written word, this seeming disjuncture is of little consequence to most Muslims. Repetitions are seen as God's repeated reminders, legal texts in the middle of a narrative as God drawing our attention to what has to be learnt from the text, breaks in a narrative reflects God's freedom from human literary patterns or suggest that the information contained therein is often incidental, while the mode, the sound patterns and inner rhythm are central. Most Muslims see the seeming absence of structure or classification in its *surahs* itself as signalling a demarcation value and as reflective of the Qur'an's role in the universe. Kenneth Cragg, notwithstanding his own attempts to give the Qur'anic revelation an irrefutable sense of the here and now, of revelation in context, says:

> We are being properly, divinely discouraged and frustrated if we mistakenly endeavour to "incidentalize" Qur'anic meaning, to link *what* it is with *when* and *where*. We must needs follow, in memorizing, reciting, perusing and expounding, the sequence of the surahs, serial and inward, as they stand in the dissonance of dates, that we may better apprehend the music of their truth" (1971, 113).

THE LANGUAGE OF THE QUR'AN

In general, both Muslim and critical scholarship hold that the Qur'an first appeared in the Arabic language. In its own words, "We have sent it down as an Arabic *qur'an* in order that you may learn wisdom" (12.2). The Qur'an also describes its own Arabic as "*mubin*" ("clear"). In an interesting insight into the dialectical relationship between the Qur'an as the word of God and society as the work of God, the Qur'an explains why it was revealed in Arabic:

> Had we sent this *qur'an* [in a language] other than Arabic, they could have said: "Why are its verses not explained in detail? What [a book] not in Arabic [a messenger] and an Arab?" Say: "It is a guide and a healing to those who believe" (41.44).

Traditional Muslim scholarship holds that the Qur'an was written in the dialect of the Quraysh, the tribe of the Prophet, for it was also the classical language known to and understood by all the Arabs. Some Western scholars have argued that the Arabic of the Qur'an was not peculiar to any tribe but was a kind of *hochsprache* that was understood by all throughout Hijaz – the identical position of classical Arabic today. Others have again suggested the "arabiyy" referred to in *Surah* 12, *ayah* 2 is a reference to the "arabiyya", the literary language of the Bedouins. Based on this, they argue that the Qur'anic Arabic is more akin to the language used by classical Arab poets of that era. Karl Vollers, for example, in his *Volksprache und Schriftsprache im alten Arabien* (1906) argued that the Qur'an was first recited by Muhammad in a colloquial Arabic without the case endings and the current language of the Qur'an was the fabrication of later philologists who attempted to put the revelations in classical Arabic. A yet untranslated recent German publication by a scholar writing under the name of "Christoph Luxenborg" modestly titled, *Die Syro-Aramaische Lesart des Koran – Ein Beitrag zur Entschlusselung der Koransprache* (The Syro-Aramaic Reading of the Qur'an – a Contribution to Deciphering the Language of the Qur'an) will probably be a major contribution to revisionist scholarship – particularly with regard to the language of the Qur'an. He suggests that a Syriac rendition of numerous words, normally rendered in Arabic, will throw a lot of light on texts which scholars have had difficulty trying to understand from a linguistic perspective. Through a careful process of alternately trying to replace "obscure" Qur'anic

Arabic words or phrases with Syriac homonyms, changing the diacritical marks (on the assumption that they were possibly misplaced by the "editors"), or retranslating it into Syriac to gather from those roots the most "logical" explanation, Luxenburg provides radically different meanings for a number of texts, which are at variance with any reading premised on the idea that the Qur'an is essentially an Arabic text.

The Qur'an itself repeatedly asserts that it is a unique and inimitable "Arabic Qur'an" (12.2, 13.37, 16.103) in order to communicate its meaning in a perfect manner to a people who took great pride in the expressive quality of their language. Much of the early discussion about the linguistic components of the Qur'an centred on the presence, or otherwise, of non-Arabic words in it – of course, based on the premise that it was an essentially Arabic text. The verses referred to above became the key supportive texts for those who argued that the Qur'an did not contain any non-Arabic terms. The earliest exegetes, particularly those associated with 'Abd Allah ibn 'Abbas (d. 68/67–68), a cousin of Muhammad, freely discussed a large number of non-Arabic words in the Qur'an.[12] Hadith literature credits Ibn 'Abbas and "his school" with having a special interest in seeking their origin and meaning.[13] Later eminent scholars of the Qur'an such as the philologist/exegete Abu 'Ubayd (d. 838), however, continued to argue that the Qur'an contained foreign words. Others such as Ibn 'Atiyyah (d. 541/1146), Suyuti (d. 911/1505), and 'Abd al-Rahman al-Tha'labi (d. 1468) tried to reconcile theology with linguistic principles. They argued that the foreign words in the Qur'an came into Arabic through the ancient Arab's contacts with other languages in foreign travel and commerce but that they had been thoroughly Arabized by the time of the Prophet. Various theories were evolved to resolve the contradiction between the notion ascribed to Ibn 'Abbas and the one which subsequently gained greater acceptance, i.e., that the Qur'an does not contain any foreign terminology. To deal with actual occurrence of words in the Arabic language that were also found in non-Arabic languages, some of these scholars, such as Muhammad ibn

12 Most books dealing with Qur'anic Studies have a section dealing with the occurrence of non-Arabic words in the Qur'an. The most exhaustive is probably that of Suyuti whose *Al-Itqan fi Ulum al-Qur'an* (1973, 135–141) contains a long list of such words and their likely origins. Suyuti has also given an extensive summary of the discussion on the employment of non-Arabic words in the Qur'an in the introduction to his *Al-Muhadhdhab fi ma waqa'a fi'l-Qur'an min al-mu'arrab* (1988). Critical scholarship has devoted considerable attention to this subject. Until Luxenberg (2000), the most significant work, albeit not without theological biases, is that of Arthur Jeffrey (1938). Its bibliography (pp. xi–xiv) has a full listing of earlier relevant works.
13 Recent research seems to indicate that much of the supposed early works of Ibn 'Abbas dealing with the presence of non-Arabic words in the Qur'an may be "fiction designed to give the texts more credence by assigning them an early and prominent figure" (Rippin, 1981, 24).

Idris al-Shafi'i (d. 204/819) and Tabari, developed the notion of *tawafuq* (coincidence). They argued that both Arabic and other languages employ the same words with identical meanings and that this uniformity of meaning was purely coincidental.

The idea of any language or discourse being absolutely free from expressions or words used in another language is alien to one of the most basic linguistic principles, i.e., the inter-relatedness of human speech. While this may sound trite, two factors, however, ensured that this notion was rejected by the "orthodoxy": first, the Qur'an is not really regarded as human speech but rather as God's and God's speech cannot be subjected to any linguistic principles. Indeed, as is commonly known, Qur'anic Arabic became the standard of Arabic grammar. (The problem of God's speech of necessity having to coincide with human speech for effect and meaning remains.) Second, for the "orthodoxy", God's own eternalness and self-subsistence fused with those of His revelation. The Qur'an and its language thus came to be viewed as equally timeless and independent of any "non-divine" elements, non-Arabic included. The fact of God's revelation occurring in Arabic (or any other language for matter) alongside the insistence that this is the unmediated medium which was used by God raises an interesting question: If all comprehensible language and speech is the result of social interaction then does this imply that God is also "limited" or confined to the limitations of language? If so, then what does this imply for the all-powerful nature of God?

THE LITERARY STYLE OF THE QUR'AN

The difference in various appreciations of the Qur'an's style is truly a tale of "two looked out from behind prison bars; the one saw mud, the other saw stars": Ruhl speaks about how "to Muslims, the absolute perfection of the language of the Kur'an is an impregnable dogma, the acknowledgment of which is not easy to a reader with some stylistic training and a certain amount of taste" (1987, 1067). The question, of course, arises as to whose "training" and whose "taste"? According to Ruhl's taste, the Qur'an shows that "the Prophet becomes fond of wearisome repetitions of long stories interspersed with religious and moral platitudes which have an unpleasing effect ... or crude psychological explanations, or polemics which prove little to those who do not share his premise" (ibid.). Ayoub writes about the same text in the following vein:

Qur'anic language is at times rhapsodic. The opening verses of *surah* 36 (*Yasin*, [two of the disjointed letters]), for instance, move rapidly and with great dramatic force in relating the unknown stories of bygone ages and the dramatic encounter of human beings with God on the Day of Judgment; its awe inducing power is such that is recited over the dead. In other places, the language is smooth and calming, as in *surah* 55 (*al-Rahman*, The Merciful) which describes the flowing rivers of paradise, only imperfectly realized on earth, and which has been recognized to have hypnotic qualities. A good reciter often has the power to carry his listeners into moods of excitement or transports of bliss as they become totally engrossed in the words (Ayoub, 1987, 12:176–77).

Much of the Qur'an comprises rhymed prose (*saj'*) that consists of two or more short sections of the utterance being linked together by a rhyme and usually without metre. This is particularly true for the shorter *surahs* and parts of the longer ones. This "distinctive feature is closely related to its oral and liturgical function" (Welch, 1986, 5:40). In a number of texts there is a kind of rhythm or metre for stress (e.g., 74.1–7 and 91.1–10). "This feature is due to the shortness of the rhyming verses and the repetition of the same form of phrase rather than to any effort to carry through a strict metrical form" (Bell, 1970, 61). An example of *saj'* is reflected in the following rendition of *Surah Al-Duha* (The Morning Hours, *Surah* 93) by Arthur Jeffrey:

I swear by the splendour of the light
And by the silence of the night
That the Lord shall never forsake you,
Nor in his hatred take you
Truly for you shall be winning
Better than all the beginning
Soon shall the Lord console you, grief no longer overwhelm you,
And fear no longer cajole you
You were an orphan boy, yet the Lord found room for your head
When your feet went astray, were they not to the right path led?
Did he not find you poor, yet riches around you spread?
Then on the orphan boy, let your proud foot never tread,
And never turn away the beggar who asks for bread,
But of your Lord's bounty, ever let praises be sung and said.

The Arabic of the Qur'an though, deviates fairly frequently from finer rules of the rhymed poetry such as when it repeats rhymes or uses "false rhymes". In the longer chapters, particularly the ones regarded as entirely Medinan, "the rhyme is set formulas that are attached loosely to the end of verses, often with little or no connection of thought with the contexts" (*EI*, see "*Al-Kur'an*"). Whereas this represents a lack of taste to some critical scholars, confessional Muslims argue that the Prophet had never claimed to be a poet and that the Qur'an is beyond the rules of poetry. "And when God wished to speak in the same language as man, He turned his mind towards that flexible and elegant form of style, and not towards figures of speech appreciated by one people and not another, ... neither towards norms which may change with time" (Wali Allah, cited in Baljon, 1986, 140). The Qur'an is relentless in its denial that it is poetry and of any suggestion, indeed accusation, that there was a relationship between Muhammad and professional soothsayers and singers (the *kahins*) that were characteristic of Meccan society at that time. From the Qur'an it would also appear that Muhammad was deeply stung by these accusations.

> "Nay", they say, "[Muhammad propounds] the most involved and confusing of dreams!" – "Nay, but he has invented [all] this!" – "Nay, but he is [only] a poet!" (21.5). "Shall we give up our deities at the bidding of a mad poet?" (37.36).

> Exhort, then [O Prophet, all people] for, by your Lord's grace, you are neither a soothsayer nor a madman. Or do they say, "[He is but] a poet – let us await what time will do unto him"? (52.29–30).

Some of the other literary devices that the Qur'an uses are narratives and similes. Many of the narratives of the Qur'an are in an allusive style and presume that the hearers have some prior knowledge of the story or allegory, that the details will reach them through some other means, or that they are not of pivotal consequence. The longest of these narratives is that of the Prophet Joseph and covers his father's dream, his abandonment by his brothers, his imprisonment and dreams during it, his way into the court of the king, rise to power and, finally, reconciliation with his family. Often direct expressions of the subjects of these narratives appear in the text. In *Surah Taha*, which deals mostly with Moses' encounter with Pharaoh, for example, more space is devoted to the direct speech of the actors than to the narrative. Although, in the popular imagination of Muslims, the figures alluded to in the narratives are "real" in the sense that they believe that these are historical figures who really existed, there is little or no concern with the details of this existence. The lessons (*al-'ibrah*) from their lives and struggles, Muslims suggest, are the only issues of any substance. While others may lament the scanty and "bitty" nature of these narratives, for Muslims they are quite adequate. They serve to emphasize the continuity of Muhammad's prophethood and that of earlier Prophets, as moral lessons and warnings to others who may also want to ignore or reject God's commands, they encourage the Prophet in the correctness of his own path by informing him that adversity had met each of God's previous Messengers; and finally they act as a polemical device against his adversaries. Other than the narratives of previous Prophets and peoples, the Qur'an also recounts some of the incidents that occurred during the Prophet's lifetime.

Another favourite rhetorical devices of the Qur'an is the simile. These are often simple but effective and pointed comparisons.

> And yet, after all this, your hearts hardened and became like rocks, or even harder: for, behold, there are rocks from which streams gush forth; and behold, there are some from which, when they are cleft, water issues; and, behold, there are some that fall down for awe of God. And God is not unmindful of what you do! (2.74)

The gifts of those who spend of their possessions for the sake of God are compared to "that of a grain out of which grow seven ears, in every ear a hundred grains" (2.261). Those who take other than God for their protectors are compared to "a spider which makes for itself a house: for, behold, the frailest of all houses is the spider's house" (29.41). The prayers of the rejecter of faith are described thus: "He stretches his open hands towards water, [hoping] that it will reach his mouth, while it never reaches him" (13.14), and their works are like "ashes which the wind blows about fiercely on a stormy day" (14.18–21). The Qur'an describes the last day as the Day when We shall roll up the skies as written scrolls are rolled up ... (21.104).

> When the sun is shrouded in darkness,
> When the stars lose their light,
> And when the mountains are made to vanish,
> And when she-camels big with young, about to give birth, are left untended,
> And When all beasts are gathered together,
> And when the seas boil over,
> And when all human beings are coupled [with their deeds],
> And when the girl-child that was buried alive is made to ask for what crime she had been slain,
> And when the scrolls [of people's deeds] are unfolded,
> And when heaven is laid bare (81.1–11).

Other similes are more difficult to grasp.

> God is the Light of the Heavens and the earth. The parable of His light is, as it were, that of a niche containing a lamp; the lamp is [enclosed] in glass, the glass [shining] like a radiant star: [a lamp] lit from a blessed tree – an olive-tree that is neither of the east nor of the west – the oil whereof [is so bright that it] would well-nigh give light [of itself] even though fire had not touched it: light upon light! (24.35).

Traditional Muslim scholarship makes a neat and unbridgeable distinction between the words of the Prophet and those of God as communicated by the Angel Gabriel regardless of what the content of those words may be suggesting. The notion of God as a single entity being the direct speaker is quite common in the Qur'an's dramatic form. The following are some examples of this:

> And believe in that which I have [now] bestowed from on high, confirming the truth already in your possession, and be not foremost among those who deny its truth; and do not barter away My messages for a trifling gain; and of Me, of Me be conscious! (2.41).

Many passages are addressed to the Prophet directly as is evident from both the context as well as the use of the second person in the singular form. These are sometimes of personal relevance to the Prophet's own emotional or spiritual state and at other times advice is given on how to deal with a particular situation.

> O Prophet! Why do you, out of a desire to please [one or another of] your wives, impose [on yourself] a prohibition of something that God has made lawful to you? But God is much-forgiving, a dispenser of grace (66.1).

More than two hundred verses of the Qur'an ask the Prophet to "Say" this or that to his followers or detractors. This seems to emphasize the externality of the Qur'an to the Prophet: he is instructed to say and, therefore, the one instructing him must of necessity be someone other than he. Often though, the first person plural is invoked where evidently God is the speaker and some have suggested that this is the plural of the majesty.

> Say [to the Jews and the Christians]: "Do you argue with us about God? But He is our Sustainer as well as your Sustainer – and unto us shall be accounted our deeds, and unto you, your deeds; and it is unto Him alone that we devote ourselves" (2.139).

There are also numerous occasions though where God is referred to in the third person even though the Prophet is clearly the person being addressed. This poses difficulties for those engaged in critical scholarship and these texts have been invoked in support of the notion that the Qur'an is not entirely the product if a single entity. There are also several cases where the speaker alternates between singular and plural forms adding to the notion that the Qur'an was compiled in an incoherent manner. An example of this is *Surah* 6.98–99:

> And He it is who has brought you [all] into being out of one living entity, and [has appointed for each of you] a time-limit [on earth] and a resting place [after death]: clearly, indeed, have We spelt out these messages unto people who can grasp the truth!
>
> And He it is who has caused waters to come down from the sky; and by this means have We brought forth all living growth ...

Rather than God alternating between the use of the first person singular and the first person plural representing incoherence, others have argued that however disorienting this may be at a superficial perusal, these sudden shifts have an important literary and theological dimension.

> The shifts prevent the deity from becoming defined in anthropomorphic terms. Given the finite human characteristics built into the structure of language, a single constant form of reference would lead to a reified deity – an intellectual idol in the terms of Islamic theologians and mystics. In the Qur'an the divine voice is heard in a variety of manners through an extraordinary range of emotions and tones, but the form or image of the speaker, is never defined – a literary feature that mirrors the Qur'anic affirmation that the one God is beyond being fixed in any delimited form or image (Sells, 1999, xxix).

Besides God, though, numerous *ayat* suggest that the Angels or the Prophet himself are the direct speakers and it is only the interpolations of translators or the comments of exegetes that suggest otherwise. *Ayat* such as 19.64–65, for example, if read without the interpolation of the translator, clearly suggest that the Angels are the speakers:

> And [the Angels say]: "We do not descend [with revelation], again and again, other than by the command of your Sustainer; unto Him belongs all that lies open before us and all that is hidden from us and all that is in-between. And never does your Sustainer forget [anything] –

The Sustainer of the heavens and the earth and all that is between them! Worship, then, Him alone, and remain steadfast in His worship! Do you know any whose name is worthy to be mentioned side by side with His?"

In a few *ayat*, such as 27.91, the obvious speaker seem to be the Prophet and then a sudden switch occurs when he becomes the one being addressed.

[Say, O Muhammad:] "I have been bidden to worship the Sustainer of this City – Him who has made it sacred, unto whom all things belong; and I have been bidden to be of those who surrender themselves to Him, and to convey this Qur'an [to the world]." Whoever, therefore chooses to follow the right path, follows it but for his [her] own good; and if anyone wills to go astray, say [unto him (her)]: "I am only a warner!"

The fact that these *ayat* are often characterized by a later addition of "say" (*qul*) suggests that the entire section may have been preceded by the unarticulated instruction "say". Muslims have always understood it in this manner. In other words, the fact that they are the direct words of the Prophet or of the Angels does not detract from the other-worldliness of the Qur'an. They were merely repeating words that in the first instance came from God.

CATEGORICAL (*MUHKAMAT*) AND ALLEGORICAL (*MUTASHABIHAT*) VERSES

Traditional Qur'anic scholarship has evolved a number of categories whereby the *surahs* and *ayat* are divided and knowledge of these divisions is regarded as indispensable to understanding the Qur'an. One of these divisions, the categorical and the allegorical, as we have seen above, in fact, relates to whether a certain text lends itself to being understood by human beings or not. All the other divisions really pertain to how that text is to be understood and whether it is to be currently applied or not. These latter divisions I shall discuss in the following chapter as part of the Qur'an's principle of progressive revelation: i.e., the text was revealed within a particular historical situation over a period of time and in response to specific needs. For the moment, I confine myself to the categorical and allegorical verses. The following *ayah* was discussed above within the context of the problem of ascertaining where an *ayah* stops and the serious implications that it has for the understanding the text – in this case, even if one has permission to try to understand the text.

> He it is who has bestowed upon you from on high this divine writ, containing messages that are clear in and by themselves – and these are the essence of the divine writ – as well as others that are allegorical. Now those whose hearts are given to swerving from the truth go after that part of the divine writ which has been expressed in allegory, seeking out [what is bound to create] confusion, and seeking [to arrive at] its final meaning [in an arbitrary manner]; but none save God knows its final meaning. And those whose hearts are deeply rooted in knowledge say: "We believe in it; the whole [of the divine writ] is from our Sustainer – albeit none takes this to heart save those who are endowed with insight" (3.7).

The categorical verses are generally viewed as those verses whose meanings are explicit and/or have a legal significance whereas the allegorical are viewed as those verses where the meaning is obscure or inexplicable.

There are, however, a number of different opinions regarding the definitions of the categorical (*muhkamat*) and the allegorical (*mutashabihat*). There are undoubtedly a large number of verses that do not easily lend themselves to more than one interpretation and there are several which one can only attempt to understand by entering into the realm of wild speculation. An example of this is "the Most Gracious, established on the Throne" (20.5). The larger part of the text, though, falls somewhere in between and its meanings has been vigorously contested throughout the history of Islamic legal, philosophical, moral, and theological thought. What is clear to one may not be so clear to another, what is "evidently true" to me may not be the case to someone else. What constitutes "wild speculation" to me, may be "insights based on an intuitive or gnostic links with God", for others. Asad, offers a somewhat helpful appreciation of these categories in his definition:

> [The allegorical] may be defined as those passages of the Qur'an which are expressed in a figurative manner with a meaning that is metaphorically implied but directly in so many words stated. The [categorical] comprise the fundamental principles underlying its message, and in particular its ethical and social teachings; and it is only on the basis of these clearly enunciated principles that the allegorical passages can be correctly interpreted (Asad, 1980, 67).

Given the fact that language is an extension of the human world, it is inevitable that images pertaining to this world be invoked to give us a sense of the infinite. Thus when the Qur'an speaks of God being on a throne, or in the heavens on the one hand, and, on the other, being emphatic that God is everywhere, then we can appreciate that *ayah* only in an allegorical sense. When the Qur'an describes God as all-seeing or all-hearing, then it only intends to convey a sense of God's omnipotence. It would not really serve any person to speculate on the nature of God's being on the throne or of God's hearing or sight (cf. Asad, 1980, 989–992).

As for the permissibility of reflecting on the allegorical verses, as I indicated in chapter two, this depends on one's opinion as to where one places the letter "*waw*". If one terminates one's reading before the *waw* as Asad, whose translation I have used above, has chosen to do, then it is not permissible. If, however, one reads the *waw* as a conjunctive (and), then both God and those whose hearts are steeped in knowledge would be able to have that knowledge.

4 GATHERING THE QUR'AN

In the previous chapter we have seen how the Qur'an was revealed in seemingly disjointed verses and chapters. How were these parts gathered to form a coherent whole – even if that "whole" defied conventional literary understandings of coherence before the emergence of post-modernism and post-structuralism? How did the spoken word from Gabriel to the Prophet become transformed into a canon that is composed, recited, read, taught, and disseminated?

According to Muslim scholars, and several others, the "gathering" of the Qur'an took place in three overlapping periods: during the period of Muhammad's prophethood, the period of Abu Bakr (d. 13/634), his immediate successor; and finally the period of 'Uthman ibn 'Affan (d. 35/656), the third Caliph after Muhammad's demise. Others hold that this process was much more diffuse and prolonged. The universal Muslim consensus today is that, in terms of content, the current version of the Qur'an is the sole authentic one which was read during the time of the Prophet and was left with the community at the time of his departure from the world. The current consensus though is not one that has always existed. The Shi'i mainstream agree with this consensus although they argue that a copy that 'Ali ibn Abi Talib produced immediately after the demise of the Prophet had a different diachronical arrangement. A minority among them have also argued that that copy also contained additions that were deleted or omitted during the process of compilation.[1]

---

1 The Rafidis, usually described as "a group of extremist Shi'is" alleged that 'Uthman had expunged some verses from the Qur'an (Zarkashi 1972, 1:240). Literally, meaning "repudiators", the term was also used as a term of abuse used by some Sunni theologians for all Shi'is. None of the ealier Shi'i groups that rejected the authenticity of the 'Uthmanic canon are still in existence.

GATHERING THE QUR'AN DURING THE PROPHET'S LIFETIME

One of the problems in discussing the gathering of the Qur'an objectively is that the most easily accessible sources are nearly entirely "Muslim" and based on prior assumptions about the authenticity of the text itself and that – even if of lesser authenticity – of the prophetic traditions. The kind of argument that "the Qur'an is free from any interpolation because God says 'And We [i.e., God] are its guardians'" illustrates the point; to base one's argument on "God says", in fact, implies *a priori* recognition of the authenticity of the Qur'an as a true reflection of God's word. This is also reflected in the way the verse "And none shall touch it except the pure" (56.79) is used to support the belief that the Qur'an must have existed in a coherent written form. This circular reasoning also applies to Hadith literature in understanding the process of gathering the Qur'an. The basic Muslim appreciation of the process of memorization, transmission, and transcription is based on the following texts from the Qur'an:

> Move not your tongue in haste, [repeating the words of revelation] for, behold, it is for Us to gather it [in your heart] and to cause it to be read [as it ought to be read]. Then when We recite it, follow its wording [with all your mind]: and then, behold, it will be for Us to make its meaning clear (75.16–19).

> ... And do not approach the Qur'an in haste, ere it has been revealed unto you in full, but [always] say: "O my Sustainer, cause me to grow in knowledge!" (20.114).

Apparently the Prophet, in his anxiety to retain as much as possible of the revelation, hurried in his repetition of the words recited by Gabriel. The above verses were revealed both to allay his fears that he will give some revelation a miss and to indicate clearly that the responsibility of ensuring the Qur'an's retention in his heart and to give it textual coherence was God's. The fact that in the first text the notion of God gathering the Qur'an appears immediately after the reprimand of the Prophet's means of guarding against forgetfulness, seems to imply that memorization was also part of God's "gathering" of the Qur'an. The expression "gathering of the Qur'an" (*jam' al-qur'an*) thus acquired a very broad meaning that encompasses memorization, understanding, consolidating, transmission, and transcription. The first text cited above is also the basis for the predominant Muslim belief that the Qur'an was protected from any loss or addition in the Prophet's memory and in the subsequent process of transcribing it. The notion of divine providence in securing the authenticity of the Qur'an is also affirmed in several other verses dealing with different dimensions of this "authenticity".

> We shall teach you and you will not forget, save what God may will [you to forget] (87.6–7).

> Behold, it is We Ourselves who have bestowed from on high, step by step, this reminder: and, behold, it is We who shall truly guard it [from all corruption] (15.9).

In addition to the actual revelation, Muslims believe that Gabriel also acted as a teacher to the Prophet and this is born out in the following tradition narrated by 'A'ishah and Fatimah, a wife and daughter of the Prophet, respectively: "Gabriel would present the Qur'an to me once every year ..." (Suyuti, 1973, 1:40, Zarqani, 1996, 1:198).

> 'Abd Allah ibn Mas'ud said: the Prophet was the best of persons; And he was even better in the month of Ramadan when Gabriel met him. Gabriel used to meet him every night to teach him the Qur'an (cited in 'Inayah, 1996, 1:240).

The Companions, in turn, it is said, "gathered" the Qur'an from the Prophet in a very comprehensive sense. The following verse is seen to be referring to this task:

> He it is who has sent unto the *ummiy* (unlettered) people an apostle from among themselves, to convey unto them His messages, and to cause them to grow in purity, and to impart unto them the divine writ as well as wisdom – whereas before that they were indeed, most obviously, lost in error (62.2).

> We have sent you but as a herald of glad tidings and a warner, bearing a discourse which we have gradually unfolded so that you may read it out to humankind by stages, seeing that we have bestowed it from on high, step by step, as one revelation (17.105–6).

After receiving the revelation the Prophet would declare it to his Companions and instructed them to memorize it. There are several traditions indicating that the Companions would memorize and study five verses – some accounts say ten – at a time. They would reflect upon them and try to implement the teachings contained therein before proceeding with the next set (Zarkashi, 1972, 2:157).[2] This was also the putative beginning of a tradition of *hifz* (entrusting to memory) that continues today whereby hundreds of thousands have learnt to memorize the entire Qur'an.

While the vast majority of Muslims believe that the Prophet was unlettered – thus enhancing the miraculous nature of the Qur'an – this belief has not gone entirely undisputed.[3] There is, however, no evidence to suggest that the Prophet engaged in the actual writing of the Qur'an. While writing was not a common skill in the Prophet's time, Mecca, being a commercial center, had a number of people who could write. The Qur'an was written down by a number of scribes acting either on their own initiative or upon the instruction of the Prophet, who called for a scribe after every revelation. The following tradition, narrated by Al-Bara' ibn 'Azib (d. 690), a Companion, recounts a typical example of this:

> There was revealed "Not equal are those believers who sit [at home] and those who strive and fight in the cause of Allah" [4.95]. The Prophet said, "Call Zayd and let him bring the board, the ink pot and the scapula bone." Then he said: "Write: 'Not equal are those believers' ..." ('Asqalani, n.d., 9: 22).[4]

An interesting story relating to the transcription of revelation during the Prophet's time gives some insight into the different approaches to the history of the text. *Surah* 23, *ayah* 14 deals with the various processes of human conception and birth and details how God transforms "the essence of clay" into a fully shaped human being.

> Now indeed, We create humankind out of the essence of clay, and then We cause it to remain as a drop of sperm in [the womb's] firm keeping, and then We create out of the drop of sperm a germ-cell, and then We create out of the germ-cell an embryonic lump, and then We create within the embryonic lump bones, and then We clothe the bones with flesh – and then We bring [all] this into being as new creation: hallowed, therefore, is God, the best of artisans! (23.12–14).

Fakhr al-Din al-Razi (d. 606/1209), one of the great commentators of the Qur'an, cites 'Abd Allah ibn 'Abbas, on the authority of Kalbi, that 'Abd

2 It is somewhat difficult to understand these traditions for the assumption is that five or ten verses dealt in a neat fashion with a particular injunction or set of injunctions: something not borne out by the order of verses that we currently have with us. The notion of managing a large and ever increasing group with each individual memorizing a few verses in a coordinated manner seems rather strange for that period.
3 This is further discussed in the following chapter.
4 Suyuti also reports that the material upon which the revelation had been written upon was stored in the Prophet's house (1973, 1:81).

Allah ibn Abi Sarh often acted as a scribe to the Prophet and transcribed this verse. When he reached the section "And then we bring [all] this into being as a new creation" (23.12), he is said to have exclaimed: "Hallowed, therefore, is God, the best of artisans!" The Prophet is then reported to have said: "Write this [what you have just exclaimed] down for this is what has been revealed." Ibn Abi Sarh then doubted the Prophet's veracity, saying "if Muhammad speaks the truth, then I can also be regarded as a recipient of revelation and if he is untruthful then I do not really want to have anything to do with an imposter" (Razi, 1990, 23:86). He is said to have abandoned Islam and fled to Mecca where, according to some accounts, he re-embraced Islam when the city was taken over by the Prophet and according to others he died in a state of unbelief. Some Muslim accounts attribute a similar incident to 'Umar who, upon hearing the first part of the verse dealing with the process of human conception, made an identical exclamation. In contrast to Ibn Abi Sarh, 'Umar rejoiced in his affinity with revelation. "This [the different responses of 'Umar and Ibn Abi Sarh] is the meaning", says Razi, "of God's word 'Many are lead astray by it [i.e., the Qur'an] and many are guided by it [2.26]'" (ibid). The same incident with Ibn Abi Sarh is rendered in the following manner in the *Shorter Encyclopedia of Islam*:

> According to a curious story 'Uthman's foster-brother 'Abd Allah ibn Abi Sarh, often acted as Kur'an scribe to him [Muhammad] and he had the honour of having an enthusiastic exclamation of his on listening to the dictation of Sura 23 adopted in it. ... He boasted before the Kuraysh that he had often induced the Prophet to alter the wording of the revelations whence it ultimately came to be said that he had falsified the Kur'an (*SEI*, see "Kur'an", 277).

In contrast to the Muslim view of a blessed coincidence between the word of God and that of a human being, the *Shorter Encyclopedia of Islam* presents the one as authentic (Ibn Abi Sarh's) and makes the assumption that his word was, in fact, "adopted" by the Qur'an.[5]

Muslims hold that the Qur'an was written down in its entirety at the time of the Prophet's death. When exactly the process of transcription commenced is unclear. It would seem that at the earliest stage the Qur'an was only gathered in the Prophet's memory and that later various scribes copied his dictations. The two verses below also suggest that the Prophet forgot some of the revelations, albeit by the will of God. The fact that there

---

5 It should be noted the *surah* wherein this verse occurs is also regarded as entirely Meccan, which casts a bit of a shadow over the accuracy of this entire account.

is no record of any prophetic instruction that any text ought to be destroyed may suggest that the texts forgotten were never put in a written form:

> "We shall teach you, and you will not forget [anything of what you are taught], save what God may will [you to forget]" (87.6–7).

> Any message which We annul or consign to oblivion We replace with a better or similar one. Do you not know that God has the power to will anything? (2.106).

There are several indications of the Qur'an existing in a written – even if not textually compiled – form during the life of the Prophet and the traditions give the names of various scribes. Up to forty-eight of them have been mentioned by Azami (1974, 56), with the most prominent being Zayd ibn Thabit (d. 665) and Ubayy ibn Ka'b. Hassan ibn Thabit (d. 674), another Companion, also speaks of *khatt al-wahi* (the script of revelation) on smooth paper (papyri) while other traditions speak of the script on the bark of date palms and skin. (Zarqani, 1996, 1:203). The Qur'an refers to itself as a scripture which is handled by people: "... Behold, it is a truly noble discourse, in a well-guarded divine writ which none but the pure [of heart] can touch; a revelation from the Sustainer of the worlds" (56.76–80). 'Abd Allah ibn 'Umar narrates that the Prophet said: "Do not take the Qur'an on a journey with you, for I am afraid lest it should fall into the hands of the enemy." There was, however, no material collection of revelations in one place or form (Suyuti, 1973, 1:41).[6] Given the progressive nature of revelation that terminated only a few days before the demise of the Prophet, it could not be otherwise. These officially transcribed texts, along with what people had retained in their memories, formed the scriptural Qur'an (*mus-haf*) in its earliest stage. In a tradition which seems to post-date the demise of the Prophet and cited by Suyuti, 'Abd Allah ibn 'Umar is reported to have said, "Let none of you say, 'I have got the whole Qur'an.' How does he know what all of it is? Much of the Qur'an has gone (*d-h-b*). Let him say, instead, 'I have got much of what has survived'" (Suyuti, 1973, 3:72).

From the perspective of critical scholarship, some have argued that memorizing a narration as long as, say, the story of Joseph in the Qur'an, would not have been possible on a single recital by Gabriel (Nöldeke, 1909, 599). Muslims argue that it is created by God who is free to alter the capacity

---

6 Burton (1977, 118) cites Zayd ibn Thabit, as saying, "The Prophet died and the Qur'an had not been assembled in one place". The reference that he supplies is Ibn Hajar, 1939, 9:9. The closest that I could trace this in Ibn Hajar was ibn Hajar himself saying that the Qur'an was completely transcribed during the time of the Prophet albeit not collected in a single place (*ghayr majmu' fi mawdi'in wahid*) and with the *surahs* unsorted (*wa la murattab al-suwar*).

of whatever or whomever He wills.[7] Questions are also raised about the ability or otherwise of the Prophet to hold the process of transcribing and collating the Qur'an – even in oral form – together with a large and often varying number of scribes over a period of twenty-three years when he was also engaged in many other activities. This is seemingly a very fragile project involving all the inevitabilities of the human condition such as memory, interpretation, selection, and recollection. Referring more specifically to the writers of the Qur'an, Mohammed Arkoun raises the question thus:

> The authority of scriptural tradition is conditioned by the value of each testimony. Only the generation of the *Sahaba* [Companions] has seen and heard the circumstances and the words which are reported as the Qur'an in the Hadith and the *Sira* [prophetic history]. Historically, it is difficult, if not impossible, to assert how each reporter saw and heard the object of his report (1988, 64).

Muslims link the claim of the Prophet's absolute veracity and of God's overall protection of the process of gathering the Qur'an. The few Muslim scholars who are familiar with and even participate in critical Qur'an scholarship, while engaging in historical and textual criticism, continue to hold on to the Qur'an as the word of God, albeit in a wider sense of the expression than that understood by the vast majority of Muslims. While many respond in a defensive manner whenever the established Muslim appreciation of the Qur'an's earliest history is challenged, others go about quietly reflecting on the challenges which critical scholarship presents to Qur'anic studies. For them it is ultimately a struggle of *a priori* faith (*iman*) seeking to live in fidelity to both the Qur'an as the word of God and to one's intellect as the work of God.

A significant question here is that of the shift from the Qur'an as essentially an oral discourse to a written one. While Muslim scholarship has focused primarily on efforts to prove the textual veracity of the Qur'an, little or no attempt had been made to deal with the implications of this shift that saw the Qur'an emerging as an "Official Closed Corpus" (Arkoun, 1987a, 15). Quite a number of scholars who look at religion and scripture from a phenomenological perspective have "underscored this dichotomy between word and writ by pointing out that although the written word fixes and lends permanence to the spoken word, it also threatens to kill the originally vital spirit of the oral word by

7 Many Muslims regularly invoke developments in science and technology to support their claims. In this case, the phenomenal memory of minute computer chips is invoked to suggest that if this is what humankind are capable of creating surely the Creator of humankind can create something much more spectacular.

incarcerating it in the 'letter'" (Graham, 1980, 26). Arkoun is one of the few Muslim scholars who has dealt with the implications of this shift.

> Whatever the original form of the initial revelation, the oral discourse originally pronounced by the mediator between God and mankind has been written down on parchment or paper to become a *book* [italics in original] which I open, read, and interpret. This book itself has become the "Holy Scriptures" which means that it has been sanctified by a number of rituals, discursive strategies and methods of exegesis, related to many concrete and known – or knowable – political, social and cultural circumstances (Arkoun, 1987a, 6).

Arkoun spells out some of the consequences when an oral discourse is transformed into a written text: the sacred nature of the divine discourse is extended to the book "as the material receptacle and vehicle of the 'revelation'" (ibid., 15) and "the book" becomes an instrument of culture. This results in another significant change, i.e., "the increasing role and finally the domination of written, learned culture over oral folk culture". One of the consequences of this is the emergence of a social group called *'Ulama*, specialists in charge of exegesis of the holy texts and the orthodox elaboration and use of law and beliefs" (ibid.). These "specialists", while often functioning independently of the state, were also frequently an extension of the ruling class and employed by the state. Arkoun then argues that this invariably resulted in Qur'anic text being used as "pre-text" or a vehicle to justify state ideology, rather than a text that yields meaning independent of a particular group's agenda.

THE QUR'AN BECOMES A CANON

The Qur'an as canon is referred to as *"mus-haf"*. From the word *"suhuf"* (lit. fragments of writing material such as paper, skin, papyrus, etc.), *"mus-haf"* means the collected *suhuf*, compiled into a fixed order "between two covers".[8] Sunni scholarship on the canonization of the Qur'an is based on approximately twenty-two extant hadith pertaining to post-Prophetic compilation and transcription of the Qur'an, many of them in apparent contradiction to others. In most of these accounts the Battle of Yamamah (12/633),[9] with the resulting death of numerous

---

8 The word *"mus-haf"* is said to have been agreed upon through a consultative process soon after Abu Bakr had the compilation completed (Suyuti, 1973, 1:89).

9 The Battle of Yamama resulted from a insurrection led by one Musaylimah, who claimed prophethood for himself after Muhammad's demise, in a central district of Arabia, well to the east of Mecca and Medina. This was one of several such insurrections soon after the death of Muhammad, all of which were put down by the Muslims, albeit with heavy casualties.

qurra (Qur'an reciters), is regarded as the turning point in the textual gathering of the Qur'an. A lengthy account of this initiative undertaken by Abu Bakr, the Prophet's immediate successor, and 'Umar al-Khattab can be found in a tradition contained in Bukhari and narrated by Zayd ibn Thabit, regarded as the pre-eminent scribe of revelation:

> Abu Bakr sent for me after the casualties among the warriors of Yamamah. 'Umar was present with Abu Bakr who said; "'Umar has come to me and said: 'The people have suffered heavy casualties on the day of Yamamah, and I am afraid that there will be some casualties among the reciters of the Qur'an at other places, whereby a large part of the Qur'an may be lost, unless you collect it. I am of the opinion that you should collect the Qur'an.' Abu Bakr added: "I said to 'Umar, How can one do something which God's Apostle has not done?" 'Umar said [to me], 'By God, it is [indeed] a good thing'. So 'Umar kept on pressing, trying to persuade me to accept his proposal, till God opened my bosom for it and I had the same opinion as 'Umar".
>
> 'Umar was sitting with him [Abu Bakr] and was not speaking. Abu Bakr said [to me], "You are a wise young man and we do not suspect you of telling lies or of forgetfulness; and you used to write the divine inspiration for God's Apostle. Therefore, look for the Qur'an and collect it [in one manuscript]". By God, if he [Abu Bakr] had ordered me to shift one of the mountains it would not have been harder for me than what he had ordered me concerning the collection of the Qur'an. I said to both of them "How dare you do a thing which the Prophet has not done?" Abu Bakr said: "By God, it is [indeed] a good thing."
>
> So I kept on arguing with him about it till God opened my bosom for that which He had opened the bosoms of Abu Bakr and 'Umar. So I started locating the Qur'anic material and collecting it from parchments, scapula, leaf stalks of date palms and from the memories of people. With Khuzaymah I found two verses of *Surah al-Tawbah* [the chapter titled "Repentance"] which I had not found with anybody else (and they were); "Indeed there has come unto you an Apostle from among yourselves: Heavily weighs upon him [the thought] that you might suffer [in the life to come]; full of concern for you [is he, and] full of compassion and mercy towards the believers (9.128) (Asqalani, n.d., 9:10).

Zayd reportedly brought together all the revelations into the *suhuf* from both the oral and written sources and handed them to Abu Bakr.[10] The compilers under the leadership of Zayd are purported to have insisted on a number of conditions before accepting any text as suitable for

---

10 There are a number of traditions praising Abu Bakr for this initiative including one attributed to 'Ali; "May Allah have mercy upon Abu Bakr, he is the first to have gathered the Qur'an" (Zarkashi, 1972, 1:239).

inclusion. These conditions included the requirement that at least two witnesses should testify that they heard the recital directly from the Prophet[11] and it must have been originally written down in his presence. Furthermore, the accepted sections ought not to have represented sections of the Qur'an that the Prophet had declared as abrogated. If the above account is to be believed then, given that Abu Bakr's caliphate lasted approximately two years, it may be assumed that a single complete copy was available within two years after the demise of the Prophet.[12] Abu Bakr is reported to have bequeathed these *suhuf* to 'Umar al-Khattab, his successor. Upon Umar's death in 644 they are said to have come into the possession of his daughter Hafsah who was also a widow of the Prophet (Bukhari, 1981, 6:477–478).

It is likely that Zayd was engaged in more than one process and in different periods: the first, during Abu Bakr's reign, when he had undertaken the material collection of the *suhuf*, and another, during the period of 'Uthman, when he undertook its arrangement and editing. The second process also commences with concern about ordinary human frailties – recollection, memory, pronunciation, retention, etc., – which became particularly acute as the Muslim empire began to spread and time moved on. This is reflected in the following statement attributed to Abu Qullabah on the authority of Malik ibn Anas, a Companion:

> During the Caliphate of 'Uthman, different teachers were teaching different readings to their students. Thus it used to happen that that the students would meet and disagree. The matter reached the point that they would take their dispute to their teachers, who would denounce each other as heretics (*kaffara ba'duhum ba'da*). This situation reached 'Uthman's ears. He delivered an oration saying: "You are here by me, yet you disagree on the reading and pronunciation of the Qur'an. Therefore, those who are far away from me in the provinces must be in greater dispute ... (ibn Abi Dawud, cited in Zarqani, 1996, 1:210).

11 Zayd was evidently not always able to find more than one witness as an account by Ibn Shihab indicates. "A verse from [*Surah*] Al-Ahzab was left out when we copied the *mus-haf*. I had heard the Prophet of God, peace be upon him, read it but did not find it with anyone except with Khuzaymah. [It was the verse] 'among the believers are men who have [always] been true to what they have vowed before God' and I inserted it in its *Surah*. Thus Khuzaymah al-Ansari's witness was the equivalent of two witnesses" (Zarkashi, 1972, 1:234). "Furthermore,", says Zarkashi, "Khuzaymah's testimony was really in addition to that of Zayd's" (ibid.).

12 *The Shorter Encyclopaedia of Islam* argues that according to lists handed down of the martyrs of the Battle of Yamamah, most were new converts to Islam and it is unlikely that they had any extensive knowledge of the Qur'an. Furthermore, the period between the Battle of Yamamah (633) and the death of Abu Bakr (634) is "too short" for the accomplishment of such a task (Gibb & Kramers, 1974, 278).

This statement casts a further shadow around the putative finality of the earlier process which Zayd had engaged in and the notion of an official codex lodged with Hafsah.[13] While a loose collection may have been completed then, the arrangement and editing seem to have taken place much later. During the time of 'Uthman's reign, a major impetus for this task was the concern expressed by Hudhayfah ibn al-Yaman, who led the Muslim forces against the Armenians in Azerbaijan. He was deeply perturbed at the quarreling that had broken out among soldiers from different areas of the then Muslim world. Upon his return to Medina he urged the Caliph to ensure the proper collection of the Qur'an. 'Uthman then selected Zayd for this task. Traditional Muslim scholarship holds that Zayd took the *suhuf* in Hafsah's possession and, with the assistance of a group of scribes comprising 'Abd Allah ibn Zubayr, 'Abd al-Rahman ibn al-Harith, and Sa'd ibn al-'As, prepared a text faithful to the language/dialect of the Quraysh, the Prophet's tribe (Zarkashi, 1972, 1:236). Copies of this new version were sent to Damascus, Basra, and Kufa and another copy was kept at Medina.[14] Orders were given to destroy all other versions, and, as indicated earlier, the extent of compliance with these orders seems to vary in different places. Given the conflict ridden nature of 'Uthman's rule, it would seem somewhat strange for such a process to be undertaken and completed in the neat manner that later Muslim writings hold. The vehemently apologetic nature with which most Muslim scholars, even the earlier ones, present this account suggests that the battle for the authenticity of this process as well as its final product may have lasted longer than what traditional opinion may suggest. This is also evident from some traditions attributed to 'Ali ibn Abi Talib, which were meant to respond to accusations against 'Uthman. "O People! Fear Allah and desist from exaggeration and your assertions that 'Uthman destroyed the *mus-haf*. By God, he did not destroy it except upon the advice of the companions of the Prophet of God" (cf. Zarqani, 1996, 1:214; see also Zarkashi, 1972, 1:240). As-Sa'id cites Ibn Qayyim al-Jawziyyah on an interesting justificatory parable for 'Uthman's actions:

> A house may have many roads leading to it. If it is the ruler's judgment that allowing people to use all the roads causes conflicts and confusion then he may decide to permit the use of one road only, forbidding the

13 There is no record of Zayd's initial collection gaining public circulation. This could be attributed to other intervening factors other than that it did not exist. The absence of public circulation and the fact that it ended up with Hafsah, who was not a public figure, is another indication of its lack of official public status.
14 Some accounts suggest that seven copies were produced including ones supposedly destined for Mecca, Bahrain, and Yemen (Zarkashi, 1972, 1:240).

others. He does not thereby abolish the roads as such, as they could still lead to the house; he merely forbids their use (1975, 25).

THE SHI'I PERSPECTIVE

There is consensus around the fact that 'Ali produced a copy of the Qur'an that differed at least in arrangement from that subsequently accepted as the authenticated canon (Suyuti, 1973, 1:62) and mainstream Shi'ism, both Seveners and Twelvers, hold that this was the only difference between the 'Uthmanic codex and that produced by 'Ali. Some twenty traditions[15] suggest that the canon produced by 'Ali's predecessors willfully excluded all explicit references to his legitimate prior claim to the Prophet's mantle. The following two traditions traced to Abu 'Muhammad ibn 'Ali Baqir (d. 114/732) and another to Jabir, a companion of the Prophet, and cited by Abu'l Qasim al-Khu'i (1998, 156), are examples of this:

> a) The Messenger of God prayed in Mina. Then he said: "O People, I leave among you al-thaqalayn [the two stable/weighty ones]. If you hold on to them, you shall never be misguided. [These are] the Book of God and my family,[16] and the Ka'bah is the Sacred House." Then Abu Ja'far [al-Baqir] added: "As for the Book of God, they have altered it; the Ka'bah they have destroyed and the family they have slain. All these trusts of God they have abandoned and from them they have rid themselves."

> b) Three [entities] will come complaining on the Day of Resurrection: the Book [Qur'an], the mosque [the Sacred Mosque in Mecca] and the Family [of the Prophet]. The Book will say: "O Lord, they have altered me and rented me." The mosque will say, "O Lord they have abandoned and wasted me." The Family will say: "They killed, rejected and dispersed us."

A small group of early extremist Shi'i's questioned the integrity of the 'Uthmanic codex alleging that two surahs, "al-Nurayn" (The Two Lights) and "al-Walayah" (The Guardianship) – both supposedly dealing with the virtues of the Prophet's family – were excised and that a "true copy" was secretly transmitted by each Imam until a clear exposition of it will emerge with the coming of the Hidden Imam. Al-Khu'i (d. 1992), a great contemporary Shi'i scholar of the Qur'an, painstakingly examines

15 These traditions are largely invoked by those who supported 'Ali's claims to the Caliphate over that of Abu Bakr, 'Umar, and 'Uthman, and the pre-eminence of the Prophet's family,

16 The Sunni version of this same hadith speaks about the "the Book of God and the practice of His Prophet" (Sunnah). One can thus see how the Prophet's family becomes a source of law for Shi'i Muslims whereas for Sunnis, it is the Prophet's practice.

all the relevant hadith in Sunni sources and argues that their account above opens the question of the Qur'an's authenticity to a number of problems. He argues for the authenticity of the Qur'an on the basis that it was compiled during the lifetime of the Prophet and that the distinction between the oral collection (*jam'*) and transcription (*tadwin*) is an unfounded one (1998, 105–176). Al-Khu'i basis his arguments on several traditions where the Prophet reportedly played an active role in the arrangement of the text and where the Qur'an was recited as a composite whole. Above all, he relies on a hadith, often referred to as the *"thaqalayn* tradition". ("I leave among you two things of high estimation: the Book of God and my descendents. These two will never separate until they return to me by the pond [*kawthar*])"; (Al-Khu'i, 1998, 29).[17] Al-Khu'i is evidently motivated by a deep desire to uphold the authenticity of the Qur'an and possibly also by the ideological need or sectarian impulse to detract from 'Uthman's pivotal role in the Sunni account of the collection process. However, it remains difficult to understand the proliferation of various and conflicting accounts of the Qur'an's compilation and transmission if there were indeed a single undisputed copy of the text available during the Prophet's lifetime, even allowing for some flexibility about the place where the very last revelations before his death had to be located. Sunni scholars argue that the notion of "'Ali's own version", which supposedly differed in arrangement from the dominant readings, is disproved by the fact that neither did 'Ali oppose the dominant readings during the period of the Prophet's successors who preceded him – Abu Bakr, Umar, and 'Uthman – nor did he seek to impose his version upon his own assumption of that office when he was in a position to do so.[18] Like the work of John Burton, *The Collection of the Qur'an*, which arrives at the conclusion that the Qur'an was really fully gathered during the time of the Prophet, Al-Khu'i's conclusion may, at a superficial glance, lead to a firmer belief in the authenticity of the Qur'an. The problem though is in the methodology which both apply. The methods of both Burton and Al-Khu'i, which emphasize the internal contradiction of Muslim sources, must inevitably lead to a questioning of the entire hadith literature upon which the history of the Qur'an's compilation is based.[19]

17 The pond is a reference to a well where the believers will seek refuge from the thirst on the Day of Judgment.
18 Shi'is generally argue that 'Ali and his supporters had remained silent on this issue to in order to preserve the unity of the community (cf. Tabataba'i, 1996, 100),
19 The correspondence between Burton and Al-Khu'is arguments and source material is astounding and would provide fascinating material for one studying the way critical scholarship feeds on Muslim confessional scholarship without acknowledgment.

NON-MUSLIM CRITICAL QUR'ANIC SCHOLARSHIP

The area of criticism ranges from the very notion of the Prophet having been the recipient of divine revelation – rather, challenging any notions of divinity and all notions of divine revelation – to the compilation, transcription, and dissemination of the Qur'an. Some of these scholars also refer to a number of debates around the authenticity of various parts of the Qur'an among some sections of the early Muslims. These included the rejection by some of the Kharijites[20] of the twelfth *surah* (*Joseph*) as a "silly love story", the early Shi'i questioning of the integrity of the Uthmanic version, the accusation that two *surahs* were deliberately omitted by 'Uthman, and the supposed additional *surahs* in Abu Musa and Ubayy's recension. Others have argued that the idea of the Qur'anic text reaching finality under 'Uthman is essentially motivated by dogmatic factors rather than historical evidence. While all of this leads to the conclusion that there was no definitive canon at the time of 'Uthman's death, others such as John Burton (1977) argue that the Prophet himself had prepared and sanctioned a complete written Qur'an that he had left behind upon his demise. Burton, ignoring the fact that the Qur'an is not really a book of legal precepts but one of moral guidance and that very few of the variations on the 'Uthmanic canon have an actual legal significance, advances the theory that the Muslim jurists found themselves deprived of flexibility in their rulings by the need to honor this original text. In response they invented both the notion of variant readings and the account of 'Uthman's collection. "The exclusion of the Prophet from the collection of the Qur'an was a prime desideratum of the *usulis* [legalists] wrestling with the serious problems generated by some of their own theoretical positions" (Burton, 1977, 160).

In a broader sense and with the exception of Burton, these scholars have challenged the idea of any neat compilation and transcription of the Qur'an, arguing that it evolved gradually in the seventh and eight centuries and that the reason no original source material from that period has survived is quite simply because none ever existed. As I said in the introduction, they regard Islamic tradition as just another example of salvation history whereby the story of the origins of one's religion is

---

20 The Kharijites are one of Islam's earliest sects which played an important role in continual insurrections against 'Ali and the Umayyads. They first emerged during the conflict between 'Ali and Mu'awiyah which culminated in the Battle of Siffin (July, 657). They refused to allow the matter to be resolved by mediation, instead insisting that "judgment belongs to God alone".

invented afterwards and projected back in time in order to accommodate current socio-cultural or political needs. Crone and Cook (1977), following Wansbrough, conclude that the Qur'an "is strikingly lacking overall structures, frequently obscure and inconsequential in both language and content, perfunctory in its linking of disparate materials and given to the repetition of whole passages in variant versions." On this basis, they argue that the Qur'an is the product of the belated and imperfect editing of materials from a plurality of traditions, initially it – or rather components of what later came to be the Qur'an – was just part of an extensive corpus of the prophetical *logia* (Wansbrough, 1977, 1). Their problems with the traditional Muslim account of the transcription of the text are also reflected in three major areas: (1) the development of the Arabic script; (2) the existence of several variant copies of the Qur'an; and (3) the variant readings of the text.

THE GRADUAL DEVELOPMENT OF THE ARABIC SCRIPT

The notion of the Qur'an being transcribed by Zayd ibn Thabit (or a committee) in the dialect of the Quraysh is challenged by the fact that the means did not exist at that time to "indicate the subtle differences that would differentiate one dialect from another" (Adams, 1987, 12:163). The Arabic script as we know it today was unknown in the Prophet's time and the Qur'an was recorded in a *scripta defectiva* made up of simple lines and strokes. Early Qur'anic Arabic thus lacked precision because distinguishing between consonants was impossible given the absence of diacritical marks (*a'jam*) by which one recognizes these in modern Arabic. Furthermore, the vowelling marks (*tashkil*) to indicate prolongation or vowels were also absent. All of this made for endless possibilities in meanings and error in transcription. An example of this is the case where a simple "*u*" on the pronoun "*h*" (his) after word *rasul* (prophet) in 9.3 led to the following reading: "That God dissolves obligations towards [*both*] the pagans and his Prophet." When the vowel "*u*" on the pronoun is replaced with the vowel "*i*" the meaning is as follows: "That God and his Apostle dissolve obligations with the pagans." While some form of the *a'jam* or diacritical marks were known in pre-Islamic times they were rarely used. It is widely believed that they were first introduced for wider usage by the Caliph 'Abd al-Malik al-Marwan (d. 705). Even then only dots were used above, below, or at the beginning of a letter to indicate vowels. The Arabic script as we know it today, the *scripta plena*, with its pointed texts and being fully vowelled was not perfected until the middle of the ninth century.

THE EXISTENCE OF SEVERAL VARIANT CODICES

'Uthman's project to compile the Qur'an was clearly in response to the proliferation of "unauthorized copies" during his time – partly as a result of the problems of the Arabic script of that time. Early Muslim scholars such as Ibn Ashtah (d. 360/970–971), Ibn Abi Dawud (d. 316/928–929), and Ibn al-Anbari (d. 328/939–940) also dealt with these variant codices. Some of these codices seem to have been in use well after the official canon was produced and up to well into the fourth Islamic century. In Kufa, for example, the version of 'Abd Allah ibn Mas'ud remained in vogue for some time and there are indications that he refused instructions to stop teaching his version and to destroy copies of it. Traditional Muslim scholars argue that the period of Ibn Mas'ud's version's persistence and its strength had been exaggerated and that the wisdom of 'Uthman's course of action had become apparent to Ibn Mas'ud fairly early (Zarqani, 1996, 1:214, cf. 224–228).[21] The extra-canonical texts never gained general approval and were viewed by Muslims as the personal copies of individuals worth retaining for their exegetical value.

VARIANT READINGS OR MODES

One of the ways that traditional scholarship has dealt with the variety of readings of the Qur'an is the notion that the Qur'an was revealed in seven "modes." The legitimacy for the variety of modes can, in fact, be traced back to several traditions of the Prophet through a number of Companions which suggest that these various readings are an expression of the Divine will. 'Umar is said to have complained to the Prophet that Hisham ibn Hakim recited *Surah al-Furqan* (*The Criterion*) in a way different from what he had heard from the Prophet. The Prophet sent for ibn Hisham and after the latter read the text that 'Umar had disputed, the Prophet told 'Umar "... this Qur'an has been revealed in seven different

---

21 Among the better known ones were those attributed to Zayd ibn Thabit (Hijaz), 'Abd Allah ibn Mas'ud (Kufa), Abu Musa al-'Ash'ari (Basra), Miqdad ibn Amr (Hims), and Ubayy ibn Ka'b (Damascus). The version attributed to 'Abd Allah ibn Mas'ud, for example, did not contain the *Fatihah* (*The Opening*) and some versions lacked the last two chapters. Labib as-Sa'id argues that this was in all likelihood because these *surahs* were so well known that that did not warrant being written down in a private text (1975, 35). Jeffery has listed fifteen primary codices and a large number of secondary extra-canonical recensions, while Von Denffer's *Ulum al-Qur'an* has a detailed list of the differences in various recensions recorded by classical scholars and commentators (1983, 46–52).

ways, so recite of it whatever is easier for you". (Asqalani, 9:94) In another tradition cited in Bukhari, 'Abd Allah ibn 'Abbas narrated that the Prophet said: "Gabriel recited the Qur'an to me in one way ('ala harfin). I then requested him [to read it in another way] and continued asking him to recite it other ways and he recited it in several ways till he recited it in seven different ways." (ibid., 23). Some scholars have attempted to make a distinction between a variety of modes (ahruf) and a variety of readings (qira'ah), both having settled at the number seven with the idea that "modes" relate to interpretation and qira'ah to recitation (cf. Al-Nimr, 1983, 152–159). The immediate impact that any change in recitation has on the meaning of the verse, though makes such a distinction rather futile. In most earlier writings the two words were used interchangeably alongside "wujuh" (facets) and lughat (dialects or languages), suggesting that the Qur'an had several facets to it. All of this seems to point to the fact that the Qur'an was read in a variety of ways and its meanings were seen as multifaceted before the subsequent more rigid ways inherent in canonization.[22] A major problem for traditional Sunni scholarship is the lack of unanimity around explanations of the meaning of various modes, their extent and impact. Abu al-Hatim ibn Hubban, in fact, says that there are at least thirty-five different opinions on this issue (cited in Zarkashi, 1972, 1:214). Some of these are listed as follows:

1. That this hadith is nearly impossible to understand because the Arabs used the word "harf" to described a coherent word, a single letter, a facet, and the meaning of a word.
2. The seven ahruf are synonomous with the seven readings, all of them encapsulated in the canon of 'Uthman.
3. The Qur'an employed words with identical meanings from different languages or dialects.
4. Different dialects had different ways of pronunciation among the various tribes and this impacted upon the spelling of the words, e.g., al-tabuh and al-tabut (2.248), hiyaka for iyyaka (1.5), and atta for hatta (12.35).
5. The use of synonyms, e.g., irshida for ihdina in 1.6 when both mean "guide us".
6. The variety of injunctions or themes of the Qur'an.

---

22 Wansbrough holds that the "companion codices" which contained the variant readings were really "manufactured from exegetical material in support of an argument central to the traditional account of canonization, namely the 'Uthmanic recension. Much of the material persisted anyway in the form of standard deviations from the canon, accommodated by the ahruf doctrine" (1977, 204). See also pp. 208–227.

7. Various ways of reading the same word, such as the word *amanah* in 23.8 which can be read as both "trust" (*amānatihim*) and "trusts" (*amānātihim*).

8. Different wordings of a particular passage such as 9.100 – "Gardens under which rivers flow" – which others read as "Gardens from under which rivers flow" because they adhere to the grammatical implication of the insertion of the word "*min*" (from) to the text.

Some scholars such as Tabari and Zarkashi hold that the Qur'an currently with Muslims comprises only one of the seven *ahruf*; this being the last repeated reading done by the Prophet in the presence of Gabriel and which served the purpose for abrogating the rest, a subject dealt with in chapter six. Others argue that the current codex is capable of bearing all seven *ahruf*. In an attempt to make a distinction between the "divinely sanctioned" various modes and the later developed "readings", Von Denffer concludes his discussion on the seven modes by saying that "they are the basis of several distinct ways of reciting the Qur'an, reflecting the different usage at the time of revelation, comprising variations in pronunciations and even minor differences in wording." Although much of what the seven contain is also found in the seven *ahruf* (modes) they are not identical and came about at "a later stage" (1983, 117). In a description of the seven variant readings (*qira'at*), in which there are hardly any significant deviations from the seven variant modes (*ahruf*), Von Denffer explains the readings as "different forms of oral recitations of the Qur'an as well as punctuation of the written text which corresponds to the oral recitation" (ibid.).

In an interesting example of how non-confessional scholarship would see confusion at best and contradiction at worse and confessional scholarship sees the uniqueness of the Qur'an, Abu'l 'Ala Mawdudi uses two texts from the Qur'an to show how different readings, in fact, elucidate the meaning of the text. The word "*maliki*" [on the Day of Resurrection] in *Surah Fatiha* (*The Opening*) can be read with or without prolonging the "*a*" sound. Without a prolongation the word means "sovereign" and by prolongation it means "master" or "owner". Mawdudi concludes that there is no contradiction between the two; quite the contrary, "These two readings make the meaning of the verse all the more clear" (cited in Von Denffer, 1983, 118). The second example comes from *Surah 5, ayah* 6 where a seemingly insignificant matter as reading a word with an accusative ending rather than a genitive ending could determine the nature of the ablutions before prayers. The verse reads as follows: "When you arise for prayers then wash your faces and your hands up to your elbows; rub [your wet hands (*mas-h*)] over (*bi*) your heads and your feet up to your ankles." When the word "your feet" is read as "*arjulakum*", then it is the third object of "wash" and the implication is that one's feet must be washed as a part of ablutions. Reading it as the second genitive of the preposition *bi*, as in "*arjulikum*", means that one can merely pass a wet hand over them. Mawdudi argues that both versions are acceptable for, under normal circumstances, you are required to wash your feet as part of the ablution and, under exceptional circumstances, such as when you are on a long journey, you are allowed to just wipe them with a wet hand. Thus God is able to supply you with two injunctions for separate circumstances by allowing flexibility in the reading (paraphrased from Von Denffer, 1983, 118).

Within the different versions of the codex in circulation there were also a diversity of readings in particular verses and this has been acknowledged by Sunni classical commentators and scholars of the Qur'an. The systematization of the various readings and a significant stage in its more definite canonization was achieved by Abu Bakr Ahmad ibn Mujahid, (d. c. 935) the Baghdad linguist who fixed a single system of consonants and placed a limit on the variations of vowels which were employed in the text. His systematization resulted in the acceptance of seven variant readings with each of the seven readings being traced through two chains of narrators and where the reading through the one chain may have differed somewhat from that of the other.[23] These seven variant readings are as follows:

1. Nafi from Medina (d. 785) as transmitted through Warsh and/or Qalun;
2. Ibn Kathir from Mecca (d. 737) as transmitted through al-Bazzi and/or Qunbul;
3. Ibn Amir from Damascus (d. 736) as transmitted through Hisham and/or Ibn Dhakwan;
4. Abu Amr from Basra (d. 770) as transmitted through al-Durri and/or al-Susi;
5. Asim from Kufa (d. 744) as transmitted through Hafs and/or Abu Bakr;

---

23 The notion of seven variants took a considerable while to become the dominant. Some claimed that there were ten variant readings and others claimed that there were fourteen.

6. Hamza from Kufa (d. 772) as transmitted through Khalaf and/or Khallad;
7. Al-Kisa'i from Kufa (d. 189) as transmitted through al-Duri and/or Abu al-Harith.

With the passing of time three variants predominated: those of Warsh transmitted via Nafi, Hafs transmitted via Asim, and Al-Durri transmitted via Abu Amr. Currently, with the exception of large parts of West and Central Africa where the reading of Warsh is widespread, elsewhere in the Muslim world, the reading of Hafs, popularized during the reign of Egypt's King Fu'ad (d. 1936), and first printed in 1925, is virtually the only one known to Muslims. All the other variants though are still studied and practiced by the *qurra*, those who specialize in the reading of the Qur'an. Given that the Qur'an is not only a recited scripture but also one that forms the basis of Muslim philosophy and law, the variant readings are also significant for exegesis and more so for Islamic law.[24]

WORLDS APART

Much critical scholarship is necessarily based on empirical proof or the lack thereof. Of course, the fact that something cannot be proven to have existed by one's own peculiar standards of measuring the veracity of the sources does not mean that it did not exist. Critical scholarship relies – understandably, though perhaps – unduly – on assumptions flowing from the absence of hard evidence. And of course, if there were such indications in the hadith literature then they would be subjected to other tests and in all likelihood be dismissed as part of "salvation history". Yet this hadith literature yields much "usable" material for the same group of scholars whenever the case against the traditional account of the Prophet's life or the Qur'an's revelation and transmission can be

24 Al-Khu'i has devoted two chapters to systematically examine all the Sunni traditions on the variety of readings and modes. He moves from the premise that "differences in the reading ... cause confusion between what is from the Qur'an and what is not, and make it difficult from the point of form and vocalization ..." (1998, 111). By a somewhat polemical deconstruction of these accounts he concludes that the idea of a variety of readings is unfounded in the "true" prophetic traditions. None of these readings, he argues, have "reached through single narrations" and some of them "have neither been acknowledged nor confirmed as trustworthy" (ibid., 105). Like his arguments on the collection of the Qur'an, al-Khu'i's conclusions really result in circumventing a morass of exceptionally difficult arguments and contradictory claims about diverse readings and a firmer belief in the soundness of the *mus-haf* which Muslims currently posses. Yet, the way he marshals all the putative traditions and then systematically goes about attacking their authenticity invariably places the entire corpus of traditional material on an even more unstable footing.

challenged. Examples of these are the account of the Satanic verses, and
'Abd Allah ibn Abi Sarh's supposed apostasy examined earlier, which are
invariably accepted as "certainly reliable because they go against the
grain of Muslim tradition". Similarly, the *Encyclopaedia of Islam*
contains a long list of "incidents" and arguments against the Muslim
account of canonization, much of it based on Hadith material.[25]
Humphreys puts the dilemma facing revisionist scholars in the following
way:

> So long as we restrict our consideration to the earliest historical tradition
> per se, we cannot get beyond circular arguments. That is, if we begin by
> asserting that the earliest Muslims could not have thought in a certain
> way, we will then reject any text which shows them thinking in that
> manner. But in fact we have no basis whatever for such assertions except
> the very texts which we are trying to evaluate (1991, 89).

Other than the regular defences of the Qur'an in polemical literature
and on the Internet, recent years have seen Muslim scholars seriously
considering the criticisms of their account of the Qur'an's transmission
and problems relating to it. Scholars such Muhammad 'Abdul 'Azim
al-Zarqani (1996, 1:216–236) and Ghazi 'Inayah (1996, 1:297–311),
both traditional scholars based in Cairo, have devoted chapters in their
scholarly works to a systematic rebuttal of the accusations regarding the
authenticity of the 'Uthmanic canon. Labib as-Sa'id has also devoted a
chapter in his work *The Recited Koran* to "The Defense of the 'Uthmanic
Canon". However, the overall framework of the critique offered by the
revisionists is still regrettably largely ignored by traditional Muslim and
non-Muslim scholarship. Without exception, Muslims regard the text in
their possession today as going back to the Uthmanic recension without
any change or variation of any kind. They believe this version, in turn, to
be identical to the one recited and used during the Prophet's lifetime. In
support of their position, they forward the following arguments:

1. There was a strong culture of memorization of the Qur'an (*hifz*)
   during the Prophet's lifetime and text criticism seem to ignore or
   downplay the role of memorization in the compilation of the Qur'an.
2. The entire Qur'an, however it was then constituted, was read
   during the optional prayers in Ramadan.

See also how Wansbrough makes extensive (and uncritical) use of traditional accounts of the
encounter between Ja'far ibn Abi Talib, one of the early Muslim who migrated to Ethiopia,
and the Negus, in order to advance his idea that the Qur'an comprises a collage of already
existing homilies and argument, "prophetic logia" which later found their way into the
Qur'an (1977, 38–43).

3. The process of writing the text down and its arrangement was a regular task in the Prophet's circles.

4. Many of the accounts of extra-canonical recensions seem to be exempt from critical scrutiny and are, in fact, based on unreliable sources.

All of these discussions rotate around numerous hadith, their validity, chains of narration, meanings of words in the text itself, the definitions of technical terms such as *naskh* (abrogation/annulment/suspension) and the legitimacy/usefulness of, or need for, sources external to the Muslims, etc. A detailed discussion on these questions is outside the ambit of this work. Somewhere between the confessional insistence on a neat and clinical collection process and the critical position that the process of compiling the Qur'an took several centuries one may find a way of reconciling some of these tensions; and the faithful may retain the deep seated belief in the authenticity of the text while being able to look the facts of history in the eye. Alas, the facts are never as uncomplicated as the fundamentalist (religious or secularist) may want to insist; even if they are, they still require a person to approach them and people, like facts, also exist within history and carry their own histories within them. Any scripture should be understood in terms of its relation to its audience at any given point in time. As William Graham has pointed out "So long as one uses 'scripture' unreflectively to refer to a document rather than to a document as it is understood by those for whom it is *more than a document,* the meaning of scripture as an important phenomenon in religious life and history will be inaccessible" (1980, 27).

5 THE PROPHET AND THE BEGOTTEN-NOT-CREATED QUR'AN

For Muslims the Qur'an is the literal word of God. It is God speaking, not merely to the Prophet in seventh-century Arabia, but from all eternity to all humankind. It represents, as Wilfred Cantwell Smith says, "the eternal breaking through time; the knowable disclosed; the transcendent entering history and remaining here, available to mortals to handle and to appropriate; the divine become apparent" (Smith, 1980, 490). As we have seen in the previous chapter, the predominant Muslim thinking is emphatic about the otherness of the Qur'an. A neat distinction is thus made between the words of God – regarded as rehearsed or recited revelation (*wahi matlu'*) – and the words as well as works of the Prophet – regarded as unrehearsed or unrecited revelation (*wahi ghayr matlu'*). While the former is used in recitation, and can be relied on for authenticity in both its words and meaning with absolute certainty, the latter is not recited, its wording is conjectural and is reliable only for its meaning. Suyuti describes the differences in the two forms of revelation as follows:

> As to the first kind, God says to Gabriel: "Tell the Prophet to whom I sent you that God tells him to do such and such". And he ordered him to do something. Gabriel understood what his Lord had told him. Then he descended with this to the Prophet and told him, but the expression [which Gabriel used] is not the same [as God's original] expression, just as a king says to someone upon whom he relies: tell so and so: the king tells you: "Do not fail in my service, and do not let the army break up, and call for fighting, etc.". In this case, [the Messenger] has not lied, nor abbreviated [the message].

> And as to the other kind, God says to Gabriel: "Read to the Prophet, this [piece of] writing and Gabriel descended with it from God, without altering it in the least, just as [if] a king writes a written instruction and hands it over to his trustworthy servant and says to him: "Read it to so-and-so."

The Prophet's life and the Qur'an are really thoroughly interwoven and many, including Muslims scholars, have argued that there is much more to this relationship than the neat distinction which is drawn by traditional scholarship between the two forms of revelation: Qur'an and Hadith. We return to the theme of interwovenness after a discussion on the dogma around the Qur'an, the developments leading thereto, and a note on the putatively non-recited revelation – the *sunnah*.

RECITED REVELATION: DEVELOPMENT OF DOCTRINE REGARDING THE QUR'AN

In order fully to appreciate confessional Muslim scholarship's refusal to deal with this area of grayness it is necessary to understand the two key doctrinal developments that have shaped Muslim, particularly Sunni Muslim, appreciation of the Qur'an and Qur'anic scholarship. These are the doctrines of the Qur'an's eternalness (*detain*) and its inimitability (*'ijaz*). While the eternal relevance of the Qur'an has for long been regarded as synonymous with a Qur'an divested of time and space, the history of the Qur'an and of its interpretation prove otherwise, as anyone concerned with the Qur'an as a functional or contextual scripture will soon discover. In order to relate Qur'anic meaning to the present, Muslims are compelled to relate to it from the distance of some historical moment. Both the doctrines of the Qur'an's eternalness and its inimitability have profoundly affected the nature of Qur'anic scholarship and account for the absence of historico-literary criticism in Qur'anic Studies (*'Ulum al-Qur'an*). Reflections on these two doctrines also show a consistent trend in the early period of the formation of Islamic theology from a broader interpretation of dogma to a narrower one and a clear relationship between doctrine and socio-political reality or history. While I shall focus on two key doctrines and their role in the shaping of Qur'anic scholarship, it will be important to remember that these doctrinal developments converged with others in the field of tradition and jurisprudence to systematically increase the space of the unthinkable in Islamic theology.

THE DOCTRINE OF INIMITABILITY ('IJAZ)

Theological formulae, notwithstanding their "truth" or otherwise, and the intensity of the believer's commitment to them are, in addition to whatever else they may be, the result of intellectual labor which has often endured for centuries. This labor is invariably accompanied and often also shaped by religio-political disputes and it is thus logical to conclude that these disputes will affect theological developments to a considerable extent. From the beginning of Islam, Muslims have upheld the notion of the miraculous and inimitable nature of the Qur'an as proof of Muhammad's prophethood. "Indeed", says Muhammad al-Baqillani (d. /1013), "(his) prophethood is built upon this miracle" (1930, 13), a miracle which "abides from its revelation up to the day of resurrection" (ibid.). The belief that the Qur'anic revelations cannot be equaled or surpassed by any human power in its eloquence and its contents acquired a more precise form in the teaching that each Prophet was given a verifying miracle and that the Prophet Muhammad's miracle was the Qur'an.[1] Muslims maintain that the Prophet was illiterate and, therefore, incapable of producing any literary work, least of all such "exquisite literary perfection" as the Qur'an. The Qur'an refers to the Prophet as *"al-nabiyy al-ummiy"*, which Muslims have interpreted as the "unlettered Prophet". The etymology of the word *"ummiy"* is disputed by some critical scholars who maintain that the Prophet's supposed illiteracy was a later Muslim invention to lend polemical support to the concept of the Qur'an's uniqueness (cf. Bell, 1970, 34–36). The doubts raised by critical scholarship are supported by some of the early scholars of the Qur'an. Tabari, citing the case of the Prophet actually writing some parts of the Treaty of Hudaybiyyah, says that the Prophet could write "albeit not well" (cited in al-Baqillani, 1930, 37). Baqillani, despite suggesting that *"ummiyyah"* implies illiteracy, cautiously describes the Prophet's *ummiyyah* as "he could not write and did not read well" (*ibid.*).

From the beginning of announcing his prophethood Muhammad encountered intense and bitter opposition to his mission from his tribe, the Quraysh. One of the forms that this opposition took was to denounce the source of his claims and thereby, his truthfulness. He was at various times accused of being bewitched, possessed by a demon (*jinn*), a lunatic

---

1 Ibn Qutaybah gives a larger polemical context to these claims when he says that the miracles of Moses reflected an era of sorcery (*zaman al-sihr*), those of Jesus, an era of medicine (*zaman al-tibb*), and those of Muhammad an age of eloquence (*zaman al-bayan*) (1954, 10).

and thus unworthy of being followed. Furthermore, as we saw in the previous chapter, the new literary style of the Qur'an had little in common with the Arabic poetry of the time. It was thus dismissed as fabrication produced with the assistance of others. The Prophet's opponents were challenged by the Qur'an to "produce another discourse like it" (52.34), "ten *surahs* of similar merit" (11.13), or even "just one *surah*" (10.38). The Qur'an then confidently declared that "they would not be able to produce the like thereof, even if they were to exert all their strength in aiding one another" (17.88). The apparent failure of the Prophet's opponents to take up the challenge – Suyuti says "none of them has been recorded as having busied himself with this" (1973, 117) – was regarded as vindication of the Qur'an's divine origin. Muslim tradition identifies very few such attempts. "What remain of these attempts", says Boullata, "understandably suppressed by orthodoxy, are snippets of ludicrous parodies that have a hollow ring to them and that do no credit to their authors" (Boullata 1988, 141).[2]

The necessity to prove the truthfulness of the Prophet's mission within the concrete religio-social situation of proclamation and rejection thus "necessitated" or "occasioned" the texts dealing with this challenge. After the Prophet's demise this necessity merged with the need to provide the Muslim community with a waterproof authority for doctrine. The result was a systematic concept of *i'jaz*, i.e. the unique and miraculous nature of the Qur'an. While the supernatural nature of the Qur'anic revelation had, from the beginning, been the "primary postulate and justification" for Muhammad's prophethood, the term *i'jaz*, acquired its technical meaning only at the time of Ahmad ibn Hanbal (d. 855). Most scholars agree that it was first elaborated fully by the Mu'tazilites, the pioneers of scholastic theology in Islam, about whom I shall say a bit more shortly. The apparent unanimity around the doctrine of uniqueness is not always well-founded in early Qur'anic scholarship and what exactly formed the core or basis of its inimitability was never really resolved (cf. Von Grunebaum 'I'djaz' in *Encyclopaedia of Islam*, 1987, 3:1018–20). Some of the Mu'tazilite scholars, the pioneers of scholastic theology in Islam, argued that the Qur'an was not unique by itself but that any actual attempt to imitate it is rendered futile by God. This

2 Wansbrough locates these challenges within an expectedly Judeo-Christian context when he suggests that it was tied to a project to develop Arabic as a *lingua sacra* and the "elaboration of Islam characterized by its exclusively Arabian origins" (1977, 81). "Exegesis of the *tahaddi* (challenge) verses, in order to underline the complete failure to meet the challenge (*mu'arada*: the absence of logic in that reasoning was never admitted), presupposed the specifically Arabic eloquence of all contestants. When this failed, as indeed they must, how could the claim to inimitability be denied?" (ibid).

concept of deflection, *sarfa* (lit. "turning away"), described by Wansbrough as a "slightly unrealistic" and "unsatisfactory" argument "whose very terms were self-defeating" (1977, 80), was rejected by the majority consensus which insisted that the intrinsic linguistic, stylistic, and meaning supremacy of the Qur'an was an inseparable component of the idea of uniqueness. Dissent, however, loomed for a long while to come. 'Ali ibn Hazm (d. 1064), the famous Spanish-Arabic theologian, for example, refused to acknowledge the aesthetic qualities of the Qur'an as proof of its uniqueness and denied that the word of God could in any way be compared to human speech (Ibn Hazm, n.d., 3:15 ff.), while 'Abd al-Malik al-Juwayni (d. 1085), who served as an imam of both the sacred mosques in Mecca and Medina and was a teacher of Abu Hamid al-Ghazali, arguably the most acclaimed Islamic scholar since the medieval period, refused to recognize its unqualified aesthetic superiority altogether (al-Juwayni, 1948, 54–55).

The most widely accepted basis for the uniqueness of the Qur'an is its linguistic and aesthetic character: "Its eloquence and rhetorical beauty, and the precision, economy and subtlety of its style" (Ayoub, 1984, 2). After much discussion a broad consensus emerged on a comprehensive combination of characteristics to form the basis of the Qur'an's inimitability, rather than any single characteristic. Ibn 'Atiyyah and others have broadly categorized these under "its literary arrangement, soundness of its meaning and eloquence of its words" (1954, 278). Some have again suggested that the Qur'an's inimitability is located in the quality of its guidance.

A few observations are appropriate here in reflecting on the question of the Qur'an's inimitability:

1. The Qur'anic revelation – of which the *tahaddi* (challenge) verses are an early example – was intrinsically linked to the concrete religio-social situation of Prophetic proclamation and rejection of it. It is quite obvious that the doctrine of its uniqueness is also tied to history.

2. It is evident that early Qur'anic scholarship was not characterized by the closed certainties that came to dominate it subsequently. This is borne out by the diversity of views on the various elements comprising the Qur'an's *i'jaz*: soundness of meaning, eloquence of words, and rhetorical style, and the theological discussions surrounding each of these.

3. The Qur'an itself and Qur'an scholars have always conceived of language as simultaneously speech and act: God is encountered by humankind through language. This performative–informative function of language was recognized by all the early scholars and accounts for the agreement that the Qur'an's uniqueness is located in both its message as well as its medium. The word–event that occurs in revelation, as well as in proclamation, is itself regarded by the Qur'an as a salvific event (2.19–20, 13.31, 17.107, 39.23, 85.21–22; etc.).

4. Would the "literary arrangement, soundness of its meaning and eloquence of its [the Qur'an's] words" have been employed as components of its uniqueness if the Qur'an were to have been revealed in a non-Arab society? The achievement of the Qur'an is that it does this so successfully and still engages numerous adherents from countless other cultures in an entrancing manner.

THE DOCTRINE OF THE QUR'AN'S UNCREATEDNESS AND ETERNALNESS (*QADIM*)

The connection between the way dogma develops and the socio-political environment wherein it develops is also demonstrated in the theological developments around the question of the nature of the Qur'an as God's speech. These developments eventually led to the Sunni doctrine of the Qur'an's uncreatedness and eternity. Initially the debate centred on the question of the Qur'an as the speech (*kalam*) of God in the sense of whether it was a divine attribute or not. Subsequently another dimension of that question gradually acquired greater significance: Is it created (*makhluq*) or not (i.e., *laysa bi makhluq*)? Finally, in the first half of the ninth century the somewhat non-assertive "not really created" (*laisa bi makhluq*) was replaced by a more definitive "*ghayr makhluq*" ("uncreated"). The question now at stake was: Does the Qur'an co-exist with God in all eternity? No controversy has influenced Islamic scholarship in general and Qur'anic scholarship in particular as decisively as this one. While this problem was the outcome of a post-prophetic theological discipline, i.e., *Kalam*,[3] it must be acknowledged

---

3 The Arabic word "*kalam*" normally means "speech". In its technical sense it may be rendered as speculative, dogmatic, or scholastic theology. The word is applied not only to the dialectical method but also to the discussions in which it was used and to the body of doctrine that emerged from it (*Encyclopaedia of Religion* s.v. "*Kalam*" [Anawati]).

that this discipline itself arose out of questions implicit in the Qur'an. Reflections on how the doctrinal positions were transformed during and subsequent to the *Mihnah* (833–848), a kind of "inquisition" or trial instituted by the Mu'tazilite benefactor, the Caliph Abu'l-Abbas al-Ma'mun (d. 198/833), are very important in trying to understand how theological diversity was virtually eliminated in opinions regarding the Qur'an. The changing theological position of ibn Hanbal in this debate, particularly, mirrors this transformation.

THE MU'TAZILITES AND THE EMERGENCE OF *KALAM*

Shortly after its emergence, Islam, not unlike other religions, saw a period of intense theological speculation. This period was invariably accompanied by a "tangle of dogmatic commentaries" (Goldziher, 1981, 67) which removed the text from the "spirit that pervades its true essence" (ibid.). "More intent on proof than on elucidation" (ibid.), the defenders of the faith ended up being its subverters. This was true of the initiators of *Kalam*, the Mu'tazilites, as well of their fiercest opponents – and subsequent annihilators – the *Muhaddithun*, the Traditionists (scholars in prophetic tradition, i.e., Hadith). What is self-evident is that *Kalam* as a definitive discipline is rooted in the earliest socio-political struggles within the Muslim community.[4] It was, however, not solely intra-Muslim polemics that shaped the emergence and development of *Kalam*: contact with the world of non-Islam was equally responsible. It was inevitable that the development of Islamic thought would be influenced by other cultures. With the spread of Islam – itself also, at least in part, a product of its earlier social environment – contact with non-Muslim thought and institutions of learning accelerated and left its mark on Muslim institutions and ideas. In being confronted with Christological literature and their underlying ideas, for example, Muslims could no longer confine themselves to the Qur'an; it

---

4 Nyberg argues that Mu'tazilite teaching in general can only be "perfectly understood" as "the theoretical crystallization of the political program of the Abbasids before their accession to power" (cited in Gimaret, 1986). (The Abbasids were the second dynasty of Islam and followed the Ummayads in 749. Their dynasty ended in 1258.) This may be overstating the political nature of the relationship between Mu'tazilite teachings and the political program of the Abbasids. However, while ideas are not always born with an awareness of their political implications, they are never shaped in an ideological vacuum. Given that, from its origins, Islam had been inseparably religion and polity, it is not surprising that the political struggles among the early Muslims should also have led to the elaboration of theological problems. It was inevitable that political issues were clothed in religious garments. Given the subsequent explicit co-operation between Abbasid political ideology and Mu'tazilite theological discourse, it is quite tenable that there was considerable convergence between them in their formative stages.

was at this point that Greek conceptions and intellectual tools were employed.[5]

The focal point of Mu'tazilite theology was their emphasis on the absolute unity of God and on God's justice – they described themselves as the "people of divine unity and justice" (ahl a-tawhid wa'l-'adl). In dealing with the issue of God's attributes, therefore, and in particular with the attribute of speech, their primary concern was to uphold God's absolute unity, uniqueness, and immutability. To suggest that anything, even divine revelation, shared in any of these characteristics, they argued, would detract from God's utter beyondness. Their principle of divine justice resulted in a rejection of notions of God's arbitrary rule and predestination. If the Qur'an were eternal, they reasoned, it followed that all the events narrated therein were pre-ordained; the players in all of these events would thus all have had their fate sealed, even before birth.

There is considerable uncertainty as to when exactly serious theological discussion commenced on the nature of God's speech and the Qur'an's createdness or otherwise. It is generally agreed that the affirmation of the uncreated nature of the Qur'an chronologically followed the assertion of its created nature by Jad ibn Dirham (d. 743) and Jahm ibn Safwan (d. 745) and that this discussion was confined to a few scholars until the time of the Mihnah. An increase in state interest in Kalam is, however, discernible from the time that the Abbassids came to power; the period of the Caliph Harun al-Rashid (d. 809) especially saw debate on this issue becoming quite extensive. This controversy reached new heights – intellectually, politically, and emotionally – during the reign of al-Ma'mun (d. 198/833). The compelling nature of the controversy is evident from the establishment of the Mihnah towards the end of al-Ma'mun's reign in 833. Most leading officials and other prominent personalities were forced to publicly profess the createdness of the Qur'an. With a few exceptions, most theologians and jurists submitted. A large number however, continued in secret to uphold the doctrine of an uncreated Qur'an and a few even openly refused to submit to official doctrine. The most prominent among the latter was Ibn Hanbal who was publicly flogged and imprisoned for his beliefs.

---

5 That these external factors were invariably seen as only having influenced the genesis and development of the ideas of one's adversaries, and never one's own, does not alter this. This "foreign influence" was the subject of much discussion among Muslim scholars and was confined to passing references which attempted to disparage the ideas of opponents by suggesting that the matrix of these ideas are foreign to the Islamic world. Quite frequently the persons of Muslim opponents were also attacked by suggestions that their Christian, Jewish, or Magian backgrounds may have had a role in their interpretation of doctrine (Watt, 1950, 29).

The *Mihnah* aroused fierce opposition among the inhabitants of Baghdad, whose populist and anti-intellectual bias rejected what it regarded as the intellectual acrobatics of *Kalam* in favour of the more simple and literal Hadith. The *Mihnah* continued intermittently under the next two Caliphs until it was abandoned in 234/848, shortly after the accession of al-Mutawakkil (d. 247/861). The repression unleashed during the *Mihnah* polarized the various protagonists to a hitherto unknown degree and the new "orthodox" Islam asserted its ideas with a rigidity that was alien to the Muslims in the period preceding the *Mihnah*. The Mu'tazilites were now denounced as Jahmites[6] and the intermediary position that the Qur'an is uncreated but an event originated in time (*muhdath*) was denounced as heresy. Subsequently the denunciations transcended even this level to "*man shaka fi kufrihim faqad kafar*" ("whoever doubts their disbelief also denies the faith"). This unstoppable march of "orthodoxy" into the terrain of the "thinkable" and its conversion into "unthinkable" territory is evident from the following. First, prior to the *Mihnah* it was acceptable to most Traditionists of undoubted "orthodoxy" to suspend judgment on the question of the Qur'an's createdness or otherwise; some even regarded it as necessary and virtuous to do so. Ibn Hanbal was evidently among those who refrained from any addition to the statement that "the Qur'an is the speech of God". He is even quoted as having said: "Whoever asserts that the Qur'an is created is a Jahmite and whoever asserts that it is uncreated is a heretic innovator" (cf. Madelung, 1985, 521). Later Ibn Hanbal is reported to have said that "the one who suspends judgment is worse than the one who maintains that it is created" (ibid., 509). Thus we observe that during and after the *Mihnah* this attitude of tentativeness was transformed into a dogmatic insistence that everyone had to declare their belief in the Qur'an's uncreatedness and even a bitter denunciation of those who maintained silence. Second, before the *Mihnah* the notion of the Qur'an's createdness was not regarded as synonymous with its temporality. Here Madelung refers to the intermediate positions ascribed to Ja'far al-Sadiq (d. 765) and Abu Hanifah (d. 767), both among the luminaries of "orthodox" Islam. Both al-Sadiq and Abu Hanifah accepted the Qur'an as God's speech while

---

6 So named after Jahm ibn Safwan, a follower of Jad ibn al-Dirham, who was executed for his "heretical" views during the last years of the reign of the Umayyad Caliph Hisham (d. 745). Al-Shahrastani, the heresiographer, says that al-Jad was the first to espouse the concept of the createdness of the Qur'an. The Jahmites, unlike the Mu'tazilites, denied that Allah really speaks. Their name came to be eternally associated with all those who denied the createdness of the Qur'an.

ignoring or rejecting respectively its uncreatedness (ibid., 508 and 512).[7] After the *Mihnah*, however, "created" came to be regarded as essentially meaning "temporal" and "uncreated" as meaning "co-eternal with God (*qadim*)".

The new refined orthodox doctrine on the nature of the Qur'an is expressed epigrammatically in a sentence attributed to Ibn Hanbal: "What lies between the two covers is the Speech of Allah" (Ibn Hanbal, 1959, 1:415). It specifies that the Qur'an, the Speech of God, is eternal, and uncreated in its essence and sense, (but) created in its letters and sounds (*harf wa jarh*). Soon it came to pass that that "which is read in the prayer niches as it emerges from the throats of the believers" was upheld as inseparable from God's eternal and uncreated word. The expression "my uttering of the Qur'an is created" was denounced as heretical and even Muhammad ibn Isma'il al-Bukhari (d. 256/870), the great compiler of Prophetic tradition who considered such pronouncements permissible, was not saved from denunciation. As the scope of the doctrine of the eternal and uncreated Qur'an expanded, the position articulated by Ibn Hanbal and later the Ash'arites,[8] came to occupy the center and their doctrine triumphed as the intermediate position.

THE IMPLICATIONS OF THE *MIHNAH* FOR QUR'ANIC SCHOLARSHIP

In our discussion on the nature of the Qur'an we have attempted to demonstrate that both the epistemological tools, i.e., the discipline of *Kalam*, as well as the direction of the discourse on scripture, were shaped by "external" historical forces. The issue was thus not so much what the Qur'an or God says but what He was willed to say by the believers. From the regular resort to the Qur'an for legitimization by all sides it is evident that the plausibility of both its createdness and non-createdness may be inferred from there.[9] We may summarize the consequences of these theological developments as follows. First, intermediate theological positions and ideas of doctrinal tentativeness were virtually eliminated. The earliest Muslims did not discuss the issue despite attempts to

---

7 There is much dispute as to whether Abu Hanifah finally upheld the doctrine of the Qur'an's uncreatedness (cf. Momen, 1986).

8 The Ash'arites, named after Abu'l-Hassan al-'Ash'ari (d. 324/935), the famous Basra theologian, are the theological heirs of Ibn Hanbal and used the *Kalam* methods denounced by him to arrive at his conclusions.

9 It is said that al-'Ash'ari wrote a commentary on this issue in which he explained every verse employed by his opponents in such a way that his new interpretation supported his own views.

fabricate hadith to indicate the contrary. For more than a century the vast majority of Muslim scholars, including the Traditionists, did not pronounce on this question. When the matter became an issue of political and public debate it was resolved with an inflexible "true" doctrine of the Qur'an's uncreatedness and eternity. Second, the Mu'tazilites were reduced to a heretical fringe and, with them, the progressive content of many of their ideas. The intolerant spirit with which they ruthlessly pursued their ideas – and their opponents – and the reason which they brought to bear upon questions of belief were, however, to abide with Muslims until this day.[10] Accompanying these two consequences was the re-emergence of an "orthodox" position with a vengeance and armed with the all-purpose doctrinal weapon of *bila kayfa* (lit. "without how", i.e. "without further enquiry"), which is to unquestioningly accept matters of dogma.[11] The consequence of the debate about the Qur'an's createdness on the creativity of Muslim thinking is seen in the following lament by Muhammad Iqbal (d. 1938), the great philosopher poet of the Indo-Pak Sub-continent:

> Are the words of the Qur'an created or uncreated?
> In which belief does lie the salvation of the Muslim Ummah?
> Are the idols of al-Lat and al-Manat[12] chiseled out of
> Muslim theology not sufficient of the Muslim of these days? (tr. and cited
>   by Rahman, 1978, 67).

What are the hermeneutical implications of the idea that the Qur'an as scripture exists outside of history? First, traditional Islamic scholarship has made a neat and seemingly unbridgeable distinction between the production of scripture on the one hand and its interpretation and reception on the other. This distinction, if it is to continue – as indeed seems to be the case – is the crucial factor in the shaping of Qur'anic hermeneutics for it implies that the only hermeneutics, which Islam can cope with is that pertaining to how the Qur'an has been received and

10 The Mu'tazilites were far from the enlightened liberals which earlier Western scholarship made them out to be. Their overwhelming arrogance and self-righteousness is evident in their notion of *takfir al-awam*, i.e., proclaiming the masses unbelievers due to their lack of scholarly sophistication. A devout Mu'tazilite, Abu Musa al-Murdar's belief that only he himself and three of his followers would be able to enter Paradise, while being somewhat exceptional, remains a logical consequence of Mu'tazilite arrogance (cf. Shahrastani, 1961, 1:51).
11 With the notion of *bila kayfa* Ibn Hanbal attempted to resolve the conflict between reason and revelation and this was particularly employed to "explain" the apparently anthropomorphic expressions in the Qur'an. This is now the accepted view of orthodoxy. Ibn Hanbal, however, more than any of the other three prominent Sunnite jurist eponyms, came to signify a particular theological position: literalism and the acceptance of dogma without enquiry.
12 Al-Lat was a goddess worshipped at Tai'if, Al-Uzza and Nakhlah, near Mecca, and Manat at a shrine between Mecca and Medina.

interpreted by its listeners and adherents, i.e., reception hermeneutics. Whether this is adequate in coping with the challenges of post-modernity is doubtful. It would seem, however, that it will only be a matter of time before Muslims are confronted with the interconnectedness of these issues and the fruits – however bitter – of critical literary and historical scholarship. Like the futile distinction between the technological benefits of modernity and their underlying value system – and this is not suggested judgmentally – we will have to face the consequences of our myopia. Second, unlike early biblical scholarship that was at least unanimous about the Bible being a "work" – God's or that of men – in Islam the transcendentalist perspective went beyond this; the Qur'an's being a "work" was itself disputed as was the question of its (historical) "event-ness" (*muhdath*). Anything remotely conceding any aspect of Qur'anic revelation is summarily dismissed as making "conceptual room for posing a potentially dangerous question about the authority of scripture" (Akhtar, 1991, 97). To the extent that hermeneutics also deal with the birth and nature of a text, it is thus difficult to foresee Muslim scholars of the Qur'an taking it on board in the foreseeable future. In this respect Qur'anic scholarship may follow the path walked by early biblical scholarship whereby classic Christian exegesis and polemics around the Reformation were characterized by accusations of exegesis being a product of human systems going wrong without questioning the genesis of scripture. There was thus considerable debate about the historical setting of scripture and how that setting influences interpretation without touching the nature and genesis of scripture. Third, the way in which the formula of the Qur'an's eternity found expression, the doctrine of *i'jaz* as well as the historical factors which occasioned it, and the Qur'an's claims to be a guide to people who are located within history mean that revelation remains related to history. Muslims, like others, have connected with a reality transcending history and that revelation, putative or real, has taken place within history and has been conditioned by history. Thus, as Smith so cogently argues "scripture, whatever else it may additionally be, is also an historical phenomenon" (1980, 489).

THE *SUNNAH*: UNREHEARSED REVELATION

Presented as distinct from the Qur'an, is the Hadith (lit. report, news, narration, pl. *ahadith*) – the Prophet's own deeds, speech, and silence in the presence of others while they were doing something (indicating approval) encapsulated in a collection of Traditions. In the classical period of Islam, these became the sole bases for determining the *sunnah*.[13] The pattern of a gradual rigidification of religious thinking and reification of religious terminology is also evident in the transformation in the concept of *sunnah* as initially understood by the earliest Muslims into a very specific legal category inherently tied to putative traditions of the Prophet. For the first two generations of Muslims, the Qur'an and *sunnah* (lit. "path", "precedent"), both viewed as interrelated parts of a revelatory event, were seemingly adequate as the religious bases whereupon they could construct their religious lives. There are a number of indications during the earliest years of Islam that the Muslims were guided by an essentially undefined and undifferentiated body of tradition – the Qur'an, the *sunnah*, the Prophet, and the *sunnahs* of the Companions and early Caliphs, which was viewed as related to revelation. It was only after A.H. 150 that scholarly legal theory began to emphasize the *sunnah* of the Prophet as "an ex post facto confirmation of the living sunnah of the community" (cf. Rahman, 1966, 43–67; Graham, 1977, 9–19).

In the early years of Islam the term "*sunnah*" was widely used to denote socio-religious precedent and included precedents set by any of the first four Caliphs who succeeded Muhammad or even more broadly, the practice of a particular community. Hence the "*sunnah* of Medina" or the "*sunnah* of Baghdad". Equally significant is the fact that the term was often used in early Islam to denote a broad pattern of just dealings that was characteristic of the period when the Prophet lived in Medina. Tabari records that the expression "*kitab Allah wa sunnat nabiyyihi*" ("the book of God and the *sunnah* of His Prophet") was the rallying slogan for major revolts, regardless of the ideological or theological persuasion of those who revolted. Later, largely due to the efforts of al-Shafi' (d. 204/819), *sunnah* came to be used exclusively for the precedent set by the Prophet which could be authenticated by reliable Hadith. Al-Shafi' argued that the *Sunnah* – which now gets a capital letter – was to be regarded as co-equal to the Qur'an in authority "for the command of the Prophet is the Command of God".

Al-Shafi' represented a strand that was referred to as the "*ashab al-hadith*" or "*ahl al-hadith*" (the people of hadith). From the polemical works of al-Shafi' we note that his position was opposed by at least two

---

13 Wansbrough, in line with his overall framework of locating Muslim approaches to revelation within a Jewish scriptural framework, describes the *Sunnah* as "*Mishna*" and "yet another element in . . . the Mosaic syndrome of Muslim prohetology" (1977, 57).

strands of thinking among his contemporaries: First, and preceding the *ashab al-hadith*, there was the *ahl al-ra'y*, the legal pragmatists from the earlier legal schools who believed in the *sunnah* as a living tradition which could not be calcified in the Hadith. The prophetic *sunnah* was one of several sources for them and they were far more concerned with the inner coherence of their own various legal reasoning systems. Second was the *ahl al-kalam*, the scholastic theologians who rejected any reliance on Hadith and insisted that the Qur'an alone should be relied on. For them acceptance of any hadith was premised on it having an inner coherence, being logical and conforming to the Qur'an.

As we have seen in our discussion on the Qur'an's createdness, the early centuries after the Prophet's demise were characterized by an enormous diversity of opinion on every conceivable political and theological issue and more often than not these were interrelated. As the Muslim empire expanded and brought along with it a host of complex legal and ideological issues both the Qur'an and the *Sunnah* became contested terrain in the various struggles for authority and legitimacy. The emerging orthodoxy both spearheaded and, in a sense, was the product of attempts to define, gather, codify, and authenticate the *Sunnah* of the Prophet. The various and often varying accounts of the Prophet's words, deeds, and approval by silent consent multiplied rapidly and it is possible to find more than tens of thousands of hadith attributed to a Companion who was in his early teens when the Prophet passed away.[14]

With *Sunnah* now equated with the *sunnah* of Muhammad and elevated to the level of a source of religio-legal authority, and with Hadith established as the only means to authenticate *Sunnah*, the various disputants attempted to justify their views and to strip their opponents of legitimacy on the basis of Hadith. This contributed to the emergence of both a corpus of Hadith literature and an entire science around it, much of it based on the growing informal hadith manufacturing industry.[15] In a widely disputed hadith, the Prophet discouraged the Companions from

14 Tens of thousands of hadith were, for example, attributed to Abu Hurayrah (d. 57 or 58/ 676–677), a Companion who had spent just three years in the company of the Prophet. Muhammad Mustafa al-'Azami estimates that there are about three quarters of a million hadith (1978, xix).

15 Brown notes that the "extent of forgery was dramatic. Forgers became active even during the lifetime of Muhammad, in spite of the warning that whoever spreads lies about him would burn in hell. In the Caliphate of 'Umar, the problem became so serious that he prohibited transmission of hadith altogether. Forgery only increased under the Ummayads, the first dynasty of Islam that reigned from 661 until 750. They considered hadith a means of propping up their rule and actively circulated traditions against 'Ali in favour of Mu'awiyah [ibn Abi Sufyan (d. 680), the founder of the dynasty]. The Abbasids [who succeeded them]

taking any notes when he advised them on anything for fear that these notes would be conflated with the written revelation. "Whoever has written anything from me, other than the Qur'an, let him erase it." This was the supposed cause of the reluctance by some of the Companions, including the first four Caliphs, to record anything said by him, although the oral rendition of the prophetic sayings remained common.[16] This hadith seemed to have been surpassed by several later hadith wherein the Prophet renders specific approval for such recording. 'Abd Allah ibn 'Umar (d. 73/692), for example, reported that he was in the habit of writing down everything that the Prophet said until he was warned against it. He approached the Prophet for guidance and the latter responded: "Write ... I say nothing but the truth" (Busti, 1981, 4:184)[17] With the passing of time the writing of hadith gained wider acceptability and certain criterion were fixed to determine the authenticity or otherwise of hadith.

Hadith consists of two parts: the chain of narration and its content. The vast majority of Hadith scholars focused on the first part to ascertain the authenticity of a hadith. An entire science, investigating the backgrounds of each transmitter to identify the weakness or strength of a chain developed from this process. The preponderance of this science – at the expense of examining the inner coherence of a hadith and its compatibility with Qur'an – is seen in the following categories of demarcating the authenticity or otherwise of the hadith: (1) *sahih* (sound): a faultless hadith in whose chain of narration there is no weakness; (2) *hasan* (beautiful, good): a hadith whose chain of narration is not entirely complete or whose reliability is in doubt; (3) *da'if* (weak): a hadith against which there are serious doubts because either the narrator or its chain is known to be unreliable or of doubtful orthodoxy. In many ways, the hadith literature and Muslim approaches to the hadith

followed the same pattern, circulating Prophetic hadith which predicted the reign of each successive ruler. Moreover, religious and ethnic conflicts further contributed to the forgery of hadith. The *Zanadiqah* (those who professed Islam while holding Manichean ideas, as we are told by the heresiographers), for example, are reported to have circulated 12,000 fabricated traditions. The degree of the problem can be seen from the testimony of the *muhaddithun* themselves. Bukhari, for example, selected 9,000 traditions out of 700,000.' (1999, 96).

16 Al-'Azami suggests that the earlier instruction referred to a prohibition to write down the Qur'an and non-Qur'anic material on the same sheet, "because that might have led to misunderstanding"; or that the people were forbidden to write down hadith in the early days of Islam as "all attention was to be paid to the Qur'an and its preservation" (1978, 23–24).

17 Some Muslims who reject the authority of hadith entirely insist that the prophetic prohibition on recording his own utterances remained valid. The vast majority though, argue that this prohibition was effective early in the Prophet's mission because he feared that Muslims would confuse them with divine revelation, thus compromising the integrity of the Qur'an. When the Qur'an was well-established as an emerged written corpus, the prohibition was lifted.

literature resemble those of Christian approaches to the New Testament: a corpus of sacred literature acknowledged to have been developed and gathered by a number of persons over an extended period of time.

There is another kind of hadith where the Prophet seems to be quoting God verbatim without this quotation being in the Qur'an. These hadith are called "*ahadith qudsi*" (divine traditions). The most explicit reflection of what William Graham terms "extra-Qur'anic revelation" is believed to have emanated from Gabriel or one of the Prophet's dreams. Their chains of transmission are often untested, varied, and sometimes contain weak links such as an untrustworthy source in them. The following is one such example:

> God says: Whosoever is kept from petitioning Me [for help] because of preoccupation with reciting and constant mentioning/remembrance of Me (*al-qur'an wa-dhikr*), him shall I give far better that what I give to those who ask things of me. (Maliki, 1980, 6:46)

The phenomenon of the divine traditions is one relatively unexplored and highlights a number of issues pertaining to the intersection between prophetic word and divine word and, perhaps more importantly, the fluid nature of their relationship with each other before Muslim crystallization in the period when theology was written in books and its dogma fixed.

THE PROPHET MUHAMMAD AND THE QUR'AN

What was the relationship between Muhammad and the Qur'an as a divine text and between his *sunnah* and the Qur'an as a book of guidance? The ontological otherness of the Qur'an, as I have said earlier, is a given for the Muslim "orthodoxy". To ensure this otherness though, the messenger had to be absolutely reliable and therefore free from the ordinary human limitations intrinsic to humanness – such as forgetfulness or error – that could possibly impair the faithful transmission of this message from beyond. Besides, if he were to be the transmitter of guidance for humankind, ought he not to be the personification of following that guidance – a perfect human being? In freeing the Prophet from these limitations does one then not run the risk of conflating his personality with that of the One who sent him? In describing the prophetic precedent (*sunnah*) as "unrehearsed revelation", does one not get into some difficult waters in terms of defining religious authority beyond God? In the second chapter I narrated an incident whereby the son of Halimah, the Prophet's foster-mother, reported that two men came dressed in white and opened his breast and stirred their hands inside. Later Muhammad explained that the visitors were angels who had washed a dark spot from his heart with snow. This incident was subsequently to become a key one in the much debated doctrine of *isma'* – prophetic infallibility.[18] While there was little agreement on all the implications of the doctrine, there was unanimity around the notion that all Prophets who were also messengers with divine revelation entrusted to them were free from any error related to the transmission of divine revelation. In this way the inevitability of a human element in the gathering of revelation was acknowledged and confronted.

However, the problem persists at two levels. First, Muhammad was also an ordinary human being and if the divine revelation entered upon "his heart" then does one assume that that heart – located in his unique person which, in turn, was located in sixth-century Arabia – did not impact upon what entered it and later emerged from his tongue as uttered revelation? Second, how does one confine his *isma'* (infallibility) to his verbal transmission of the divine revelations and not to his personal explications of its message. Yet, if one extends it, then where does one draw the line, given that he was also an ordinary human being who was even on occasion admonished in the Qur'an? (cf. 80.1–4). A hadith recorded in the collection of ibn Hanbal says that "Gabriel used to descend to the Prophet with *sunnah* just as he descended with the Qur'an." This ought to have presented significant problems if one were to view the matter of revelation in purely rational terms.[19] How did the Prophet, for example, always distinguish between rehearsed Qur'anic revelation and non-rehearsed revelations which were to become manifest in his behaviour or in his own sayings such as the *hadith qudsi* which commences with "God says"? If, on the other hand, God was in charge of the entire process, then it does not present any difficulty at all: God simply wills the mind and/heart of Muhammad to distinguish between the two categories of revelation.

18 "A Prophet of God must possess the quality of inerrancy" says Tabataba'i. "In receiving the revelation from God, in guarding it and in making possible its reaching people, he must be free from error" (1995, 144). Sunni Muslims extend this infallibility to all the Companions in matters of Qur'anic transmission, notwithstanding the differences in their accounts and Shi'i Muslims believe that, in addition to the Prophets, only the Imams are infallible (ibid., 185).
19 Wansbrough argues that this distinction between rehearsed (*litteratum*) and unrehearsed (paraphrasitic) modes of revelations was "purely theoretical". "In practice, Sunna as revelation, was transmitted with infinite care and was the primary instrument by which the Qur'anic revelation was linked with the historical figure of an Arabian prophet" (1977, 52).

Muslim orthodoxy does not address the first question. The late Fazlur Rahman, a Pakistani scholar and the doyen of contemporary modernist Muslim scholarship, developed an interesting position around this question. He insists that revelation intends obedience rather than information and believes that "the Qur'an is the divine response, through the Prophet's mind to the moral and social situation of the Prophet's Arabia, particularly the problems of the commercial Meccan society of his day" (Rahman, 1982, 5). He affirms the ontological otherness of the Qur'an as *verbally revealed* [italics in original] and not merely in its meaning and ideas" (1966, 30–31). According to him, this "divine message broke through the consciousness of the Prophet from an agency whose source was God" (1988, 24). Rahman insists that while the Qur'an "itself certainly maintained its otherness ..., objectivity and the verbal character of the revelation, [it had] equally certainly rejected its externality vis-à-vis the Prophet" (ibid). He argues though that

> orthodoxy lacked the necessary intellectual tools to combine, in its formulation of the dogma, the otherness and verbal character of the revelation, on the one hand, and its intimate connection with the work and religious personality of the Prophet, on the other; i.e., it lacked the intellectual capacity to say both that the Qur'an is entirely the Word of God and, in an ordinary sense, also entirely the word of the Prophet. (1966, 31).

Although, Rahman's views were regarded as novel, even as innovation, he was merely articulating what others had done a long time ago. In the following chapter I shall be looking at the model of progressive revelation suggested by Shah Wali Allah Dehlawi (d. 1762), a leading reformist scholar from the Indo-Pak Subcontinent. It should be noted that his ideas that "verbal revelation occurred in the words, idiom and style already present in the mind of Prophet" imply that revelation is also the product of Muhammad's mind.

> When God wished to communicate a guidance to abide till the end of the world He subdued the mind of the Prophet in such a way that in the pure heart of the Prophet He sent the Book of God in a nebulous and undifferentiated manner (*ijmalan*) ... The Message comes to be imprinted in the pure heart of the Prophet as it existed in the supernal realm and thus the Prophet came to know by conviction that this is the word of God. ... Subsequently as the need arose well-strung speech was brought out from the rational faculties of the Prophet through the agency of the angel (ibid.).

As for the second question, that of prophetic infallibility, jurists (*fuqaha*) and theologians (*mutakallimun*) developed two distinct ways of dealing with it. The jurists viewed the issue from the angle of applying the law. What in the prophetic precedent – based on prophetic infallibility – was binding and what was not? A criterion was evolved to distinguish between the actions of the Prophet that emanated directly from his mission as God's messenger (*sunnah al-huda*, i.e., *sunnah* of guidance) and his actions as mortal (*sunnah al-'adiyah*, i.e., *sunnah* of habit). Most of the theologians agreed that the Prophet was free from error in matters pertaining to guidance. Widespread disagreement persisted on all other matters, with the majority holding on to the notion that while all Prophets are free from major sins, they are nevertheless capable of human errors of judgment in worldly matters and even of committing minor sins.[20] The *Sunnah*, in fact, became a significant manifestation of extra-Qur'anic revelation as is clear from a hadith in Abu Dawud: "I was given the Book and alongside it something akin to it *(wa mitlahu ma'ahu)*." This also meant that all of the Prophet's actions deemed to flow from his prophetic mission acquired an obligatory character and had a significant impact on the question of the Qur'an's authority.

Given that Muhammad's religious life was seen as an explication of the Qur'an's message and that the Qur'an was actually "in need" of the *Sunnah* to verify it, the dictum that the Qur'an is in need of the *Sunnah* and not vice versa – and that the *Sunnah* can, in fact, abrogate the Qur'an – became widespread and is still upheld by mainstream Muslim jurists. For them this does not contradict the authority of God because the very prophetic abrogation of a Qur'anic text emanates from God, as al-Ghazali explains:

> There is no dispute concerning the view that the Prophet did not abrogate the Qur'an on his own initiative. He did it in response to inspiration. God does the actual abrogating, operating through the medium of His Prophet. One ought thus to hold the rulings of the Qur'an as abrogated by the Prophet rather than solely by the Qur'an. Although inspiration in these cases is not Qur'anic inspiration, the word of God is nevertheless one. God does not have two words, one expressed in the Qur'an style which we are bidden to recite publicly and called the Qur'an while the other word is not Qur'an. God has but one word which differs in the mode of its expression. On occasion God indicates his word by the Qur'an, on others,

20 Muslim theology generally divides sin into major and minor categories. Major sins are defined as those for which the Qur'an has a specific legal consequence or punishment while the rest are seen as minor. Examples of major sins would be murder, theft, slander of a virtuous woman, and adultery while minor sins would include verbal abuse, cursing and lying.

by words in another style, not publicly recited, called *sunnah* (cited in Brown, 1999, 17).

Wansbrough's opinion is worthy of note in this regard. He suggests that juxtaposition of the two [forms of] revelation as equally authoritative does not have to be taken to imply that the Qur'an yielded authority to the "encroachments of the Sunnah" (1977, 54). "Indeed," says he, "it can be argued that the opposite was so. That canonization of the Qur'anic revelation could only have been effected within the community once its content could be related to that of the *prophetical* [italics in original] Sunnah and, perhaps more important, to the historical figure delineated there" (ibid.).

William Graham in his work *Divine Word and Prophetic Word in Early Islam* had detailed the evidence of how, "in the formative decades of Islam when the Qur'an was still primarily oral, rather than written facts, the distinctions between revelation and prophetic inspiration were, although present in some degree, less absolute and ... less important than the overwhelming awareness of one's being close to ... the prophetic-revelatory event" (1977, 14).[21] Remnants of this active revelatory process not entirely encapsulated in the Qur'an are to be seen in an array of revelatory "material" not found in the Qur'an itself. These include the Divine sayings, accounts of God instructing the Prophet or guiding him in a non-revelatory way, such as, for example, through dreams, the Shi'i appreciation of the continuation of revelation, albeit in a different form, to the designated imams; and indeed in the very description of the *sunnah* as "unrehearsed revelation". The collections of Muslim, Bukhari, and Ibn Hanbal contain an interesting hadith where what Graham terms "extra-Qur'anic revelation" is clearly designated as "revelation". "God continued revealing (*taba'a al-wahi*) to the Messenger of God before his death, right up to the time that he died, and most of the revelation took place on the day that the Messenger of God died."

Given the shift in the meaning of "*sunnah*" from the way it was used by the earliest Muslims and its later use as intrinsically rooted to prophetic hadith, it is not difficult to see the problem that mainstream Muslim thinking is confronted with by those who highlight the inherent limitations to the collection of hadith and what Mohammed Arkoun describes as "imperfect human procedures" in "oral transmission", the use of "imperfect graphic form", "conflicts between clans and parties"

---

21 The backdrop for Graham's views is the search for what was perceived by the early Muslim community and how the revelatory event was received by them rather than what was "really" the case; or what revelation "actually" was.

and "unreported readings" (1987a, 5). Unlike the issue of the Qur'an's authenticity to which Arkoun refers to above, the debate on the *Sunnah* as authoritative has generally been a free for all, even in Muslim circles. While the rejecters of this position, or of Hadith in its entirety, have not been spared the accusations of *kufr*, they have nevertheless remained a part of Muslim society.

While this debate was revived in the eighteenth century and vigorously pursued into the early part of the twentieth century in contemporary Muslim society, it has acquired far more nuanced tones. This is, in large measure, due to the greater sophistication of the participants and, perhaps more significantly, the fact that modernist scholars simply study and invoke the Qur'an with a far more judicious and selective usage of Hadith rather than evoke the *amour propre* of "orthodoxy" by head-on assaults on long-held doctrines.

> At a deeper level, the controversy is also about human interpreters of the Qur'an and their authority. If *sunnah* is the essential tool for under-standing revelation, then experts on *sunnah* are likewise indispensable. But if ability to contextualize revelation is needed, then those who know the modern world will be the most able interpreters of the Qur'an and knowledge of the tradition will be counted superfluous. The deep sociological rifts between traditional leadership and western educated intelligentsia, religious scholar and technocrat are thus projected on to the spectrum of Modern Muslim attitudes towards the Qur'an and its interpretation (Brown, 1999, 59).

6 UNDERSTANDING AND INTERPRETING THE QUR'AN

Although the fundamental ethical and spiritual message of the Qur'an has an ongoing revelance, much of the text in the book can be viewed as being generally addressed to the people of the Hijaz who lived during the period of its revelation. Muslim scholarship has been reluctant to explore this relationship and its implications for the genesis of the Qur'an as well as its interpretation. Instead, "they [the traditional scholars of the Qur'an] have set arbitrary limits to investigations of the myriad historical strands that, from a naturalistic perspective, coalesced in the prophetic-revelatory event that brought forth Islamic tradition and faith" (Graham, 1980, 21). Despite this unwillingness to examine the implications of the situational character of the Qur'an, the principle of contextuality itself is generally accepted by all traditional scholars of the Qur'an, and attempts to remove the Qur'an from its socio-historical birthplace both reflected and contributed to a rigidity that was alien to its earliest scholars.

PROGRESSIVE REVELATION (*TADRIJ*)

The Qur'an portrays a picture of a Diety actively engaged in the affairs of this world and of humankind. The most cogent traditional scholar of the relativistic and progressive model of revelation is undoubtedly Shah Wali Allah Dehlawi (d. 1762), a leading reformist scholar from the Indo-Pak Subcontinent who developed an elaborate theory of the relationship between revelation and its context. Following on his notion of "the unity of being" where everything is closely integrated, he emphasizes the interrelation of the cosmic, divine, terrestrial, and human powers and effects in the universe. God would thus not speak into a vacuum nor would He convey a message formed in one. Dehlawi seems to suggest some form of existential connection between history and revelation. The ideal form of religion (*din*), he says, corresponds to the ideal form of species (*fitrah*). "Actualized manifestations of the ideal form descend in successive revelations depending on the particular material and historical circumstances" (cited in Hermansen, 1985, 147) of the recipient community. Every succeeding revelation re-shapes the elements "previously found into a new gestalt which embodies primordial ideal religion, in an altered form suitable to the recipient community" (ibid.). According to Dehlawi, it thus follows that, with every succeeding context, religion has adapted "its form, beliefs and spiritual practices to the customs, previous faiths and temperaments of the nations to which it has been revealed" (Dehlawi, 1952, 1:187). In this schema of revelation, God's way of dealing with humankind is compared to a physician who prescribes different medication to his patients in the various stages of their illness; to hold on to a pre-Muhammadan religious community would, in Dehlawi's view, be tantamount to an adult using medicine prescribed for a child or using yesterday's medicine for today's ailment.

The Qur'an, despite its inner coherence, was never formulated as a connected whole, but was revealed in response to the demands of concrete situations. The Qur'an is explicit about the reasons for the progressive nature of its revelation. The "arbitrary limits" set by traditional scholars of the Qur'an in investigating the historical strands in revelation, referred to by Graham above, did not exclude the principle of gradualism (*tadrij*). This principle, which characterized the entire revelatory process, is best manifested in some specific divisions of the text and two genres in Qur'anic Studies. The divisions are Meccan as distinct from Medinan, and the genres are those of *asbab al-nuzul* (sing. "*sabab al-nuzul*", occasion of revelation) and *naskh* (abrogation).

MECCAN AND MEDINAN REVELATIONS

Although the distinction between Meccan and Medinan verses is not made in the Qur'an as presently arranged, knowledge of where each revelation occurred is regarded by all the Qur'an scholars as essential to understand its contents. The following excerpt from Abu'l-Qasim

Nisaburi's *Note on the Virtues of Qur'anic Studies* is cited with approval in numerous books on the subject:

> Among the most virtuous of the knowledge of the Qur'an is that which deals with its revelation and the chronology of what was revealed in Mecca and what in Medina, the revelations which occurred in Mecca but pertain to Medina and revealed in Medina but pertain to Mecca, the Meccan revelations dealing with the inhabitants of Medina and the Medinan revelations dealing with the inhabitants of Mecca, the revelations which resemble Meccan revelations but were actually revealed in Medina and that which resemble Medinan revelations but were actually revealed in Mecca, the revelations which took place at Al-Jahfah, in Jerusalem, in Ta'if, and Hudaybiyyah, the revelations which occurred at night and those which occurred during the day, those which occurred when [Muhammad was] in a group and those which occurred when [he was] alone, the Medinan *ayat* within a Meccan *surah* and the Meccan verses within a Medinan *surah* ... Whoever is not conversant with these twenty-five aspects and unable to distinguish between them is unfit to speak [with authority] about the Book of God ('Inayah 1996, 1:171).

This list may appear quite exhausting and even intimidating. It does, however, highlight the futility of merely asking "What does the Qur'an say?" about a particular matter and insisting on a simple answer, on the one hand, and the importance of viewing all Qur'anic revelation contextually, on the other. Another way of looking at the Meccan and Medinan divisions is to distinguish between texts revealed prior to the Hijrah and those revealed subsequent to it. Yet a third way, ascribed to 'Abd Allah ibn Mas'ud, is to look at the texts which are addressed to the Meccans and those addressed to the Medinese. Sometimes, depending on which criterion one employs to categorize a verse, it could be either Meccan or Medinan. The following verse is one such example:

> O humankind! Behold, We have created you all out of a male and a female, and have made you into nations and tribes, so that you might come to know one another. Verily, the noblest of you in the sight of God is the one who is most deeply conscious of Him. Behold, God is all-knowing, all-aware (49.13).

This verse was revealed in Mecca when the Prophet was living in Medina but while he was on pilgrimage to Mecca. Given that it addressed the Medinese and its exortation was to be lived out in Medina, it could also be described as Medinan. A few *surahs* contain verses revealed in Mecca and in Medina. In these cases, the *surah* is described by its first or major component, i.e., if the beginning of a *surah* was revealed in Medina, then the entire *surah* would be called Medinan. The texts are determined as Meccan or Medinan on the basis of a number of characteristics and scholars have usually invoked these to date a certain verse or chapter. Other than the more obvious account of a text's occasion of revelation or a direct reference in the text to a specific person or event, the Meccan verses are distinguished from Medinan ones on the basis of structure, style, and content. In terms of structure and style, the shorter *surahs*, *ayat* commencing with "O humankind"[1] or "*kalla*",[2] those instructing the believers to prostrate and those containing the genesis story, are regarded as Meccan, while the longer ones and *ayat* commencing with "O you who have attained unto faith" are regarded as Medinan. Looking at the contents of the Qur'an, the Meccan texts focus on the three essential elements of Islamic doctrine: the absolute unicity of God; the prophethood of Muhammad; and the final accountability of people in the presence of God. In support of these basic doctrines the Qur'an supplies narratives of earlier Prophets and their struggles to establish the law of God. Furthermore, it also contains responses to the philosophical, religious, or areligious arguments of opponents of the Prophet. The implications of belief in these basic doctrines are spelt out in ethico-moral injunctions that are also characteristic of this phase of revelation.

OCCASIONS OF REVELATION (*ASBAB AL-NUZUL*)

Asbab al-nuzul are those occasions ("asbab", sing. "*sabab*") of the revelation of a chapter or verse, which refer to the time and circumstances or place of its revelation. *Asbab al-nuzul* were transmitted by the Companions and are subjected to the same scrutiny for reliability as the general Hadith literature. It is thus not uncommon to find some reports regarded as "unsound" or differing reports from the Companions relating to a single revelation. In such cases, the more "reliable" account is preferred or attempts are made to synchronize the apparent contradiction in different accounts. In traditional Islamic studies, *asbab al-nuzul* forms an important element in the *maghazi* and *sirah* studies, which deal respectively with the warfare expeditions and the biography of Muhammad, in interpretation and legal matters. Despite the neglect that it has suffered as a discipline, its significance is evident from the

---

1 The exceptions to this are *Surah al-Baqarah* (*The Cow*), *al-Nisa* (*The Women*), *al-Haj* (*The Pilgrimage*), and *al-Hujrat* (*The Inner Chambers*).
2 Translated as "Nay!"; this word appears thirty three times in the Qur'an, in fifteen *surahs*, all of them in the second half of the Qur'an.

"frequency of the claim that no assistance is greater in understanding the Qur'an than a knowledge of when and in what circumstances its verses were revealed" (Burton, 1977, 16). Describing the function of *asbab* in exegesis, Rippin says that

> its function is to provide a narrative account in which basic exegesis of the verse may be embodied. The standard interpretational techniques of incorporating glosses, masoretic clarification (e.g., with variants), narrative expansion and, most importantly, contextual definition predominate within the structure of the *sabab* (1988, 2–3).

Rippin also concludes that on many occasions it seems that *asbab* (occasions of revelation) reports are cited by commentators for no apparent exegetical reason: "They are cited and then ignored" (ibid.). From the context of these citations, though, he opines that they are adduced out of a general desire to historicize the text of the Qur'an in order to be able to prove constantly that God really did reveal His book to humanity on earth; the material thereby acts as a witness to God's concern for His creation (1988, 2).[3] Given the general impression in the Qur'an of a God who is constantly involved in the affairs of humankind, this is certainly a credible reason for citing of a *sabab*. Al-Suyuti, in fact, says that the constant reminder of the presence of God in the universe is one of the functions of the *sabab* (1973, 29). "The *sabab*", as Rippin says, "is a constant reminder of God and is the rope, that being one of the meanings of *sabab* in the Qur'an, by which human contemplation ascends to the highest levels even while dealing with the mundane aspects of the text" (1988, 1). While *asbab al-nuzul* has been regarded as significant in any attempt to understand the Qur'an, it is also evident that there has been considerable skepticism regarding its use. The reasons for this range from a fear of compromising the ontological otherness of the Qur'an to an acknowledgment of the corruption that much of Hadith literature – on which all of the *asbab* accounts are based – had been subjected to (Dehlawi, 1966, 49). Dehlawi, for example, cautions against "fussing over the details of the peripheral incidents" on which there is no "significant reliability". He, nonetheless, makes a

---

3 In *Quranic Studies*, Wansbrough argued that the *asbab* material was really an extension of the Qur'an's early legal, or as Wansbrough would have it, "*halakhic* function" (1977, 408). Andrew Rippin examines a large number of the "occasions of revelation" texts and concludes that the primary purpose of the *sabab* material is in fact not *halakhic*, but *haggadic*: "that is, the *asbab* functions to provide an interpretation of a verse within a broad narrative framework" which places the origin of the *asbab* material in the context of the *qussas*: "the wandering storytellers, and pious preachers and to a basically popular religious worship situation where such stories would prove both enjoyable and edifying" (1988).

significant exception in the case of those verses wherein a contradiction (with other verses) is evident because of an incident in the prophetic period (ibid., 19).

ABROGATION (*NASKH*)

Literally *naskh* means "the removal of something by something else [and] annulment" (Ibn Manzur, 1994, 3:624). In Qur'anic Studies and Islamic jurisprudence, however, it means the verification and elaboration of different modes of abrogation. The proof text for the notion of *naskh* is Q.2.106: "Any of our messages (*ayat*) that we abrogate or consign to oblivion, We replace with a better or a similar one. Do you not know that God has the power to will anything?" The modes of *naskh* may be classified as follows:

1. Qur'anic abrogation of the divine scriptures which preceded it;
2. Repeal of some Qur'anic texts which are said to have been blotted out of existence;
3. Abrogation of some earlier commandments of the Qur'an by the later revelations, while the text containing those commandments remained embodied in the Qur'an;
4. Abrogation of a *sunnah* (prophetic practice) by a Qur'anic injunction;
5. Abrogation of a Qur'anic injunction by *sunnah*.

Textually "repealed" verses are further divided into two types: (1) those verses where both the text and law are supposed to have been repealed; and (2) those where only the text is believed to have been abrogated with the law remaining in force. The significance attached to *naskh* may be gauged from the fact that a large number of independent works were produced on the subject. Besides the literature on the theory of *naskh*, one finds a number of reports attributed to the Companions which emphasize the need to acquire knowledge of the abrogating and abrogated verses of the Qur'an. 'Ali ibn Abi Talib is reported to have seen a man in the mosque of Kufa replying to religious questions put to him by the people around him. He asked the man whether he could distinguish between the abrogating verses and the abrogated ones. When he replied in the negative, 'Ali accused the man of deceiving himself as well as others and prohibited him from speaking in the mosque again (Suyuti, 1973, 20ff.).

Despite the emphasis on a sound knowledge of *naskh*, there is probably no other genre in Qur'anic Studies to rival it in confusion regarding its validity, meaning, and applicability. This accounts for the fact that many scholars have questioned its validity beyond the first of the modes listed above, i.e., that of the Qur'an abrogating previous divine scriptures (Razi, 1990, 3:245–252). A number of latter-day reformists such as Sayed Ahmad Khan (d. 1898) and contemporary scholars such as Isma'il al-Faruqi (d. 1986) have rejected the notion that one section of the Qur'an can abrogate another. They argued that instead of viewing previous Qur'anic revelation as being abrogated by subsequent ones, it is more appropriate to continue regarding them as valid to be implemented in conditions similar to those in which they were revealed. Much of the concern of these scholars centered on the question of the authority of the text. When almost every passage or practice that is held as abrogated by one scholar is questioned by another, then there is little doubt that the question of scriptural authority itself is compromised.

The various transformations in the meaning of the term *naskh* are responsible for much of this confusion, as Dehlawi has pointed out (1966, 40). Some Companions, as Ibn Qayyim al-Jawziyyah (d. 1350) illustrates, had used the word in the sense of either *istithna'* (exception), *takhsis* (particularizing the meaning), or *tabyin* (clarifying a previous verse) (1895, 1:12). Its early usage thus did not necessarily include "abrogation", with which it subsequently came to be synonymous. These different meanings were later confused and little or no distinction was drawn between them. The use of the term *naskh* in its general sense thus enhanced the number of abrogated verses that, according to Dehlawi, had reached five hundred (1966, 40). It has been the trend among scholars of the Qur'an to reduce the number of abrogated verses (Faruqi, 1982, 40ff.; Hassan, 1965, 187). The repeal of the individual *verses* in the Qur'an was not generally favoured and various methodologies were employed to either reduce their number or to deny their actual occurrence while accepting such a possibility.[4] Abu Muslim al-Isfahani (d. 1527), for example, denied the theory of *naskh* entirely and Fakhr al-Din al-Razi (d. 1209), one of the great commentators of the Qur'an, argued that the possibility of abrogation does not actually mean that it did occur (Razi, 1990, 3:246). Suyuti reduced the number of repealed

---

4 The *Mu'tazilah* justified the doctrine of the createdness of the Qur'an on the basis of 2.106. They contend that if the Qur'an could be subjected to abrogation then it could not be eternal. However, a group of them, according to Razi, denied the theory of *naskh* (1990, 3–4: 248).

verses to twenty-one while Dehlawi, who argued that most of them can be reconciled, reduced them to five (Dehlawi, 1966, 41–46).

QUR'ANIC EXEGESIS (*TAFSIR*)

The piety and exceptionally reverential attitude of the earliest Muslim towards the Qur'an led to suggestions that there was a general aversion to exegetical activity in Islam's earliest days. Al-Mabani, mentions the response of Abu Bakr to a request that he provide the meaning of Q.4.85. Abu Bakr responded saying: "Which sky could provide me with shade and which earth could bear me if I were to say something concerning the Book of God which I do not know?" (1954, 183). Sa'id ibn Jubayr was asked to write a *tafsir* and he answered angrily: "To lose a part of my body is better than to write a *tafsir*" (cited in Ahmad 1968, 83). Harris Birkeland in his *Old Muslim Opposition Against Interpretation of the Koran* (1955) has detailed the contours of this opposition and its gradual demise. Birkeland has also shown that, personal piety notwithstanding, such opposition only arose in the second Hijri century until *Tafsir* was firmly brought "into and under the sphere of orthodox doctrine and requirements [. . . with] strict methods introduced for the transmission of information which formed the core of interpretational procedure" (Rippin, 'Tafsir' in *The Encylopaedia of Religion*, 1987, 14:237).[5]

In the earliest stages of stages of Qur'anic exegesis the term *"ma'ani"* (lit. "meanings") was the one most frequently used to denote exegesis.[6] Around the third Hijri century this term was supplanted by *"ta'wil"*, from *'-ww-l* (lit. "to return to the beginning", "to interpret", or "to elaborate"). In the following century this was gradually supplanted by the term *"tafsir"* after a long period of interchangeable usage. This is the current term used for Qur'anic exegesis. From the root *"fassara"* (lit. "to interpret" or "elucidate") or *"asfara"* (lit. "to break", e.g., *"asfara al-subh"*, the day broke), the verbal noun *tafsir*, although only occurring once in the Qur'an (25.33), came to be used technically for Qur'anic exegesis around the fifth Hijri century. Zarkashi has defined '*ilm al-tafsir* (the science of interpretation) as "that body of knowledge which deals

---

5 Nadia Abbot's work uses much of the material in Fuat Sezgin to argue for the commonness of *Tafsir* at an early period in Islam. While she acknowledges that this was an activity opposed by people such as 'Umar, the second Caliph, she argues that this opposition was confined to some specific kinds of verses, such as the allegorical ones.

6 This term, as well as *Tafsir*, was also applied to Arabic and Greek commentaries on Aristotle as well as to the explanations of lines in pre-Islamic poetry. Goldfield has demonstrated how the basic nomenclature for concepts in interpretation in Islam "point towards a much longer familiarity with these terms than just two or five score years since the time of the Prophet Muhammad could have caused" (Goldfield, 1993, 15).

with the explanation, interpretation and commentary on the Qur'an, encompassing all ways of acquiring knowledge, which contributes to the proper understanding of it, explains its meanings and extrapolating its laws and wisdom" (1972, 3:13).

Between the second and fourth centuries when the terms *"ta'wil"* and *"tafsir"* were used interchangeably, there were also attempts to particularize their application to exegesis. *Tafsir* was used to denote external philological exegesis, the exoteric, or a reference to both secular and divine books on the one hand, while *ta'wil* was taken to refer to the exposition of the subject matter, esoteric, or exegesis dealing purely with a divine scripture on the other. Muqatil ibn Sulayman (d. 150/767), an early exegete, suggested that *tafsir* denoted what could be known about the Qur'an at a human level and *'ta'wil* what could be known only by God. Later *ta'wil* became a technical term employed by both the traditionists and those outside the "mainstream" such as the Isma'ili, Mu'tazili and some Sufis to denote an interpretation which dispensed with tradition and was based on reason, personal opinion, research, and/or intuition. Today the Sunni "orthodoxy" uses the term pejoratively to denote rejection of the "obvious" meaning of a verse and adoption of another more "obscure" interpretation. In this belated sharp distinction between *ta'wil* and *tafsir* we find traditional categories at odds with the ambiguities that are intrinsic to any contemporary discourse on interpretation – and indeed with the earlier opinion in exegetical circles that did not seem to acknowledge such distinction.[7] Contemporary understanding of understanding, interpretation, and meaning rejects the neat distinction between philological exegesis and that dealing with textual substance. The meaning of even a single word that may appear "obvious" upon superficial perusal, may not stand up that description under closer scrutiny or in another generation or place. Similar difficulties accompany the traditional appreciation of the sources and typology of *Tafsir*.

SOURCES OF *TAFSIR*

The Qur'an has always been regarded as its own primary commentator and is the first source for understanding its meaning since many questions emerging from a particular verse will find answers or clarification in

---

7 Early exegetes such as Tabari and Maturidi (d. 944) used the terms interchangeably as is evident from the titles of their commentaries; *Jami' al-Bayan 'an Ta'wil Ay al-Qur'an* and *Ta'wilat al-Qur'an* respectively. In later editions, Tabari's exegesis later came to be renamed as *Jami' al-Bayan fi Tafsir al-Qur'an*, itself an indication of the subsequent pejorative connotations applied to the word *"ta'wil"*.

others. The more general statements (*mujmal*) would find clarification in the specific ones (*mubayyin*), the absolute (*mutlaq*) in the restricted (*muqayyad*) and the common (*'am*) in the particular (*khas*). This is a kind of *tafsir* that Shi'i scholars of the Qur'an put great emphasis on. The second primary source for *Tafsir* is the Prophet Muhammad, who is viewed by Muslims as the personification of the message of the Qur'an and its external commentator par excellence. There are numerous examples of prophetic commentary (*al-tafsir al-nabawi*) and the Hadith compilations of Bukhari, Muslim, Tirmidhi, and others all have chapters dealing with these specifically and arranged in agreement with the sequence of their appearance in the Qur'an. The prophetic presence was invaluable for the purposes of exegesis, for even the explanatory verses themselves were best understood if explained by the direct recipient of divine revelation. This, according to the Qur'an, was one of his prophetic functions: "And upon you have We bestowed from on high this reminder, so that you might make clear unto humankind all that has ever been thus bestowed upon them, and that they might take thought" (16.44).

The Prophet's demise deprived the Muslim community of their direct source of clarity and guidance. The Successors (*tabi'un*) – the generation following the Companions – and even some of the Companions – were often confronted with new problems and needed the guidance of those who were regarded as the masters of the Qur'an and who were closest to the Prophet in fellowship and knowledge. This group comprised the third source of *Tafsir*. Some of the latter commented freely on the Qur'an while others regarded this as the exclusive privilege of the Prophet. Among the Companions 'Umar ibn al-Khattab, 'Abd Allah ibn Mas'ud, Ubay ibn Ka'b, Zayd bin Thabit, Abu Musa al-'Ashari, 'Abd Allah ibn Zubayr, and 'Abd Allah ibn 'Abbas were regarded as the most prominent commentators of the Qur'an. 'Ibn 'Abbas was, furthermore, accepted as the most knowledgeable in the science of *Tafsir* and even during the Prophet's lifetime is said to have been referred to as "*tarjuman al-Qur'an*" (the interpreter of the Qur'an) and "*bahr al-ulum*" (the ocean of knowledge). In the early years of Islamic scholarship *Tafsir* formed an integral and indiscernible part of the science of Hadith and scholars differ as to when it became a separate science. Muhammad Husayn al-Dhahabi, a contemporary Egyptian scholar, maintains that the separation of *Tafsir* from Hadith and the growth of the former into an independent science was completed by Ibn Majah (d. 886), Ibn Jarir al-Tabari (d. 938), and others and not before then (1979, 1:144). Others argue that *Tafsir* split from the science of Hadith long before that "although the collections of Hadith and the books of *Sirah* (prophetic history) were used to incorporate *Tafsir* material regarding many verses in the form of traditions" (Sawwaf, 1979, 142).

TRADITIONAL CLASSIFICATION OF *TAFSIR*

Later Sunni scholars of the Qur'an have based their classification of *Tafsir* on the means employed by a commentator rather than on the focus or content of a particular commentary and have arrived at the following categories: (1) exegesis by transmission (*tafsir bi'l-riwayah*); (2) exegesis by opinion/reason (*tafir bi'l-ray'*); and (3) exegesis by indication (*tafsir bi'l-isharah*) ('Inayah, 1996, Zarqani, 1996).[8]

Exegesis by transmission (Tafsir bi al-riwayah)

Exegesis by transmission (*riwayah*), which is very interestingly also referred to as "*tafsir bi'l-'ilm*" (exegesis based on the knowledge), is the bedrock of what is viewed as orthodox exegesis and represents the most commonly accepted mode of interpretation. This type of *Tafsir* is supposedly based on explanatory accounts in the Qur'an itself, reliable *ahadith* of the Prophet (as defined by the "orthodoxy" and within the framework of its own theological and legal epistemology), the concrete manifestations of Qur'anic law and morality in his life, or the "authentic" narrations of the Companions. It is based on the assumption that there is an "acceptable" body of literature based on the Hadith or the views of the Companions and the Successors that was handed down from one generation to the other without the intervention of reason, discernment, selection, or rejection of the transmitters. Scholars could thus "merely repeat" on the basis of preceding authority. In this attitude they were sustained by the Qur'anic *ayah* "Ask the people of remembrance if you do not know" (16.43).

The first generation of Muslims who engaged in *Tafsir* activity based their endeavours on the first two sources of *Tafsir* mentioned above (the Qur'an and the Hadith), their own knowledge of the occasions of

8 Zarkashi, on the authority of Sufyan al-Thawri cites Ibn 'Abbas as having opined that *Tafsir* is of four kinds: (1) that what is known by the Arabs through their language; (2) the meaning which is obvious and ignorance of which is inexcusable; (3) that which is known through the scholarly reflection (*ijtihad*) of the *'ulama*, also referred to as "*ta'wil*"; and (4) that which is known only to God (1972, 2.174–180). While Zarkashi cites examples of each, the criterion for this division makes little sense. I mention his categorization, also adopted by Suyuti, to indicate the presence of divisions other than that which came to be adopted subsequently as the "orthodox" one.

revelation, pre-Islamic poetry, and their own frequent discussions with Jews or Muslims of Jewish origin. These discussions often led to the search for meanings of obscure words and gave a Judaic gloss to a large number of *ayat*. All of these views and those of the succeeding generation, the Successors, in turn, formed a part of the ever-changing and growing body of "traditional" *Tafsir* literature. In the course of time, the volume of traditional commentary increased considerably and large numbers of traditions were attributed to the Prophet as well as to 'Ali and Ibn 'Abbas, all of them being incorporated into *Tafsir*. While a number of commentaries – or compilations of "authentic" exegetical narrations – such as those of Muqatil ibn Sulayman and Sufyan al-Thawri (d. 161/778) gained prominence in the second century of Islam, none acquired the "authenticity" of Ibn al-Jarir al-Tabari's exegesis, *"Jami al-Bayan 'an Ta'wil Ayi al-Qur'an"*. Undoubtedly the pinnacle of traditional *Tafsir*, his work is the basis of the majority of the exegeses of the succeeding centuries. His work is important for two reasons: first, the extensiveness of his compilation and preservation of the various exegetical hadiths and earlier opinion regarding their soundness and applicability; and, second, he was the first to classify his material in an organized manner basing it on subject matter and their relationship to the structure of the Qur'an's verses. Despite the fact that Tabari's commentary had been hailed as the basis of *tafsir bi'l-riwayah* he still had to deal with the raw material of tradition, accepting some, rejecting some and minimizing the importance of others.[9] While it may be argued that Tabari's exegesis is entirely based on Hadith, the concomitant assumption that Tabari as a person, editor, philologist, and jurist and his social milieu played no role in his own selection or mediating process is clearly a dubious one. The wide acceptance of the first category of *Tafsir* has been paralleled by bitter theological and philosophical disputes that have characterized the second and third categories.

Exegesis by opinion/reason (Tafsir bi'l-ra'y)

The emergence of a genre of *Tafsir* that did not claim to be rooted entirely in Hadith literature and one which was committed to employing

---

9 Birkeland has noted that most of the chains of transmission in Tabari's *Tafsir* do not go back to the Companions or the Prophet but stop about 100 A.H. (cited in Smith, 1975, 59). Tabari's own acceptability really grew only after his demise and the legal school that he founded vanished soon after. He was at various times attacked by the Hanbilites of Baghdad as well as some of the Shi'is. Despite his subsequent universal acclaim by the "orthodoxy", Yaqut, the historian, reports that his funeral had to be held at night for fear of the anger of the crowd at his suspected Shi'i leanings (ibid., 58).

reason as an acknowledged and indispensable element in the hermeneutical process, was inevitable. Named *Tafsir bi'l-ra'y*, in contrast to the
supposedly *Tafsir bi'l-'ilm* (exegesis based on knowledge), by its
detractors, this description was never adopted by those supposedly
engaged in it. The permissibility of exegesis based on opinion or reason is
argued on the basis of the well-known response of the Prophet to the
answers given by Mu'adh ibn Jabal when the latter was dispatched to
Yemen as a teacher. The Prophet questioned Mu'adh about his resort
when confronted with problematic situations. Mu'adh replied that he
would judge by the Qur'an and *sunnah*. When asked "and if you did not
find the solutions therein?" He replied that he would exercise his
personal judgment. The Prophet was excited about Mu'adh's display of
initiative and praised God for it (Maliki, 1980, 3:689). Opposition to
this kind of *Tafsir* was based on the same two sayings attributed to the
Prophet that sought to legitimate the first mode of *Tafsir*, "Whosoever
speaks in respect of the Qur'an without knowledge, let him have an
abode in the fire" (Abu Dawud, cited in Suyuti, 1973, 2:179) and
"Whoever utters in respect of the Qur'an and (even if) he is correct, he
has erred" (Abu Dawud and Tirmidhi, cited in Suyuti, 1973, 2:179).

In the face of indisputable mastery by some of the luminaries of this
mode, the apparent "contradiction" in the two positions – both based on
Hadith – a number of mainstream scholars such as Al-Ghazali resolved
the "problem" by classifying *Tafsir bi'l-ra'y* into two further categories:
Tafsir mahmud – a "meritorious" commentary based on the hadith
sources of *Tafsir*, the rules of Shari'ah and the Arabic language on the one
hand, and *Tafsir madhmum* – an "objectionable" commentary based
entirely on personal opinion in disregard to the aforementioned sources
and rules, on the other. Most of the commentators of this genre rejected
the claim that earlier scholars had related a comprehensive *Tafsir* of every
single verse from the "righteous predecessors" and whose authority could
be traced to the Prophet himself or his Companions. On the contrary,
they argued that the paucity of hadith material on *Tafsir* was precisely
because the Prophet desired and encouraged the study of the Qur'an.
"A man with proof is more honorable than a lion in its lair; an imitator is
more despicable than a mangy goat," said Mahmud ibn 'Umar
al-Zamakhshari (d. 538/1075), the luminary of this genre, "for knowledge
is a city which has two doors for entry, one reason, the other tradition"
(cited in Ahmad, 1968, 87). While Al-Ghazali was among Sunni Islam's
great champions of this kind of *Tafsir*, its real protagonists were the

Mu'tazilites and in Qur'anic scholarship Zamakhshari is undoubtedly the most prominent commentator of this genre whose works are still extant. His *"Al-Kashshaf 'an Haqa'iq Ghawamid al-Tanzil'"* is grudgingly regarded by mainstream scholarship as one of the most important works of *Tafsir*. Displaying a rather casual attitude towards exegetical hadith, he places enormous emphasis on linguistic analysis, a task he "accomplishes with consummate skill" (Ayoub, 1984, 5).

Exegesis by indication (Tafsir bi'l-isharah)

In the growing intensification of the struggle between the scholastic theologians (*mutakallimun*) and traditionists (*muhaddithun*) and the overt politicization of religious life, it was inevitable that a third path would emerge: a path disdainful of both and desperate to remain faithful to the yearning of communion with God. This was the path of gnosticism or Sufism (*tassuwwuf*). The bitter theological disputes described in the fourth chapter further contributed to the rise of this tendency. The Sufis denounced the obsession with verbal arguments as void of spiritual certitude and an affinity with God, whose adoration, they insisted, is the purpose of creation.[10] The desire to escape the intellectual and philosophical formalist stranglehold exercised over *Tafsir* in the second and third centuries of Islam also contributed to the notion that the Qur'an has a deeper and more inward meaning exposed only to those who walk the path of *ma'rifah* (gnosis). The spiritual dimensions of human existence and eschatology were central themes in this genre of *Tafsir* and two core ideas formed the basis of its interpretative methodology. First, these scholars argued that just as a ritually impure person is not allowed to touch the Qur'an, similarly anyone with an unclean heart would not be receptive to the Qur'an's message. Second, while not rejecting the "obvious" and philological meaning of the text, they concentrated on discovering or, rather, being exposed to its "inner meanings".[11] *Tafsir bi'l-isharah* attaches meanings to texts that are not

10 This tendency rightly claims its origins in the aftermath of the earliest political tumult which followed in the wake of Uthman's assassination in 658. During a period which witnessed the pillage of Medina and the desecration of the Ka'bah (c. 682), many pious Muslims sought the path of renunciation of all worldly aspirations and seclusion as a means of protecting their faith. The bitter theological disputes described in the fourth chapter further contributed to the rise of this tendency. "These arid discussions," says Ahmad "usurped the role of subtle tenderness of human feelings. The concept of God thus presented could no more lend warmth and strength to the soul" (1968, 99). The disdain with these dialectical gymnastics was reflected in the saying that "the prayer of the *mutakallimun* is confined to smelling out atheism" (ibid.).

11 Gatje describes this as "parallel exegesis" whereby the character of reality of the external meaning" is maintained while seeing "allusions (*isharat*) in this, which are important to understand" (1976, 40).

perceptible – often also not acceptable – to the scholars of Islam who adhere to a more formalist and legalist approach.[12] Its philosophy is based on the idea that "nature is a fabric of symbols, which must be read according to their meaning and that the Qur'an is the counterpart of that meaning in human words" (Nasr, 1987, 24). Much emphasis is placed on the fact that the word *ayat* is consistently employed in the Qur'an to mean both its own "verses" and "signs" – the latter, in its Qur'anic context, referring to natural phenomena manifesting the Presence and Greatness of God. "Both nature and the Qur'an", says Seyyed Hossein Nasr, "speak forth the presence and the worship of God: 'We shall show them Our portents (*ayat*) on the horizon and within themselves until it will be made manifest unto them it is the truth' (41.53)" (ibid.). Umar Khayyam explains the process through which this knowledge of the Qur'an comes to the "seeker":

> [They] do not seek [it] by meditation or by discursive thinking, but by purgation of their inner being and the purifying of their dispositions. They cleanse the rational soul of the impurities of nature and bodily form until it becomes pure substance. It then comes face to face with the spiritual world, so that the forms of that world become truly reflected in it without doubt or ambiguity ... Tell unto the reasoners that for the lovers of God [gnostic] intuition is guide, not discursive thought (cited in Nasr, 1987, 34).

The pre-eminent example of this kind of *Tafsir* is the work of the Andalusian, Muhyi al-Din Muhammad ibn 'Ali ibn 'Arabi (d. 638/1240), known to his followers as *al-Shaikh al-Akbar* (the Grand Master). His major works was not on *Tafsir* but on mystical doctrine. He is widely known for his exposition of the doctrine of *wahdat al-wujud* (the unity of being), which says that all existence being ultimately nothing, is in reality nothing but God. Denounced as a heretic by the then "orthodoxy", he had many zealous defenders. "Each verse of the Qur'an", he argued, "had an external and inner sense, each expression (*harf*) has a limit (*hadd*) and there is an ascent from every limit to higher understanding" (cited in Lichtenstadter, 1974, 19). Ibn 'Arabi made frequent use of allegory and symbolism in his *Tafsir* and affirmed the Qur'an to be a treasure house from which all ideas expressed in his works are derived. He argued that he was given the key to its comprehension and to using it as the basis of his teachings (ibid.).

---

12 "As for the speech of the Sufis", says Suyuti, "it is not *Tafsir*. And if someone regards it as *Tafsir* then he is guilty of *kufr*" (1973, 2:184).

A note on the traditional typology

The Muslim "orthodoxy's" attempt at neat categorization was part of a broader pattern to secure its own legitimacy which also implies that it had to build the rejection of the "heretical" other's methods into it. In some ways, of course, this is no different from the "orthodoxy" of critical scholarship that builds its own legitimacy on the unquestioned primacy of reason and the written word and rejects as "unreliable" or "unscientific" other modes of knowledge such as intuition or the oral word. From a critical perspective, there are a number of problems with the "orthodoxy's" categorization of *Tafsir*. First, exegesis by transmission enjoys the widest legitimacy among them because it is based on the assumption that their scholars were absolutely objective and dealt with "objective" transmissions which came to them in a timeless and spaceless zone from individuals who had no interest in, and therefore no biases towards, philosophical, political, and theological issues which were raging all over the Muslim world a mere one or two decades after the death of the Prophet. Since this is hardly possible, it follows that they exercised their reason in discerning the transmissions that they dealt with as basic source material (which, in some measure, makes them "guilty" of exegesis by opinion). Second, the notion that any potential exegete must be grounded in a "deep and broad" knowledge of a wide array of requisite sciences – as distinct from the *Tafsir bi'l-ra'y* – is certainly less subjective than the latter. However subjectivity itself cannot be avoided. It is commonly accepted today that the very sciences that form the basis of this "scholarly credibility" were rooted in particular social and historical conditions. Nor has the possession of a "deep and broad" knowledge of these sciences prevented diverse opinions emerging around identical texts and numerous philosophical, theological, and jurispru-dential differences – all of them claiming to be rooted in tradition. Third, it is widely acknowledged that most of the classical exegetes who fall into the "orthodox" category were deeply pious people who engaged in frequent and regular optional spiritual exercises even if they did not follow a particular Sufi path (*tariqah*). The neat differentiation between *Tafsir* by indication and *Tafsir* by transmission would imply that these exegetes were never "touched" by their spiritual exercises and that these never resulted in spiritually illuminated insights into the Qur'an, a position untenable to "orthodoxy". Fourth, any categorization which was part of a broader struggle to legitimize some opinions as "dogma" and delegitimize others as "heresy", in order to establish an official orthodoxy, cannot escape from the undeniable gifts which the excluded other has to offer. In Zamakhshari's case, for example, "orthodoxy" resorted to a host of devices ranging from a reluctant acknowledgment of his genius, and cautious encouragement that his work be studied, to plagiarism. In the case of the latter the theologically cleansed version would then be allowed to circulate widely, in some cases bringing considerable fame to the censor-editor. Finally, the act of interpretation is far more complex than what neat exclusivist dogmatic or scientistic categories would admit to. No human being is entirely a rational animal, a spiritual being or an automaton merely repeating tradition or regurgitating scientific facts. No matter how committed to tradition a scholar may be, he or she still asks questions from that tradition and selects from it on the basis of his or her pre-understanding. Just as it was not unusual for the "traditionalist" Tabari to offer a very allegorical meaning to a certain text, it not unusual for the "rationalist" Zamakhshari to ascribe his exegetical achievements to the miraculous power of the *Ka'bah* and the *barakah* (blessing) which emanates from it.

To summarize, the meaning assigned to a text by any commentator cannot exist independently of his/her personality and environment. There is no reason to suggest that any particular generation should be the intellectual hostages of another, for even these classical commentators did not consider themselves irrevocably tied to the work of the previous generation. The emergence of *Tafsir* as a science in Islam is itself proof of the creativity of commentators who until today continue to be inspired by, assimilate, elaborate on, and, yes, even reject the work of their predecessors.

A NON-CONFESSIONAL TYPOLOGY

In contrast to the "orthodox" Muslim typology of *Tafsir* which is based on "true" or "false" methods leading to "orthodoxy" or "heresy" respectively, *Tafsir* literature has also been classified by a number of critical scholars – most which follow the typology first proposed by Wansborough in his *Qur'anic Studies: Sources and Methods and Scriptural Interpretation*. This typology has been described as "functional, unified and revealing" (Rippin 'Tafsir' in *The Encylopaedia of Religion*, 1987, 14:238) and is based on the form and function of a particular *Tafsir* work.[13] These categories are narrative (Haggadic), legal

13 I am indebted to Andrew Rippin for his summary of these types in the *Encyclopaedia of Religion*.

(Halakhic), textual (masoretic), rhetorical and allegorical. Wansborough also argued that this sequence, in addition to reflecting the content and mode of a particular *Tafsir*, exhibits a minimum of overlapping and, save for the last-named, might almost be chronologically plotted in the above sequence (1977, 119).[14]

Narrative Tafsir

This form of *Tafsir* is characterized by creating an illustrative narrative that is often supplemented by folklore from the Near Eastern World. Wansbrough says that the "obvious source for most, if not all, of this material is Rabbinic literature" (1977, 134) since the Qur'an provides little or no detail about events in the period of revelation.[15] Narrative *Tafsir* deals with ordinary questions confronting readers of a text which seldom provides a context for its many statements, and he suggests, the gaps in the Qur'anic narrative were filled from a very familiar mine of biblical folklore (ibid., 135). Wansbrough explains how, in this type of *Tafsir*, particularly in the works of the earliest commentators of this genre such as Muqatil ibn Sulayman (d. 150/767) and Muhammad Kalbi (d. 146/763), it is very difficult, "frequently impossible" (ibid., 127) to separate the text from the commentary. Furthermore, "the scriptural text was subordinate, conceptually and syntactically, to the *narratio*" (ibid., 127).

Legal Tafsir

Unlike in narrative *Tafsir* where the textual arrangement is respected, in this type of *Tafsir* material is arranged according to legal themes. One of the earliest examples of this kind of *Tafsir* is that of Ibn Sulayman's *"The Interpretation of Five Hundred Verses from the Qur'an"*. This work deals with matters such as faith, prayer, ablution, pilgrimage, the conduct of jihad, inheritance, usury, marriage, divorce, inheritance, debts, contracts. Besides the fact that all of these verses are regarded as the only verses from the Qur'an that deals with law, his interpretation provided greater juristic clarity to the text at a time when Islamic jurisprudence (*fiqh*) was not a coherent and well-defined discipline. In his

14 It is important to point out that Wansbrough does not believe that *Tafsir* is really extraneous to the text of the Qur'an, which he describes as "the Muhammadan *evangelium*" (1977, 69), itself and that the canon, in fact, in large measure grew from what later came to be regarded as *Tafsir*.
15 Only two contemporary figures are, for example, named in the Qur'an: Abu Lahab, an uncle of the Prophet, and Zayd, his adopted son.

typical way of relentlessly drawing attention to what he regards as the Jewish origin of Islam, Wansbrough argues that "the halakhists employed *Tafsir* traditions in three kinds of exegetical literature: *ahkam* (prescriptions), *ikhtilaf*, (dispute) and *naskh* (abrogation) although "the scope of each extended beyond exclusively midrashic exploitation of the text of scripture" (ibid., 183). Given the relative paucity of legal texts and the brevity of those texts, he says that "the extrapolation of law from revelation was, in the Muslim community, as in others organized on similar theocratic principles, a torturous and interminable process" (ibid.).

Textual Tafsir

This kind of *Tafsir* – Wansbrough speaks of "masoretic exegesis" – is concerned with the details of the text, is "mostly deductive" (1977, 168), and deals with "lexical explanations, grammatical analysis and an agreed apparatus of variant readings of the Qur'an" (ibid., 203). He believes that the elaboration of the text – "the Qur'anic masorah" – is "entirely exegetical, even where where its contents have been transmitted in the guise of textual variants" (ibid). Among the earliest works of this kind that Wanbrough uses to make his arguments were the *Tafsir* of al-Farra (d. 822) and Abu 'Ubyad (d. 838) titled *Ma'ani al-Qur'an* (the Meanings of the Qur'an) and *Fad'-il al-Qur'an* (the Virtues of the Qur'an) respectively. "For the textual history of Muslim scripture the activity of the masoretes was not only creative but productive: of postulates which became the foundations of both grammar and lexicography" (ibid., 208). "A feature of this type of *Tafsir* that he draws attention to was the practice of adducing and (usually) commenting on the entire text of scripture ... and concern for the integrity of the text and for the structural relevance to one another of its parts ..." (ibid., 226).

Rhetorical Tafsir

In the previous chapter we saw how the "literary genius" of the Qur'an was forwarded as Muhammad's founding miracle. Although the roots of this kind of *Tafsir* which focuses on the literary excellencies of the Qur'an are probably in the textual exegesis with a grammatical focus, its later development as a separate genre emerged from the need to prove the inimitability of the Qur'an. "As in philology, so in rhetoric, the tryranny of *lingua sacra* was not merely felt, but found expression in as a criterion of excellence (Wansbrough, 1977, 231). According to Rippin, Ibn Qutaybah's (d. 276/889) *Ta'wil mushkil al-Qur'an* was the key transition point between the earliest rhetorical analysis based upon grammatical and exegetical niceties and that of the later doctrine of the miraculous nature of the Qur'an. "In these texts attention is paid to the literary qualities of the Arabic language which place it outside the norm of Arabic prose and poetry; various poetical figures are isolated, for example, are subjected to analysis for meaning, and, in many cases, are then compared to older Arabic poetry" (Rippin, 'Tafsir' in *The Encylopaedia of Religion*, 1987, 14:239).

Allegorical Tafsir

Earlier on in this chapter we dealt with *Tafsir bi 'l-isharah*, one of the traditional categories of *Tafsir*. This mode of exegetical activity produced the genre of allegorical *Tafsir* which is based on a distinction between the *zahir* (lit. "obvious", "clear", i.e., the historically or empirically verifiable) and the *batin* (the "hidden", the allegorical). The *Tafsir* of Sahl al-Tustari (d. 896) – described by Wansbrough as "primitive and archtypal" (1977, 244) – is an early example of this. As may be expected with any work based on spiritual insights, this genre is void of an overall exegetical methodology. "Nor is any overall pursuit of mystical themes to be found; indeed its general nature is fragmented. The esoteric portions of the texts are formed around typically Sufi meditations on the Qur'an, each taking a key word from the text. Allegorical interpretation in this case becomes as much a process of thematic association as one of textual commentary" (Rippin, 'Tafsir' in *The Encylopaedia of Religion*, 1987, 14:239–240).

A note on Wansbrough

Wansbrough is at pains to present his work as tentative and yet proceeds to make assumptions premised on those very tentative conclusions. His demarcation of categories of *Tafsir* for example, besides depending on a very limited number of *Tafsir* works for each genre, is an example of his insistence that they followed each other in neat chronological order. For his category of Haggadic *Tafsir* he depends nearly entirely on the work of Muqatil ibn Sulayman (d. 150/767) and Muhammad Kalbi (763). We will recall his view that in this category the text really followed and was subject to the narrative; he cites these two works as examples thereof. When, however, he runs thin on Ibn Ishaq as actually being an example thereof, he casually resorts to unsubstantiated claims of editorial intervention – "I am tempted to ascribe this to editorial intervention" (1977, 127). Referring specifically to Ibn Ishaq's inability to fit squarely into his categorization, he says: "That this is less true of Ibn Ishaq's work could be the result of its having been drastically edited by a scholar fully conversant with the methods of and principles of masoretic exegesis" (ibid.). Wansbrough, of course, uses his typology to argue that the text evolved over nearly ten generations without offering any idea why this could not be accomplished in one generation. As William Graham has argued, "The identification of various periscopes, older prescriptural motifs, and language taken from Judaic usage is suggestive of many new interpretative possibilities, but it is not clear that it necessitates the radical conclusion that there was no generally recognized fixed Qur'anic text before A.H. 200" (Graham, 1980, 140).

In reading Wansbrough I found it curious that many of the terms that he readily applies to the Qur'anic *Tafsir* tradition, (haggadic, halakhic, masoretic, etc.) are explained in *The Shorter Oxford English Dictionary*, exclusively in terms of Jewish tradition. In other words, there is little or no meaning to them outside this tradition. Wansbrough's persistence in the employment of these terms, in addition to the intended point that the Qur'an is a product of Jewish scriptural tradition, also has the effect of highlighting the Qur'anic tradition's supposed emptiness. The message seems to be "On your own, you are nothing." Like all of us, Wansbrough is also the child of a particular mileu, even though, like all others who claim to be "disinterested scholars", he may claim to be a virgin, a disembowelled products of immaculate scholarly conceptions. He belongs to a generation of scholars wedded to a political and cultural worldview which sees the subjected people as mere borrowers and inheritors from the dominant classes. The Arabs could thus not possibly produce something remotely coherent on their own. Not that they made these claims; instead they readily acknowledged the interconnectedness of the Qur'an with other scriptures. In Mecca already Muhammad was accused of having learnt the Qur'anic messages from a non-Arab, probably a Jew or a Judaeo-Christian. "They say that it is only a man who teaches him. But the tongue of the man they allude to is foreign while this is in Arabic plain and clear" (16.103). The Qur'an does not deny that Muhammad was in contact with Christians or Jews; in fact, it claims an affinity with their scriptural traditions and describes itself as a verifier of those scriptures.

> Oh! Children of Israel, Remember those blessings of Mine with which
> I graced you, and fulfill your promise unto Me, [whereupon] I shall fulfil
> My promise unto you; and of Me, of Me stand in awe. Believe in that
> which I have bestowed from on high, confirming the truth already in your
> possession and be not foremost among those who deny its truth; and do
> not barter away my messages for a trifling gain; and of Me, of Me be
> conscious. And do not overlay the truth with falsehood and do not
> knowingly suppress the truth (2.40–42).

THE QUR'AN AND HERMENEUTICS

The term "hermeneutics" refers principally to textual interpretation and
the problems surrounding it. The problem of hermeneutics emerges from
the fact that human expressions – or divine expressions in a human
language – (texts in particular) are simultaneously familiar and alien to
the reader. Taking into account this seeming paradox, the reader – if the
text is to be understandable – has the task of transposing the meaning of
the text into his/her own system of values and meanings. Derived from
the Greek verb *hermeneuein* ("to interpret") hermeneutics is defined as the
"intellectual discipline concerned with the nature and presuppositions of
the interpretation of expressions" (Harvey, "hermeneutics" in *Encyclopaedia of Religion*, 1987, 6:279). As an interpretative activity its
essential concern is the written text and it can be described as "the theory
of the operations of understanding in their relation to the interpretation
of written texts" (ibid.). Hermeneutics deals with three major conceptual
issues: (1) the nature of a text; (2) what it means to understand a text; and
(3) how understanding and interpretation are determined by the
presuppositions and assumptions (the horizon) of both the interpreter
and the audience to which the text is being interpreted.

I am yet to come across the term hermeneutics employed in the Arabic
language. The compound *'fiqh al-tafsir wa al-ta'wil* – "the understanding
of exegesis and interpretation", however, does appeal to me. The absence
of a definitive term for hermeneutics in the classical Islamic disciplines or
its non-employment on a significant scale in contemporary Qur'anic
literature does not imply the absence of definite hermeneutical notions or
operations in Qur'anic Studies. While the term "hermeneutics" itself
dates back only from the seventeenth century, the operations of textual
exegesis and theories of interpretation – religious, literary, legal – date
back to antiquity. Traditional *Tafsir* activity has, however, always been
categorized and these categories – *Shi'ite, Mu'tazilite, Abbasid, Ash'arite,*

etc. – are acknowledged to say something about the affiliations, ideology, period, and social horizons of the commentator. Connections between the subject of interpretation, the interpreter, and the audience are rarely made. When this is the case, it is usually done with the intention of disparaging the work or the author, or they are made to underline the theological prejudices of the author. To date though, little has been written about these connections in an historical or literary-critical manner or about the explicit or implicit socio-political assumptions underlying their theological orientations; the central concern of contemporary hermeneutics.

In contemporary Muslim scholarship, Fazlur Rahman, Nasr Hamid Abu Zayd, and Muhammad Arkoun are among the rare exceptions who deal with hermeneutics. Rahman insists that "the Qur'an is the divine response ... to the moral and social situation of the Prophet's Arabia" (1986). He thus pleads for a "hermeneutical theory that will help us understand the meaning of the Qur'an as a whole so that both the theological sections of the Qur'an and its ethico-legal parts become a unified whole" (ibid.). Arkoun emphasizes the need to reconstruct the historical background of each (Qur'anic) text or period and for greater consideration to be given to "the aesthetics of reception: how a discourse is received by its listeners and readers" (1987b, 17). He suggests a critical re-evaluation of the interpretative methodology "elaborated by jurists-theologians based on rationality as founding the true knowledge and excluding the constructions of imagination" (ibid., 23). In its place he offers the "hope that semiotics and linguistics can create the possibility of reading religious texts ... in a new way" (ibid.). While both Rahman and Arkoun emphasize the historical context of the Qur'an's revelation, Abu Zayd stresses the Arabic nature of its orgin and the need to approach it as an Arabic literary work. While he does not deny the divine origin of the Qur'an ("It is a divine text in so far as its origins are concerned"), he argues that it is futile to delve into this because the divine is beyond the realm of scientific enquiry.

The Qur'an is a communicative relationship between sender and recipient that arose through the means of a code or a language system. Because, in the case of the Qur'an, the sender cannot be the subject of scientific enquiry, the study of the text must proceed from the premise of the verifiable/observable reality of the culture of the community addressed by the text as well as its primary, the recipient, the Messenger. Culture is expressed in language. The study of the text must thus proceed from the reality and culture as empirical givens. From these givens we arrive at a scientific understanding of the phenomenon of the text. The idea that the text is a product of culture (*muntaj thaqafi*) is so obvious that it does not have to be argued any further (1994, 27–28).

For Abu Zayd, however, the text is larger than the Qur'an, which he describes as the "primary text" from which all other Islamic texts sprang forth. By text in the broader sense, he refers to "that reservoir of knowledge of the Arabs at a time when they had no science; only poetry" (ibid., 41). While at a superficial glance, his methodology resembles that of Wansbrough et al. who have adopted a literary approach to Qur'anic Studies, his emphasis on the Arabicity of the text places him firmly in the camp of Arabists rather than students of Islam. "We need to win the text back as an Arabic text – and Arabic is an historical language, part of the Arabic culture which is an historical culture." While Wansbrough saw interpretation as so thoroughly interwoven with the text that that they have become indistinguishable, Abu Zayd regards interpretation of the text as "the flip side of the text" – irrevocably tied to each other and argues that only through interpretation can the text be comprehended. For this to take place, the Qur'an needs to be decoded in the light of its historical, cultural, and linguistic mileu. Furthermore, the results of this decoding must be decoded in the code of the cultural and linguistic milieu of the interpreter. Unlike Arkoun, he regards his own work as part of an Islamic renewal-cum-reform project and has utilized the results of his work to argue for human rights and gender justice, saying that in these matters the spirit of the text must take precedence over its letter (1993a).[16]

We have in these writings the beginnings of the emergence of hermeneutics as a discipline in Qur'anic studies. If previous patterns in Islamic scholarship are anything to go by then it will be a considerable while before its direction and nature become evident. Clearly though, it will be in societies where Muslims are desperate to make contemporaneous sense of the speech of God in the midst of active struggles for justice where a significant contribution to this discipline will be found.[17]

16 Abu Zayd believes that studying the Qur'an from its historical-linguistic perspective will necessarily yield progressive results for a number of social questions. He distances himself from the methodologies of the likes of Tantawi Jawhari, Rashid Rida, and Muhammad Abduh who attempted to interpret the Qur'an from the perspective of then new theories of exact sciences and/or understandings of society dealing with questions such as democracy, human rights and gender equality. They, he argues, took contemporary values as their basic premises rather than the socio-historical context of the Qur'an (cf. 1995).
17 See my own *Qur'an, Liberation and Pluralism* as an example of this contribution to Qur'anic hermeneutics.

FAREWELL TO INNOCENCE

Does the Qur'an guide in an exclusively ahistorical and universal manner or is it – interpretations and approaches to it, at least – also informed by, amongst others, socio-economic reality?

A commonly supposed presuppositionless or innocent approach to understanding the Qur'an has no basis in the history of *Tafsir* or *'ulum al-Qur'an* for all non-Prophetic human experience is essentially interpretative and mediated by culture and personality – factors which cannot be transcended. (The personal experience of "seekers of the Divine" may prove otherwise but the results of that must remain confined to the individual and cannot be of significant social import.) This has, furthermore, been acknowledged to be so – even if not always explicitly – by most of the orthodox *mufassirun* (exegetes) and *fuqaha* (jurists). Furthermore, all interpretative activity and conclusions are located in a particular context. It is therefore, impossible to speak of a universal interpretation of a Qur'anic text. All interpretative activity and "meaning" are thus, of necessity, also tentative and no *tafsir* or *ta'wil* is value free. Any reading of the Qur'an is eisegetical before it is exegetical: eisegesis is really the flip side of exegesis rather that a distortion thereof.

7 BELIEF IN THE QUR'AN

The Qur'an describes its contents as an "exposition of everything, a guidance, a blessing and glad tidings for those who submit" (16.89) and declares that "no single thing have We neglected in the Book" (6.38). The contents of the Qur'an as the message of God to humankind and Muslims have been the focus of scholarly Muslim approaches to it. "How do I fulfill the requirements of God for me, in this day and age?" is the question that drives the Muslim. For most of the "engaged outsiders" and for virtually all of the "disinterested revisionists", the content of the Qur'an is really peripheral to the enquiry with the argument that the Qur'an is really impenetrable for an outsider. The works of Kenneth Cragg and more specifically that of Toshihiko Izutsu (1966) have effectively put paid to this argument. Both have produced significant – in Izutsu's case, even pioneering – studies into several aspects of the meaning of the Qur'an.

Given that the Qur'an is not divided into neat chapters dealing with a specific subject, the choice of major themes invariably involves an element of arbitrariness. I have chosen to deal with the subject matter of the Qur'an under two broad categories: belief and practice: the first is discussed in this chapter and the second in the following one. The Qur'an places an extraordinary emphasis on the binding relationship between faith (*iman*) and practice or what it describes as righteous deeds (*a'mal al-salihat*). The phrase "*alladhina amanu wa 'amilu al-salihat*" (those who have faith and act righteously) occurs no less than thirty-six times. From the Qur'an it is clear that *iman* is intrinsically connected to righteous conduct whether in the sense of such conduct actually being a part of faith, emanating therefrom or leading to it. "The separation of faith from action", as Rahman says "is, for the Qur'an, a totally untenable and absurd situation" (1983, 171). Perhaps the best elaboration of this relationship is offered by Izutsu:

> The strongest tie of semantic relationship binds *'amal al-salih* [righteous conduct] and *iman* [faith] together into an almost inseparable unit. Just as the shadow follows the form, wherever there is *iman* there is *salihat* ... so much so that we may feel justified in defining the former in terms of the latter and the latter expressed in terms of the former (1966, 204).

It is important to note that, whatever the differences in the relationship between faith and praxis, traditional scholarship has usually interpreted praxis in a very narrow sense, i.e., the rituals of reified Islam. While *iman* is often connected to the rituals in the Qur'an, this is not always the case. There are numerous other examples where the reference is to *iman* and righteous conduct in a general and unspecified sense.[1] Furthermore, the Qur'an is quite emphatic about the smallest act of righteousness being rewarded without stipulating *iman* as a condition.[2]

BELIEF IN GOD

> ... Limitless is He in His glory, and sublimely exalted above anything that people may devise by way of definition: the originator of the heavens and the earth! How could it be that He should have a child without there ever having been a mate for Him – since it is He who has created everything, and He alone knows everything.

> Such is God, your Sustainer: there is no deity save Him, the creator of everything: worship, then, Him alone – for it is He who has everything in His care. No human vision can encompass Him, whereas He encompasses all human vision, for He alone is unfathomable, all-aware" (6.100–103).

Belief in the existence of one transcendent Creator and the struggle to live with all the implications of that belief may be said to be at the core of the Qur'an's message. The Creator is arguably the single most important subject of the Qur'an. The centrality of the belief in the existence of God, for which the Qur'an uses the word "Allah",[3] is also evident from the

1 E.g., 3.56; 4.57, 122; 5.9; 6.48; 7.42; 10.9; 11.23; 13.29; 14.23; 18.30; 18.107; 19.60; 22.50; 24.55; 25.70; 27.58; 31.8; 32.19.
2 E.g., 2.281; 3.24; 4.40, 85; 12.56; 16.111; 28.84.
3 The origins of the word "*allah*" are disputed. Some believe that it is the article "*al*" ("the") and "*ila*" (deity) while others suggest that it from *lah* (secret), i.e, *al-lah*, the secret one. Abu Hanifah says that in the same manner that Allah is not derived and is in His essence unchangeable, so is His name. If the term is of Arabic origin, then it may originally have been "*al-Ilah*" ("the God"). Others have suggested that it may have been derived from the Aramaic *'alaha*-, the God (Gibb & Kramers, 1974, 33).

first article of faith: "there is no deity but God". The Qur'an uses the word "Allah" approximately 2,500 times to refer to the Transcendent. "Allah" is referred to in Islamic theology as *al-ism al-dhat* (the essential name). Other terms that the Qur'an uses for God are referred to as the *al-asma al-sifat* (the names denoting attributes). Some of the names which the Qur'an uses are *rabb* (sustainer), *rahman* (gracious), *al-malik* (the king), *al-quddus* (the sacred), *al-salam* (the peace), *al-mu'min* (the faithful), *al-muhaymin* (the protector), and *al-'aziz* (the mighty).

The expression "limitless is He in His glory, and sublimely exalted above anything that people may devise by way of definition" (*subhanahu wa ta'ala 'anma yasifun*) is one that occurs frequently in the Qur'an. At times, such as in the passage cited above, it appears within a polemical context to refute the sonship of Jesus Christ and, at other times, as a simple statement of the limitlessness of God's glory. Despite the claims that anyone may make about God, He is really free from whatever people ascribe to Him. In other words, despite what we learn about God or His nature or characteristics of God elsewhere in the Qur'an, God remains free from not only the confines of biology and paternity, but also from the confines of human language. This is also emphasized in the second part of the text cited above: "No vision can encompass Him, whereas He encompasses all vision, for He alone is unfathomable, all-aware." The Qur'anic portrayal of God is thus of a deity above the religious community that serves "Him" – and refers to God as "Him" – and which, perhaps inevitably, seeks to limit God by preconceptions and socio-religio-political horizons. God is also greater than the law and to elevate the law to the level of the divine and the immutable is, in fact, to associate others with God, the antithesis of *tawhid*. Hassan Askari has pointed out how this principle of God's Transcendence prevents the implicit tendencies in religious traditions from absolutizing themselves and claiming total equation between what they believe ("say") about God and God Himself. Second, it is a principle which prevents religious traditions from taking their differences to a point where they lose their shared ethical responsibility to serve good and, above all, their sense of orientation to God, their final return to Him (1986, 4).

God exists in and by Himself and any association with Him is rejected by the Qur'an. "[He is] God. There is no deity save Him, the Ever-Living, the Self-Subsistent Fount of All Being!" (3.2). In the text cited above we see this emerging in an indirect way: "How could it be that that He should have a child without there ever having been a mate for Him?" According to the Qur'an, ascribing paternity – of whatever kind – to God is abominable. This also applies to any notion of a shared divinity, a rejection that comes out very sharply in a short Meccan *surah* that the Prophet was wont to describe as one-third of the whole Qur'an: *al-Ikhlas* (the Perfection):

> Say: "He is the One God:
> God the Eternal, the Uncaused Cause of All Being
> He begets not, and neither is He begotten;
> And there is nothing that could be compared with Him" (112.1–4)

In affirming the absolute unicity of God, the Qur'an responds to a form of tritheism that it accuses the Christians whom Muhammad encountered of believing in.

> O followers of the Gospel Do not overstep the bounds [of truth] in your religious beliefs, and do not say of God anything but the truth. The Christ Jesus, son of Mary, was but God's apostle – [the fulfillment of] His promise which he had conveyed unto Mary – and a soul created by Him. Believe, then, in God and His apostles, and do not say, "[God is] a threesome". Desist [from this assertion] for your own good. God is but One God; utterly remote is He, in His glory, from having a son: unto him belongs all that is in the heavens and all that is on earth; and none is as worthy of trust as God (4.171).[4]

God is described as "the originator of the heavens and the earth". Elsewhere the Qur'an tells us "He it is who created for you all that is on earth and has applied His designs to the Heavens and fashioned them into seven heavens; and He alone, has knowledge of everything" (2.29).[5] The notion of God as Creator (*khaliq*) and of the creation as *ayat* (signs) of His existence and His power permeates the entire Qur'an. God is the creator of everything (6.102, 13.16); of the heavens and the earth (14.19), the sun and the moon and of day and night (41.37), the fruit, grain, and trees (55.11–12), all animals (24.45), the mountains and the rivers (13.3). Other than the visible, God is also the creator of the Angels (43.19) and the Jinn (55.15). All of the creation comes into existence by His will; "Whenever We will anything to be, We but say unto it [Our word] 'Be' – and it is" (16.40).

God is not only a Creator though, but also *rabb* (lord and sustainer). In the way the Qur'an uses the term "*rabb*" a picture emerges of a divine

---

4 Most Christians insist that the doctrine of the Trinity is not the same as Tritheism, the worship of three Gods (Kung, 1987, 90ff.; Watt, 1978, 21–22, 47–49; Basetti-Sani, 1967, 188–193). Some Christians such as the Unitarians even reject any notion of the Trinity.
5 Unlike the Book of Genesis, the Qur'an does not set out the process of the creation in any detail.

being that cares and nurtures. (These senses are also inherent in the meaning of the term *"rabb"*.) He is the *rabb* of humankind; of the heavens and the earth and all that exists in between (38.22); of the east and the west (26.28); of the universe (1.1); of everything (6.164). While "no human vision can encompass Him, whereas He encompasses all human vision ..." (6.103). The Qur'an describes a particularly close bond between God and those who serve Him: "And if My servants ask you about Me – behold, I am near; I respond to the call of those who call, whenever they call unto Me: let them, then, respond unto me and believe in Me, so that they might follow the right way" (2.186). Elsewhere, God is described as closer to persons than their jugular veins (50.16). Much of the Qur'an is devoted to the praise of God; The Qur'an holds that the entire universe is engaged in extolling the praises of God "... and there is not a single thing but extols His limitless glory and praise" (17.44), with humankind being the only created entity who choose to do so or not to do so. The following text is one of the most embracing and moving praises to God in the Qur'an:

> All that is in the heavens and on earth extols God's limitless glory: for He alone is almighty, truly wise!
> His is the dominion over the heavens and the earth; He grants life and deals death; and he has the power to will anything.
> He is the First and the Last, and the Outward as well as the Inward; and He has full knowledge of everything.
> He it is who has created the heavens and the earth in six aeons, and is established on the throne of His almightiness.
> He knows all that entered the earth,and all that comes out of it, as well as all that descends from the skies, and all that ascends to them.
> And He is with you wherever you may be; and God sees all that you do.
> His is the dominion over the heavens and the earth; and all things go back unto God [as their source].
> He makes the night grow longer by shortening the day, and makes the day grow longer by shortening the night; and He has full knowledge of what is in the hearts [of people] (57.1–6).

PROPHETHOOD

> Hence, remain patient in adversity – for, verily, God's promise always comes true. [...]. And, indeed, [O Muhammad,] We sent forth apostles before your time; some of them We have mentioned to you, and some of them have not mentioned to you. And it was not given to any apostle to bring forth a miracle other than by God's leave (40.77–78).

One of the fundamental doctrines of the Qur'an is that of the historical continuity of revelation whereby God sent a series of messengers to every nation in order to guide them to the path of righteousness. "And there is not a people but a warner had gone among them" (35.24). This continuity of revelation, according to Muslim belief, culminated in the revelation of the Qur'an and Muhammad's prophethood. All of these Messengers came with an identical message (41.43) – that of submission to the will of God – and all of humankind are required to believe in the veracity of each one of them. "Verily those who deny God and his apostles by endeavouring to make a distinction between [belief in] God and [belief in] His apostles, and who say, 'We believe in the one but we deny the other', ... they are truly denying the truth" (4.150).

The Qur'an uses two terms to denote prophethood: "*rasul*" (pl. "*rusul*") and '*nabiyy* (pl. "*anbiya*"). "*Rasul*" seems to denote a messenger with revelation who actually headed his community while "*nabi*" seems to denote an apostle who did not necessarily come with a new revelation or law. "Now every community has had an apostle; and only after their apostle has appeared [and delivered his message] is judgment passed on them, in all equity, and never are they wronged" (10.47). The following *rusul* are mentioned in the Qur'an: Nuh (Noah), Lut (Lot), Isma'il (Ishmael), Musa (Moses), Shu'ayb, Hud, Salih, and 'Isa (Jesus). The list of *anbiya'* (prophets with no new revelation) is much longer and includes figures such as Ibrahim (Abraham), Is-haq (Isaac), Ya'qub (Jacob), Harun (Aaron), Idris, Dawud (David), Yunus, (Jonas) Sulayman (Solomon), Ayyub, and Dhu 'l-Nun. Muhammad is sometimes called a *rasul* and, at other times, a *nabi*. In Islamic literature and teachings, however, little is made of these distinctions and the two terms are used interchangeably.

"God elects whomsoever He will from among his Apostles ..." (3.179) and, as the text above shows, they derive their authority solely from God: they cannot "bring forth a miracle other than by God's leave". Prophets are always chosen from among their own communities (7.35, 10.74 and 39.17) and are merely responsible for conveying God's messages (16.35). Guidance, Muhammad was repeatedly told, is not his prerogative, but that of God. Muslims also hold that all Prophets are sinless (*ma'sum*) and any wrongs attributed to them in the Qur'an are regarded as "errors" rather than sin. As for the relationship between all the messengers of God, in the following two verses, we see statements that, to some, may appear contradictory:

These are God's messages: We convey them unto you, [O Prophet,] setting forth the truth – for, verily, you are among those who have been entrusted with a message. Some of these apostles We endowed more highly than others: among them were such as were spoken to by God [Himself], and some He has raised yet higher. And we vouchsafed unto Jesus, the son of Mary, all evidence of the truth, and strengthened him with holy inspiration ... (2.252–253).

The Apostle and the believers with him, believe in what has been bestowed upon him from on high by His Sustainer: they all believe in God, and His Angels, and His revelations, and His apostles, making no distinction between any of His apostles; and they say: "We have heard, and we pay heed" ... (2.285).

Muslims generally believe that Muhammad enjoyed a distinction over all the other Prophets "inasmuch as he was the Last Prophet and the bearer of a universal message applicable to all people at all times" (Asad, 1980, 56). The expression "and some he has raised yet higher" in the first verse is thus regarded as referring to Muhammad. As for the statement "we make no distinction between any of his apostles" in the second text, Asad says: "These words are put, as it were, in the mouths of the believers. In as much as all the apostles were true bearers of God's messages, there is no distinction between them, although some of them may have been "endowed more highly than others" (ibid., 64). However, if that were the case, then one may have expected it (the statement "we make no distinction between any of his apostles") to appear after the expression "and they say", and not before it.

The Qur'an contains a number of narratives involving Prophets, often told with the intention of consoling Muhammad in the face of rejection by the Quraysh and recipients of earlier revelation. "And indeed, before your time, have Apostles been derided – but those who scoffed at them were [in the end] overwhelmed by the very thing which they were wont to deride" (6.10). With the exception of the narrative of Joseph, and to a lesser extent, that of Moses, these narratives often appear in a disjointed fashion and the Qur'an presents them not so much as history but as moral lessons ('ibrah) for humankind on the consequences of disobeying God. All of the Prophets referred to in the Qur'an are men. While Mary was the recipient of revelation, nowhere do we get any indication that she was expected or did play the social role of warner or the bearer of good tidings.[6] The following is a brief summary of some of the Qur'anic narratives that deal with the Prophets. While the details accompanying

6 The fact of the Qur'an not mentioning any women in this role is not to suggest that God

these narratives in the earlier scriptures are missing in the Qur'an, the similarities between them are manifest.

Abraham

Abraham, mentioned sixty-nine times in the Qur'an, emerges as the common father of the people of the book with the Muslim community also being the children of this great patriarch.[7] In the Meccan revelation Abraham is portrayed as an apostle of God to admonish his people and there is no mention made of him as the founder of Ka'bah or being the first Muslim, nor is the relationship with Ishmael made known. This son of Azar (6.74–79) – his mother's name is not mentioned – was a deeply reflective young person who challenged his father and community to worship the One God.

"One day when his community was away, Abraham took it upon himself to destroy all the idols, bar the major one; when his people demanded an explanation from him, he suggested that they ask the remaining one" (21.58–67). For this "crime" he was thrown into a huge fire that God decreed to "be cool and peaceful for Abraham". Later Abraham sets out for Palestine and for his indomitable commitment to monotheism earns the appellation "khalil Allah", the friend of God. Abraham was the father of two sons, both of them also regarded as Prophets in the Qur'an, Ishmael, the eldest, was borne by Hagar and Isaac was born to Sarah. The Qur'an makes no mention of their mission or community other than that they furthered the cause of monotheism. Most Muslim scholars hold that Ishmael was the son that Abraham was willing to sacrifice upon God's command. Ishmael also assisted Abraham in building and purifying the Ka'bah (2.125), replacing a temple first erected by Adam. Isaac was the result of a miraculous pregnancy at a time when both Abraham and Sarah were past their fertility age (2.120 and 90) and the tidings of his conception were conveyed to Abraham by Gabriel. In the Medinan revelations Abraham is described as "hanifan musliman" (an upright muslim), the founder and the one who named the community of Muhammad, along with his son, Ishmael, builder of "the first house determined for humankind", (the ka'bah) (3.96). Given the context of the Prophet's

never chose any women for such a function. Black, Caucasian, Latino and Chinese males are also not mentioned without any suggestion that this excludes the possibility of anyone from their ranks ever having been sent as a Prophet.
7 Increasingly, Muslims engaged in interreligious dialogue also refer to Islam in the context of it being an Abrahamic religion.

engagement with the Jews in Medina, one sees a different portrayal of the patriarch, Abraham, as the father of an "authentic" Judaism (i.e., *islam*), rather than that which was lived out by the Jews of Medina.

Moses

Moses is mentioned on approximately 140 occasions in the Qur'an, more than any other Prophet. Notwithstanding a speech impediment, he is referred to in the Qur'an as "*kalam Allah*", "the word of God", and is portrayed as the liberator of his people and a lawgiver with a new revelation which confirmed the teachings of Abraham. "Verily, [all] this has indeed been [said] in the ealier revelations – the revelations of Abraham and Moses" (87.18–19). His travails are recounted extensively in the Qur'an, many of the details similar to that found in the Haggada. If the parallels between the lives and struggle of Muhammad and those of Abraham were somewhat subtle, no such subtleties exist in the case of Muhammad and Moses. According to the Qur'an, Muhammad's emergence was foretold by Moses (7.157). Moses too had to endure false charges of being a soothsayer and magician, and of diverting his people from the faith of their forebears (10.78). He also entered the world as a virtual orphan, rescued by the Pharaoh's wife (not daughter) and then grew up in the house of the Pharaoh. Like Muhammad, Moses went into exile and during this period he received a revelation in the burning bush. Accompanied by his brother Aaron, he was sent to Pharaoh and then to the Israelites. His confrontation with Pharaoh lead to the exodus and the destruction of Pharaoh, Haman, and their army. After liberation Moses wrestled with his own community who yearned for the "better days of Egypt". While he was away spending thirty and ten nights with God (7.148 and 20.77–98) and receiving the admonitions from God, Samiri, one of the Israelites, made a golden calf for them in response to their desire to worship "a tangible god". Moses and his people ended up spending forty years in the wilderness.

Jesus

The Qur'an provides precious little detail on the life of Jesus and his mission. The focus is rather on the doctrine and Jesus' disavowal of his own divinity. Jesus, or 'Isa the son Mary, as the Qur'an names him was born of a virgin (3.45–47). He is described as "a Spirit from God"

(4.171); "a word of God" (ibid.),[8] "the Messiah, naught but a servant of God" (4.172); "one of those brought near [to God]" (3.45); "worthy of regard in this world and in the next" (3.45). The Qur'anic description "son of Mary" in a patriarchal society is indicative of his miraculous birth. Jesus was a Messenger and a Prophet who came with a book, the *Injil*. His revelations and word contained proofs and wisdom and he was assisted in his mission by God and the *ruh al-qudus*, (lit. "the sacred spirit"), understood to be the angel Gabriel. God was the essential teacher and guide of Jesus, who was bestowed with the miraculous powers of raising the dead, healing the sick, making clay birds, and, with the permission of God, breathing life into them (3.47 and 110).

Muslims in general deny the crucifixion although the Qur'an merely states: "They did not slay him, and neither did they crucify him, but it only seemed to them as if it had been so; ... nay God exalted him unto Himself and God is indeed almighty wise." Elsewhere the Qur'an says, "I am about to take you [Jesus] unto Myself and lift you toward Myself" (3.55). Those who argue that Jesus was indeed crucified say that this verse merely denies that "they" (i.e., the Jews) killed him and put paid to their boasts. The second verse is the basis for the notion that Jesus was lifted to God and that he never died a physical death. This may be difficult to reconcile with Q.5.117, where a conversation takes place between God and Jesus on the Day of Judgment and Jesus says to God: "Nothing did I tell them beyond what You ordered me [to say]: 'Worship God [who is] my Sustainer as well as your Sustainer.' And I bore witness to what they did as long as I dwelt in their midst; But since you caused me to die, You have alone have been their keeper: For you are witness unto everything." The vast majority of Muslims also believe in the second coming of Jesus. This is in part based on a somewhat obscure verse: "Yet there is not one of the followers of earlier revelation who does not, at the moment of his death, grasp the truth about Jesus" (4.159).[9] Given that this was not the case during his or Muhammad's lifetime, it is argued that this will occur during the last days when Jesus will return as the Messiah who will descend in the Holy Land and destroy all the symbols of a "corrupted" Christianity. His former community will merge

8 This is said to be a reference to the word "*kun*" (be!). God willed the creation of Jesus by merely uttering this word, rather than the natural path of conception and thus it came to be. "And when God wills anything, he merely says to it, be, and it is."

9 Asad holds that the "his" in "his death" refers to Jews and Christians. All believing Jews and Christians realize at the moment of their death that Jesus was truly a prophet of God – having been neither an impostor, nor the son of God' (1980, 135). Yusuf 'Ali also suggests that the emphatic form of the verb "believe" in this case may suggest that it is a duty upon the Jews and the Christians before death rather than a fact (1989, 236).

with the Muslim community and after forty years he will die a physical
death and be buried at Medina next to Muhammad.

Noah

Noah is the first Prophet mentioned in the Qur'an whose community was
punished, a warner (9.25), and a true messenger of God (26.107). Along
with other Prophets such as Abraham and Moses, the Qur'an also
presents Noah as a *muslim*. His community accused him of being an
ordinary mortal like them (10.71–73) when God would have been better
advised to send an angel (223.24), of lying to them and being deceptive
(7.64), of being possessed by a Jinn (54.9), and of attracting only the
lower social classes (9.27 and 24.3). The pain of Muhammad's encounter
with his own community can easily be reflected in the words of Noah to
his people. "It offends you that I live among you; I seek no reward, my
reward is with God (10.71–73 and 11.29); "I do not claim to posses
God's treasures, to know His secrets, to be an angel and I cannot say to
those whom you despise, 'God shall not give you any good.'" When his
people failed to heed his message they, including his wife and son, were
destroyed in an immense deluge while Noah and his handful of followers
on the ark were saved (64.10).

Joseph (Yusuf)

The story of Joseph, the son of Jacob is the only long piece of
uninterrupted narrative in the Qur'an in a chapter called "*Yusuf*". The
narrative contains most of the details recounted in the Haggada about
the way he was abandoned by his brothers; his father's lamenting over his
disappearance; the false accusations made against him after he was
rescued from the well wherein he was thrown by his brothers, his ability
to interpret dreams, sojourn in and release from prison, rehabilitation as
a minister to the king; and his re-unification with his brothers and father.
Other than this long narrative, which is inconsistent with the general
style of the Qur'an, Joseph is mentioned on only two other occasions: as
a pious ancestor (6.84) and as someone who was rejected despite coming
with clear proofs (40.34). By his participation in a government that was
not "fully believing", Joseph represents righteous political participation
for just and noble purposes without insisting on absolute power.

Lot (Lut)

Lot acquires an importance in the Qur'an beyond that accorded in the Haggada. This may in part be due to the fact that in the Qur'an Lot emerges, like Muhammad, as a Prophet who was mocked by his people who as a consequence thereof, faced God's wrath. The Qur'an describes him as "a trustworthy Prophet who was endowed with discernment and knowledge" (26.162). In addition to the sins of rejecting God – or perhaps as a corollary thereof – a number of his community were guilty of rape, violating the rights and dignity of guests, and highway robbery. God sent two emissaries, angels, to Lot's people. When they humiliated him in front of his guests and when they attempted to sexually assault the two emissaries, God instructed him to flee the city that was subsequently destroyed.

Shu'ayb

Often identified as the father-in-law of Moses, in the middle Meccan *Surahs* (e.g. 24.176–189) the Prophet Shu'ayb appears among the people of Aykah after others such as Hud, Salih, and Lot. In later *Surahs* he appears among the people of Madyan as one of their brothers (9.84–95). Shu'ayb combined his testimony to monotheism with passionate calls against the economic exploitation of people, exhorting his community to deal honestly with weights and measures. As with the other Prophets, the powerful classes rejected him and the small groups of followers and threatened to expel them. If it were not for them considering his family they would have stoned him. After Shu'ayb and his followers fled, an earthquake struck and the morning found all the inhabitants of the village dead in their dwellings.

THE HEREAFTER

When the earth quakes with her [last] mighty quaking,
and [when] the earth yields up her burdens,
and humankind cries out, "What has happened to her?" –
on that Day will she recount all her tidings, as your Sustainer will have
    inspired her to do.
On that Day will all people come forward, cut off from one another, to be
    shown their [past] deeds.
And so, the one who shall have done an atom's weight of good, shall
    behold it;

And the one who shall have done an atom's weight of evil, shall behold it
(99.1–8).

The Qur'an speaks repeatedly about the ultimate accountability of all
human beings to God and insists that all of life and its affairs, having
originated with God, are, in fact, in a continuous state of purposeful
reversion to a just and merciful Creator, Sustainer, and Judge. "Indeed
from God [we come], and unto him is the return", (2.156). "And unto
God shall all the affairs revert" (3.109). This belief is, in fact, second
only to that of the existence of God and the belief in the Prophets of God
and can be seen as emanating from the need to establish the twin truths
of the existence of God and the ultimate accountability to Him. Physical
death is thus not the end of life but merely an evolving into another form.

This world (al-Dunya) and the next (al-Akhirah)

Both human beings and communities are placed on the earth – al-dunya –
for a predetermined period referred to in the Qur'an as "ajal musamma"
before they enter the akhirah (hereafter). "He it is who has created you
out of clay, and then decreed a term [for you] – a term known [only] to
him ..." (6.2). "For all people a term has been set: when the end of their
term approaches, they can neither delay it by a single moment, nor
hasten it" (10.49). The terms dunya [the world] and akhirah (lit. "next"
or "last") are related both to time and space and to two moral
alternatives; dunya is the geographical space and the present where
humankind are meant to prepare for akhirah, yet this abode of
preparation can also be good and fulfilling by itself. "And ordain for
us what is good in this world (dunya) as well as in the life to come
(akhirah)" (7.156). The believers are, however, cautioned about seeking
this dunya at the expense of the akhirah: "To the one who desires a
harvest in the life to come (akhirah), We shall grant an increase in his
harvest; whereas to the one who desires [but] a harvest in this world
(dunya), We [may] give something thereof – [but] he will have no share in
[the blessings of] the life to come (akhirah)" (42.20).

The intermediate stage between dunya and akhirah is the barzakh –
the period in the grave. "[As for those who do not believe in the life to
come, they go on denying] until, when death approaches anyone of them,
he prays: O my Lord Sustainer! Let me return [to life] so that I may act
righteously in whatever I have failed. Nay, it is indeed but [a
meaningless] word that he utters; for behind those [who leave the

world] there is a *barzakh* until the day when all be raised from the dead!" (23.99). From this verse it would seem that all those in this stage are in fact conscious and already experiencing the consequences of their deeds in the *dunya*. Q.40.45–46 speaks about the people of Pharaoh experiencing chastisement every morning and evening and when the Hour [shall] come to pass.[10]

The Resurrection (Al-Qiyamah)

The various names which the Qur'an applies to the resurrection are themselves rich in imagery and convey a dramatic sense of the end of life as we know it. The most frequently employed term – it occurs no less than seventy times – is the term *yawm al-qiyamah* (the day of resurrection). This is followed by *al-sa'ah* (the hour) which appears forty times; and *al-yawm al-akhir* (the last day), which appears twenty-six times. Some other terms are *yawm al-din* (the day of requital), *yawn al-fasl* (the day of decision), *yawm al-hisab* (the day of reckoning), *yawm al-fath* (the day of victory), *yawm al-talaq* (the day of gathering), *al-qari'ah* (the sudden calamity), *al-ghashiyah* (the overshadowing event), *al-sakhkha* (the deadening calamity), *al-haqqah* (the great truth), and *al-waqi'ah* (the great event). From the Qur'an it would appear that there is a particular moment in time when the hour will strike and Muslim eschatological literature is filled with the signs of the hour (*isharat al-sa'ah*). It is also not uncommon to hear Muslims, whenever faced with a new ethical issue such as, for example, cloning, that "we can see that we are living in *akhir zaman* (the last period)". The Qur'an only says "People ask you about the Last Hour. Say, 'Knowledge thereof rests with God alone'" (33.63). "Nonetheless, it seems that the early Muslims would be surprised to find that after fourteen centuries Muslims are still in expectation of those signs portending the cataclysmic conclusion of time" (Smith and Haddad, 1981, 65). The arrival of the hour is captured in a very dramatic manner in Q.81.1–14.

> When the sun is shrouded in darkness
> And when the stars lose their light
> And when the mountains are made to vanish
> And when the she-camel big with young, about to give birth, are left
>   untended,

10 Muslim eschatological literature contains abundant material on life in the grave and, more specifically, on the punishment in the grave. Much of this has been rejected by groups such as the Mu'tazilites, Ikhwan al-Safa, and many Shi'i scholars who deny any resemblance of occurrences in the grave to the earthly experience.

And when all beasts are gathered together and when the seas boil over
And when all human beings are coupled [with their deeds]
And when the girl child that was buried alive is made to ask for what
  crime she was killed
And when the scrolls of [humankind's deeds] are unfolded
And when the heaven is laid bare
And when the blazing fire [of hell] is kindled bright
And when paradise is brought into view
[on that Day] every human being will come to know what he/she has
  prepared for him/herself.

The hour itself shall commence with the sounding of the Trumpet. Q.69.13 mentions a single blast while Q.39.68 mentions two blasts. "Hence, [bethink yourselves of the Last Hour,] when the trumpet [of judgment] shall be sounded with a single blast, and the earth and the mountains shall be lifted up and crushed with a single stroke!" (69.13–14). "As human moral degeneracy has been seen to be one of the signs of the impending hour, so now cosmic disintegration signals the end of the world and the imminence of resurrection" (Smith and Haddad, 1981, 71). The second blast heralds the final collapse of the entire cosmos and reflects the utter aloneness and oneness of God. "There is no Deity save Him, Everything is bound to perish, save His [eternal] self. With Him rests all judgment; and unto Him shall you be brought back" (28.88).

The Qur'an is unclear about the exact chronology of the blowing of the horn and related events. It would appear that when resurrection commences bodies will be reconnected to their spirits and be brought into the presence of God for the ultimate reckoning. The Qur'an suggests that this resurrection is a bodily one, yet it is also a day when the earth shall be changed into non-earth (14.48). Everyone will be in desperate need of support and the Qur'an repeatedly emphasizes the simultaneous disintegration of ties of kinship along with that of the cosmos; a more horrific plight to a people who hardly knew of any existence as individuals and saw themselves essentially as members of a broader social unit is difficult to contemplate: "And so, when the piercing call [of resurrection] is heard on a Day when everyone will [want to] flee from his brother, and from his mother and father, and from his spouse and his children: on that Day, to every one of them will his own state be of sufficient concern" (80.33–35). While several prophetic sayings suggest that some sinners will be saved on the basis of the intercession of the

Prophets and other righteous people, the Qur'an is emphatic about the notion of individual responsibility because each person's deeds have been recorded in his or her "book":

> Now as for him whose record shall be placed in his right hand, he will exclaim: Come you all, Read, this my record! Behold, I did not know that [one day] I would have to face my account. And so he will find himself in a happy state of life ... But as for him whose record shall be placed in his left hand, he will exclaim: O, would that I had neither known this my record, and neither known this my account. O, would that this [death] had been the end of me ... (69. 19–27).

One's deeds are placed in a balance (*mizan*) before one is sent to Paradise or Hell.[11] While the word *mizan* appears several times in the Qur'an and Muslims commonly refer to it in the singular form, only in its plural form (*mawazin*) is there a direct connection made to the Day of Judgment. The word seems to carry both the meanings of "scale" and of "balance" in the sense of an account. Interestingly, deeds will be weighed rather than counted, a theme that recurs throughout the Qur'an.

> And true will be the weighing on that Day: and those whose weight [of good deeds] is heavy in the balance – it is they, they who shall attain to a happy state; whereas those whose weight is light in the balance – it is they who will have squandered their own selves by their willful rejection of Our Messages (7.8–9).

Paradise and Hell

The Qur'an is explicit about two alternatives for each person in the Hereafter, *jannah* (Paradise) or *jahannam* (Hell), and at various junctures spells out the deeds which will earn one a place in the one or the other. While Muslim scholars hold different opinions about the exact nature of these two abodes and the experiences that a person will undergo there, ordinary Muslims generally adopt a literal approach to the texts that portray the two abodes in vivid terms and explicit imagery which are quite overwhelming. Mainstream Muslim thinking accepts that these texts are a portrayal of real events to come but do not insist that that reality must correspond to the one human beings know. Modernist interpreters of the Qur'an also increasingly suggest that these verses are essentially of an allegorical nature. "Many of the details of the Fire, as of the Garden, are reminiscent of the New Testament; others reflect on

---

11 Muslim eschatology is filled with reference to the *sirat*, a bridge over Hell which one must cross for entry into Paradise. The Qur'an, however, makes no explicit reference to this.

occasions the tone of early Arabic poetry. On the whole, however, the picture afforded by the Qur'an is uniquely its own, articulated in a generally consistent and always awe-inspiring fashion" (Smith and Haddad, 1981, 84).

As for Hell itself, seven different words are used to describe it in the Qur'an, the most frequent being "*jahannam*" which indicates a place of great depth.[12] Reflecting the relationship between deeds performed in this life and their consequences in the hereafter, Hell is generally connected to various levels of descent in the same way that Paradise is connected to various levels of ascent. The key element of Hell is the torture of fire. In fact, the Qur'an often uses the term fire (*al-nar*) as synonymous with Hell. The flames of this fire crackle and roar (25.14), it has fierce boiling waters (55.44), scorching wind and black smoke (56.42–43); it roars and boils as if it would burst with rage (67.7–8). The companions of the fire are sighing and wailing, wretched (11.106), drinking festering water, and, though death appear on all sides, they cannot die (14.16–17).

The Qur'an at various junctures indicates the sins which earn a person consignment to Hell; these include, lying, dishonesty, corruption, ignoring God or God's revelations, denying the resurrection, refusing to feed the poor, opulence and ostentation, the economic exploitation of others, and social oppression. The fire, however, is not the only consequence that the wrongdoers have to face on the Day of Judgment: "And those who earned evil, the punishment of evil is the like thereof, and abasement will cover them – they will have none to protect them from God – as if their faces had been covered with slices of dense darkness of night" (10.27).[13] Denial of water (7.50) and of light (57.13) are also spoken of as forms of punishment for the inhabitants of Hell.

Muslims scholars are divided on the question as to whether the inhabitants of Hell will remain there forever. A somewhat arbitrary distinction is made by most "orthodox" scholars between the believing and unbelieving inhabitants of Hell. The Qur'an uses the words kh-l-d and a-b-d to denote permanency with reference to Hell and applies it to both believers (4.13–14) and others who have committed evil. However, when it comes to the believers, "the orthodoxy" holds that these words

12 Another word which the Qur'an uses to denote a similar meaning is "*hawiyah*", i.e., an abyss or a bottomless place.
13 The blackening of faces is elsewhere also mentioned as the chastisement of Hell. On the Day when some faces will turn white and some faces turn black. Then as to those whose faces are black: Did you disbelieve after your belief? So taste the chastisement because you disbelieved (3.105) See also Q.80.40–42.

have a limited meaning while, in the case of the "unbelievers", "forever" means forever. Others such as Muhammad 'Ali (1990, 229–231) and Fazlur Rahman Ansari have argued – also on the basis of certain Qur'anic texts – that the essential function of Hell is both punitive as well as remedial and that after a time Hell will be emptied of all its inhabitants.

> The man who lives in sin is debarred from the Divine presence, but being purified by fire, is again made fit for divine service. Hence hell is called the friend of the sinners (Q. 83.15) and their mother in another (Q. 57.15). Both descriptions are a clear indication that Hell is intended to raise up man by purifying him from the dross of evil, just as fire purifies gold of dross ('Ali, 1990, 231).

The word "paradise" (*firdaws*) occurs only twice in the Qur'an (18.107 and 23.11), while the word "garden" (*jannah*) is used far more frequently and then usually in the plural (*jannat*). The Qur'an makes it clear that the blessings of Paradise cannot be perceived by physical senses. "No soul knows what refreshments of the eyes is hidden for them, a reward for what they did" (32.17).[14] The most frequent description of *jannah* is that it is a garden underneath which rivers flow. "The parable of paradise promised to those who are conscious of God [is that of a garden] through which running waters flow: [but, unlike an earthly garden,] its fruits will be everlasting, and [so will be] its shade" (13.35). The elusiveness of what *jannah* really entails is also seen in provision of shade (53.14–16) and abundant sustenance as among the most significant gifts of *jannah*. Yet there will be no sun (76.13) in the Hereafter and neither shall the body be subjected to the biological needs of sustenance that belongs to the physical world. In the same way that the Qur'an portrays a very graphic image of Hell, it presents Paradise in a similar manner which has often led some to suggest that the Qur'anic Paradise is actually a very materialistic and sensuous one, which does not always appeal to the more noble instincts of men.

> But the foremost shall be [they who in life were] foremost [in faith and good works]: they who were [always] drawn close unto God! In gardens of bliss [will they dwell] ... [They will be seated] on gold-encrusted thrones of happiness, reclining upon them, facing one another [in love]. Immortal youths (*wildan*) will wait upon them with goblets, and ewers, and cups filled with water from unsullied springs, by which their minds

14 The concealing or elusive nature of Paradise is contained in the word itself. From *j-n-n*, it means the concealing of a thing so that it is not perceived by the senses. *Jannah* in ordinary usage means a garden because the ground is covered by grass and trees.

will not be clouded and which will not make them drunk; and with fruit of any kind that they may choose, and with the flesh of any fowl that they may desire. And [with them will be their] companions pure (*hur*), most beautiful of eye, like unto pearls [still] hidden in their shells. [And this will be] a reward for what they did [in life]. No empty talk will they hear there, nor any call to sin, but only the tidings of inner soundness and peace (56.10–26).

Besides the ordinary believing and righteous adult male, three other categories of inhabitants are also mentioned in the Qur'an – two in the verse cited above – and, at a superficial glance, are seemingly there for the pleasure of its male inhabitants: the *azwaj*, *hur*, and *ghilman* or *wildan*. *Azwaj* is the plural of *zawj* which literally means partner. The fact that it is normally attached to the male form of the possessive pronoun (*azwajuhum*); i.e., their partners leads to the idea that the women who are in Paradise are there in the secondary role as partners to their earthly husbands. Yet, at other times the Qur'an is specific that women shall enter paradise on the basis of their own deeds. "Whereas anyone – be it man or woman – who does [whatever s/he can] of good deeds and is a believer, shall enter paradise" (4.124, 40.40). The second entity, the *hur* which is mentioned four times in the Qur'an, has particularly been the subject of derision by some Non-Muslim scholars. Normally portrayed as "young virgins with eyes like guarded pearls" or simply as "pure beautiful ones", they are presented in much of Muslim eschatological writing as a new type of creation with boundless sexual energy and incredible beauty for the sensuous pleasure of the male inhabitants of Paradise. Others, particularly more contemporary and apologetic Muslim scholars such as Muhammad Asad whose translation is used throughout this work, have presented them as merely the resurrected earthly partners of the males, synonymous with *azwaj*. The third category is that of *wildan* (youthful males or boys), the word used in the *ayah* above or "*ghilman*", which carries a similar meaning (cf. 52.24, 56.17, 74.19). In an undisguisedly apologetic twist, after rendering these words as "children", Muhammad Ali suggests that these are really "the off-spring of the faithful" … "who have died in childhood". As if in belated awareness of the leaps in translation and his conclusions, he then acknowledges that "there is however, a possibility of these boys are only a blessing of Paradise, as boyhood is, like womanhood, an emblem of purity and beauty" (224).[15]

15 It is curious that boyhood and not girlhood is presented as a symbols of innocence and the absence of similar pleasures for women does reinforce the notion that the essential addressees of the Qur'an are men.

From the text cited above it is evident that the Qur'an appeals to the various senses of men and not only the sensuous and material ones. The emphasis on Paradise being an abode of peace is reflective of this: "Enter this [paradise] in peace; This is the day on which life abiding begins!" (50.34). "They hear therein no vain talk or sinful talk but only the saying 'peace! peace!'" (56.25–26). More significant though is that the Qur'an presents something completely different and beyond Paradise as the ultimate reward for righteousness; the meeting with God. "So whoever looks forward to meeting his [her] Sustainer [on Judgment Day] let him [her] do righteous deeds, and let him not ascribe unto anyone or anything a share in the worship due to his [her] Sustainer!" (18.110). "On that Day, faces will be radiant, looking towards their Lord" (75.23). "And seek aid in steadfast patience and prayer: and this, indeed, is a hard thing for all but the humble in spirit, who know with certainty that they shall meet their Sustainer and unto Him they shall return" (2.45–6).

8 RIGHTEOUS CONDUCT IN THE QUR'AN

In terms of content, the bulk of the Qur'anic message contains exhortations dealing with righteous conduct, and the consequences of following or ignoring them. These are framed within the backdrop of the all-pervading presence of God and humankind's ultimate accountability to Him. Although Muslim jurists have made a distinction between what it regards as the "rights of God" (i.e., what is owed to God) and the "rights of the servants" (i.e., what is owed to the creation), the reality is that from the Qur'an's perspective, they are inseparable. Furthermore, in the same way that faith and righteous deeds are intrinsically connected, so are the personal, social, and ritual dimensions of praxis. For convenience though, I have classified righteous deeds under three headings, viz. "Personal", "Social", and "Religious".

PERSONAL CONDUCT

The Qur'an regards the human being as a carrier of the spirit of God and a sacred trust from Him who is in a continuous state of journeying towards Him. This state of returning to God requires a ceaseless struggle of preparation for that encounter. The following are some of the qualities that have to be developed as a part of that struggle.

Spiritual well-being

The most important obligation that the Qur'an places on the believer is probably that of pursuing the pleasure of God and desiring the ultimate encounter with Him.

... And of humankind are such who would willingly sell his [her] own self in order to please God: and God is most compassionate towards His servants.

And [the righteous have in their minds] no favour from anyone for which a reward is expected in return, but only seeking the countenance of his [her] sustainer, the Lord, the Most High (92.19–20).

The pleasure of God is attained by cultivating a direct relationship of love and adoration of God as well as leading a life characterized by a struggle to fulfill His commandments. Other than the rituals and, for many Muslims, more important than the rituals, the Qur'an often speaks about the adoration of God is an important part of a Muslim's ideal personality and pursuit.

And remember your Sustainer's name, and devote yourself unto Him with utter devotion. The Sustainer of the east and the west is He! There is no deity save Him (72.8–9).

O you who have attained unto faith. Remember God with much remembrance and glorify Him early and late (3.41).

And when you have finished your prayer, remember God – standing and sitting and lying down ... (4.103).

... And hold fast unto God. He is your Lord Supreme: and how excellent this Giver of Succour! (22.78).

The tremendous emphasis that the Qur'an places on God as the focus and objective of a believer's life has led many a contemplative Muslim to regard the law as merely a means of facilitating closeness to God in the same way that railings may help one up the stairs. While condemned by the "orthodoxy", they feel capable of dispensing with the aid of the railings as long they are on "the ascending path."

Physical and aesthetic well-being

"And do not cast by your own hands to ruin", says the Qur'an (2.190, cf. 4.29). Thus Muslims are to avoid whatever injures one's sense of well-being – spiritual, emotional, or physical. The prohibition on the consumption of alcohol explicitly stated in the Qur'an (5.90–91), and that of tobacco, implicit in the above verse, are examples of this. Other examples are the following injunctions: "O humankind, eat of whatsoever is on the earth; lawful and wholesome" (2.168) and "Partake

of the good things which We have provided for you as sustenance ..."
(20.81). While the Qur'an cautions against excess and wasteful
consumption, it nevertheless, encourages a sense of joyful living and asks
the believers not to impose burdens upon themselves that are unwar-
ranted: "O you who have attained to faith! Do not deprive yourselves of
the good things which God has made lawful for you" (5.87). Other
dimensions of this sense of personal well-being that the Qur'an refers to
are physical cleanliness and sexual pleasure: "... Verily, God loves those
who turn unto Him in repentance and He loves those who keep
themselves pure" (2.222). "And among His wonders is this: He created
for you mates, out of your own kind, so that you might incline towards
them, and He engenders love and tenderness between you ..." (30.21).

God, Himself the possessor of beauty and "the light of the heavens
and the earth" (24.35) is also the one "who makes most excellent
everything that He creates" (32.7). He created humankind in "the best of
patterns" (40.64) and whatever is on the earth has also been placed here
as a source of beauty (28.7). All of these are meant to enrich and beautify
the life of the believer when she recognizes the beauty of God in these
signs of nature and in her own being. The believer's conduct is to mirror
the beauty of the world around her as well as the submission of nature to
the will of God. As Muhammad is reported to have said in a tradition,
"God is Beautiful and loves beauty."

Intellectual well-being

While the Qur'an places great emphasis on knowledge as a value and the
pursuit thereof (49.9), it links the intellectual well-being of people to a
profound awareness of God and justice and emphasizes the compatibility
of knowledge with faith: "... Of all His servants, only such as are
endowed with knowledge who stand [truly] in awe of God ..." (35.28).
"God will exalt those who have faith among you and those who have
knowledge to high ranks" (58.11). The Muslim is also instructed to pray
"O my Sustainer, cause me to grow in knowledge" (20.144), and the
possession of knowledge is seen as leading to justice (3.18). The Qur'an
often gives the impression of a certain essential body of truth to be
acquired as "the knowledge" (al-'ilm). In numerous other ayat though,
humankind is challenged to reflect, ponder, meditate: all qualities more
connected to heurism and tentativeness and usually regarded as the basis
of wisdom ("... And whosoever is granted wisdom has indeed been

granted wealth abundant. But none bears this in mind save those who are endowed with insight" (2.269).) The Qur'anic assumption though seems to be that knowledge and reflection will invariably and inevitably lead to God: "Are the possessors of knowledge equal with those who possess no knowledge? It is the possessors of understanding that are mindful" (39.9). This is an assumption that clearly cannot stand the test of critical scrutiny unless a very specific appreciation of "understanding" is intended here. When such reflection does not lead to God, it is dismissed as conjecture: "And [since] they have no knowledge whatever thereof, they follow nothing but conjecture: yet, behold, never can conjecture take the place of truth" (53.28).

Moral well-being

The Qur'an contains a host of injunctions pertaining to the moral well-being of the individual and of society. The following two texts reflect the reproachful style of the Qur'an in respect to immorality: "... and draw not near to indecencies, whether open of secret ..." (6.151) and "... He forbids all that is shameful and all that runs counter to reason, as well as envy [...]" (16.90). While these texts are sufficiently vague to apply to numerous vices, one still has the problem of defining vice in a particular context and the inescapable reality that context shapes one's understanding of both the text and notions of morality and immorality. A pointed example is that of temporary marriages, which are regarded by the Shi'i Muslims as perfectly permissible, while the Sunnites regard it as nothing more than camouflaged prostitution. Another example is that of masturbation; while three of the four recognized and dominant Sunni schools of law regard it as reprehensible, with the punishment being witnessing one's pregnant fingers giving birth on the Day of Judgment, a fourth school regards it as virtuous.

Truthfulness

In the awareness of the all-pervading presence of God and the inevitable reckoning, people are commanded to be truthful in thought, word, and deed (33.70–71). Post-modernist notions of grayness as a value have little place in the Qur'an, which starts from the premise that there is an absolute, single, and knowable "Truth". The Qur'an speaks about "the light" (al-nur) in the singular and "darknesses" (al-zulumat) in the plural, making it convenient for traditional or fundamentalist scholars to claim that there is only one truth – usually theirs or that of their group. The believers are called upon to uphold the spirit of truthfulness by staying in the company of other truthful people (9.19) and to speak the truth in the face of falsehood. Concealing the truth is prohibited (2.42) as is distorting it with falsehood (2.42). Hypocrisy is condemned in the strongest terms and the believers are enjoined to ensure that their deeds correspond with their words: "O you who believe, why do you say that which you do not do? Grievously odious is it in the sight of God that you say that which you do not do" (61.2–3).

Humility

Given that the Qur'an starts with the premise that only God is absolutely pure and that all of humankind are ultimately dependant on the grace of God, it denounces self-righteousness and arrogance. "And ascribe not purity unto yourselves" (53.32). "Verily He [God] does not love those who are arrogant" (31.18). "Swell not your cheeks at the people and walk not in insolence through the earth for God loves not the vainglorious boastful person; be modest in your walk and lower your voice in humility . . ." (31.18–19). ". . . The men and women who possess the spirit of humility . . . for [all of] them has God readied forgiveness of sins and a mighty reward" (33.35). This humility though, is not to be confused with a polite co-existence alongside evil and injustice and is seemingly to be exercised only in respect of those who share in the values of the community of submitters to the will of God, for the believers are also those who are "fierce towards the rejecters and compassionate among themselves" (48.29). Elsewhere they are asked to be firm in the defence of their faith and their human rights (8.15 and 45).

Harmony

Notwithstanding the Qur'anic requirement that the believers must disturb the peace whenever this hides the demons of injustice and oppression, the Qur'an asks the believers to lead lives free of pointless argumentation and quarrelling. "And when the ignorant addresses them, they say 'peace' [avoiding thus all quarrel with them]" (25.63). "And keep away from all those who choose to remain ignorant" (7.199). The problem, of course, is that the Qur'anic definition of "the ignorant" (al-jahilun) is circular in that it defines the ignorant and such a definition may not be acceptable to the person so defined. One's refusal to respond to the disputations of the ignorant can thus understandably come across as intellectual snobbishness. The willingness to enter into argumentation is to be determined by its usefulness in a given context and the willingness of the other party to listen. Argumentation rooted in one's own anger is unacceptable. In dealing with the qualities of the righteous, the Qur'an says "and those who hold in check their anger ..." (3.134).

Hope

In the face of the all-pervading grace of God, the Qur'an requires the believers to remain hopeful of this grace and never to despair. In fact, the Qur'an describes deep pessimism as a sign of *kufr* (rejection). "And do not give up hope of God's soothing Mercy. Truly no one despairs of God's mercy except those who have no faith" (12.87). This verse, along with Q.2.195, has been used by many Muslim scholars to denounce suicide as an act of *kufr*. A deeper appreciation of the phenomenon of depression will hopefully bring about a more nuanced interpretation of these texts. Can suicide possibly – for some at least – be a desperate attempt to actually access that mercy of God that those so disposed have deeply yearned for and which seemingly escaped them in this life?[1]

Courage

The Qur'an uses the word *sabr* fairly frequently and this has often been interpreted to mean a passive patience. In fact, it means to persevere and to remain firm as is evident from the following verse: "Oh you who have attained to faith! Be patient in adversity, and vie in perseverance with one another, remain prepared and remain conscious of God in order that you may be successful" (3.200). In another verse "the firm and steadfast in adversity and periods of hardship" are referred to as the ones who are true [in their faith] and who are "truly righteous" (2.177). This persistence is to be exercised both in the face of physical challenges as well as verbal onslaughts. Good Muslims uphold the truth and justice "and are not afraid of the reproaches of those who find fault" (5.54). Here too one needs to tread carefully for one can easily seek refuge in self-righteousness when being challenged by others. Instead of reflecting on the accusations being made against one, the temptation is great to

---

1 The phenomenon of suicide bombings has generally been condemned under this text by Muslim jurists as prohibited. This position does not take cognizance of the fact that those guilty of this are not moved by despair and do not see it as a means of ending their lives but as act which, in their logic, extends their "real" lives in closeness to God. It is, furthermore, seen as an act of great courage.

cheerfully invoke the Qur'anic "they are not afraid of the reproaches of those who find fault" (ibid.).

Austerity

The Qur'an encourages and even commands the believers to lead an austere life and those who denounce the pleasures of this life are on much more solid Qur'anic ground than those who argue that fun and enjoyment are a part of religious life as long as these take place within the ambit of the Shari'ah (Islamic law). In describing some characteristics of Muslim conduct the Qur'an says "and those [believers] who shun all vain activity ..." (23.3) and "when they pass by some vain activity, they pass it by with dignified [avoidance]" (25.72). Of course, one can argue that recreation, laughter, and jokes are intrinsic to one's emotional well-being and there are certainly examples from the Prophet's life that he did, in fact, engage in these. From the Qur'an alone though, one cannot avoid the impression that a rather dim view is taken towards most contemporary forms of recreation. Muslim scholars in general justify the most innocuous forms of entertainment such as archery, horse riding and swimming in terms of the need for physical fitness rather than sheer enjoyment. Repeatedly the Qur'an asserts "and the next life is better and permanent".

Wealth as a trust from God

The Qur'an is contemptuous of those who are attached to wealth beyond that which one requires for one's daily subsistence. Such attachment distracts one from following the path that leads to God and provides one with an illusionary sense of eternity. "The desire for abundance and increase [in wealth, status, and other worldly possessions] distracts you until you visit your graves" (102.1–2). "Woe to every scandalmonger and backbiter who amasses wealth and counts it, thinking that his wealth will enable him to live forever! By no means! He will surely be thrown into that which breaks to pieces [hell]" (104.1–4). The notion of sustenance being properly earned (*rizq halal*) is key to the Qur'an's approach to wealth and has been imbibed by all pious Muslims. Even then, Muslims are prohibited from engaging in any wasteful and ostentatious expenses (17.26–27). The Qur'an singles out for denunciation a number of means of unlawfully acquiring money or property. This includes priests and monks devouring the property of people (9.34), gambling (5.90), and theft (60.12). While others may be the victims of these forms of ill-begotten wealth, the Qur'an also speaks about the perpetrators of dishonesty as victims in the sense that their own humanity is lessened and that they are actually a consuming fire (4.10).

Sexual fulfillment within the Confines of Committed Relationships

The Qur'an rejects all forms of sexual immodesty: "And say to the believing men that they should lower their gaze and guard their sexual organs; that will make for greater purity for them. And God is well acquainted with all that you do. And say to the believing women that they should lower their gaze and guard their sexual organs" (24.30–31). The Qur'an speaks approvingly of only two kinds of relationship for sexual fulfillment – that of marriage between a male and female and that of slave ownership – and is silent about other forms such as same-sex unions or masturbation.[2] In a text that is normally viewed as dealing with one's financial preparedness for marriage, the Qur'an does, however, say: "Those who find not the means of marriage shall keep themselves chaste." (24.33). The Qur'an also condones ownership of another person – slavery – as the basis of legitimate sexual relationship, i.e., a male freeperson may have sexual intercourse with his female slaves. This condonation is usually passed over in somewhat embarrassed silence by most contemporary commentators or placed in "its proper historical context". The insistence on marriage between a male and female as the only other legitimate basis for sexual fulfillment is, on the other hand, invested with an ahistorical immutability. Other forms of sexual fulfillment between two persons are regarded as adultery, a shameful deed. "And come not near to adultery; for it is shameful and an evil, opening the road [to other evils]" (17.32).[3]

SOCIAL AND ECONOMIC CONDUCT

The Qur'an advocates a society based on honesty, morality, generosity, justice, and equity. It takes the position that all of humankind have intrinsic socio-economic rights and concomitant responsibilities – including the responsibility to struggle for and defend those rights.

---

2 Notwithstanding a legal principle that the basis of all things is permissibility, i.e., that something is permissible unless proven prohibited, by inference of the approval of these forms of union, most scholars have, in fact, drawn opinions condemning these forms of sexual fulfilment from the Qur'an.

3 The verse is invoked to cover a wide range of activities ranging from the prohibition of opposite sexes touching with a handshake, to confining women indoors from the age of puberty, to masturbation.

The sanctity of life

All of human life is sacred for "verily We [God] have honoured the Children of Adam" (17.70) and no one is allowed to take anyone else's life "except in truth" (6.151). This is usually interpreted to mean killing during a just war, in self-defence, or in retribution after due legal process within a just social system. The diminishing of all of humankind by the murder of a single person is emphasized (5.32). While infanticide – more specifically that of the girl infant – is condemned, the Qur'an is silent on the rights of the fetus. In accordance with the social practices of pre-Islamic Arabia, the Qur'an sanctions retaliation in the case of murder and other injuries to limbs. However, it emphasizes that this must be done justly, and that a remission of the death sentence is a source of "mercy from God" (2.178). In a society where retaliatory vendettas persisted for many generations, the Qur'anic injunction can even be interpreted as progressive because the injured or his/her family was forced to limit the retaliation to the equivalent of the original crime. It is only in this sense that the verse "and in retaliation there is life for you, oh people of understanding" (2.179) can yield any coherent meaning.

Sanctity of lawfully acquired property

Overt theft is condemned (60.12) as well as other more covert forms of depriving others of their property, such as connivance in depriving someone of his/her inheritance, failing to return something entrusted to one for safekeeping (4.58), or cheating in weighing goods for sale (17.35). The Qur'an is particularly vehement in its denunciation of usury

> Those who devour usury will not stand [on the Day of Resurrection] except as stands one whom the Evil One by his touch has driven to madness. That is because they say: "Trade is like usury". But God has permitted trade and forbidden usury. Those who after receiving direction from their Lord desist, shall be pardoned for the past; their case is for God; but those who repeat the offence are companions of the Fire; they will abide therein. God will deprive interest of all blessings but he will increase the deeds of charity: for he loves not creatures ungrateful and wicked (2.275–276).

Muslims advocating diverse economic systems ranging from capitalism with a conscience to socialist control by the State have derived justification from the Qur'an. Most Muslims believe that the Qur'an is neither socialist nor capitalist but has its own unique economic doctrine.[4] The Qur'an sanctions notions of personal property with individuals being the rightful owners thereof as distinct from private property that enables individuals to keep secret the extent of their wealth and to be sole arbiters of how to dispense with it. All wealth is also regarded as a trust from God.

Generosity and the re-distribution of wealth

The Qur'an condemns greed and what is normally rendered as "hoarding" (and which can easily be understood as the more innocuous sounding amassing of wealth or "savings"):

> As for all who pile up gold and silver and do not spend them for the sake of God – give them the tidings of grievous suffering on the Day when that hoarded wealth shall be heated in the fire of hell and their foreheads and their sides and backs branded therewith; "These are the treasures which you have laid up for yourselves! Taste then, [the evil of] your hoarded treasures!" (9.35).

Greed is condemned and those free from it are regarded as "the successful ones". The Qur'an regards wealth both as a gift from God and as the product of people's labor or of their exploitation of other's labor. This provides both those who believe in communal ownership of property, as well as those who believe in private or personal ownership with a basis for Qur'anic justification. "Oh you who believe! Spend of the good things that you have lawfully earned and out of that which we have brought forth for you from the earth ..." (2.267). People are entitled only to that what they have earned. "... And humankind shall have nothing other that what is earned" (53.39–40). Elsewhere the Qur'an says, "Do not covet of the bounties which God has bestowed more abundantly on some of you than on others. Men shall have what they have earned and women shall have what they have earned" (4.32). Yet those who are given of the bounties of God are expected to spend all their superfluous wealth. "They ask you what you spend? Say 'All that which is beyond your need'" (2.219). In contrast to those who hoard, Muslims who "spend of their wealth by night and by day, in secret and in public" are promised that they "shall have their reward with their Lord; on them shall be no fear, nor shall they grieve" (2.274).

---

4 Wherever any serious practical work is being done on the putatively unique Islamic model, it invariably bears a close resemblance to capitalism with a few Arabic terms thrown into it and good care being taken that there is no direct investment in anything that is expressedly forbidden in the Qur'an, such as gambling or alcohol. The larger global networks wherein these institutions tie in though, are seldom free from these constraints.

The Qur'an takes the position that "in the possessions of the wealthy there is a right due to the poor" (51.19, 70.24–15) and places great merit on giving beyond the institutionalized wealth tax known as *zakah*. This giving will purify one's own soul and must comprise of what one really feels attached to – "You will never attain unto piety unless you spend of that which you love" (3.92), is preferably done in quiet (2.71), but can be done "day and night, in secret or in public, and must not be followed by words of injury which make the recipient feel a sense of obligation to the benefactor. Other than the commandments that slaves be treated with kindness, the Qur'an actually goes a considerable way to promote an end to slavery (90.12–13); money given to emancipate slaves is seen as an investment with God, (2.117) and this emancipation is one of the categories which the Qur'an allows for the expenditure of the obligatory wealth tax (9.60). Ways of facilitating this emancipation are spelt out and freeing a slave can serve as the price for the expiation of a major crime such as accidental homicides (4.92), nullifying a foolish utterance of divorce (58.3), or an inability to fulfill a solemn oath (5.92).

Social equality

The Qur'an takes the position that everyone is equal in the eyes of God and of the law. No human being has any inherent distinction over another on the basis of lineage or race. It does, however, recognize and condone distinction, differentiation, or discrimination on the basis of gender, religion, knowledge, and piety. Given that these four categories are very significant and their definitions difficult to verify and measure empirically, it is questionable whether one can really use the Qur'an as a standard to justify contemporary understandings of social equality or universal human rights. The following two verses, often invoked to justify this, reflect this problem:

> Oh humankind! Be conscious of your Sustainer who created you out of one living entity and out of it created its mate; and out of those two spread a multitude of men and women. And remain conscious of God, in whose name you demand [your rights] from one another, and of these ties of kinship. Verily God is ever watchful over you! (4.1).

> Oh humankind! We created you from a single pair of male and female and made you into nations and tribes that you may know each other. Verily the most honoured of you in the sight of God is he who is most righteous of you and God has full knowledge and is well acquainted with all things (49.13).

The first verse affirms the single source of our creation – "one living entity"[5] – and implies that all people are therefore equal. The reality is that the Qur'an also contains a host of injunctions detailing the differentiated way in which slaves and freepersons, men and women, those belonging to the community of faithful and those out of it, "the learned" and "the ignorant" are to be treated. The second verse has been invoked by campaigners against racism, tribalism, and xenophobia who insist that God wants us to know each other. The notion of piety as the only criteria of standing in God's eyes has been a particularly powerful rallying tool for Muslim social equality and gender activists. On the other hand, those desiring the retention of their own tribal or ethnic identity – which often implies finding and implementing ways of keeping "the other" out – also insist that tribe and nation are "givens" from God. Other than the idea that God is actually constantly re-making tribes and nations and the rather problematic question of the hand of God in the wars and genocides that invariably accompany this constant re-making, this is a difficult verse to understand.

Justice

Justice receives such prominence in the Qur'an that it is regarded as one of the reasons why God created the earth: "And we have created the heavens and the earth in Truth so that every soul may earn its just recompense for what it earned and that it may not be oppressed" (45.22). It is a quality of a God who repeatedly assures His creation that He will never deal with them unjustly by as much as an atom's weight (4.40, 10.44). Many of the injunctions of the Qur'an which come across as barbaric stem from a concern for justice for both the perpetrator and the victim.

> We ordained for them therein "Life for life, eye for eye, nose for nose, ear for ear, tooth for tooth, and wounds equal for equal". But if anyone remits the retaliation by way of charity, it is an act of atonement for himself. And if they fail to judge by what God has revealed, they indeed are wrongdoers (5.45).

> If you have to respond to an attack, respond only to the extent of the attack leveled against you; but to bear yourself with patience is indeed better for you [since God is with] those who are patient in adversity (16.126).

5 Muslim feminists have pointed out that the Arabic term "*nafs wahidah*" is feminine, thus debunking the myth that woman was created from a man and for men. The verse continues to say "and we created from 'it' (feminine), her partner."

The demands that the Qur'an makes upon individuals to uphold justice is extraordinary and transcends all social bonds. While justice is something that one demands for oneself, more importantly, it is something to be fulfilled in respect of others at whatever cost to oneself and one's own community.

> O you who have attained unto faith! Be ever steadfast in upholding justice; bearing witness to the truth for the sake of God, even though it be against your own self or your parents and kinsfolk. Whether the person be rich or poor. God's claim takes precedence over the claims of either of them. Do not then follow your desires lest you swerve from justice for, if you distort the truth, behold God is indeed aware of all that you do (4.135).

Jihad

"*Jihad*" literally means "to struggle", to "exert oneself" or "to spend" (energy or wealth)". In the Qur'an, it is frequently followed by the expressions "in the path of God" and "with your wealth and your selves". For Muslims, the term "*jihad*" has also come to mean the "sacralization of combat" (Schleifer, 1982, 122). Despite its popular meaning as a sacred armed struggle or war, the term "*jihad*" was always understood by Muslims to embrace a broader struggle to transform both one's self and society. The Qur'an itself uses the word in its various meanings ranging from warfare in self-defence (4.90; 25.52; 9.41) to contemplative spiritual struggle (22.78; 29.6), and even exhortation (29.8; 31.15). Given the comprehensive Qur'anic use of the term and the way *jihad* is intended to transform both one's self and society, one may say that it is simulaneously a struggle and praxis.[6] For many Muslims, *jihad* is the Islamic paradigm of the liberation struggle, and justice as the objective of *jihad*, rather than the establishment of Islam as a religious system, is a common theme in progressive Muslim discourse. Later Muslim scholars insisted that justice can only be established through the establishment of an Islamic order; hence the conflation about *jihad* as the means to establish an Islamic government.

Social relations

In the Qur'an, one finds two notions which govern social relations; "*huquq*" – rights which are obligations that one has upon or owes

---

6 Praxis may be defined as, "conscious action undertaken by a human community that has the responsibility for its own political determination [...] based on the realization that humans make history" (Chopp, 1989, 137).

society and which must be defended – and *ihsan*, generosity beyond obligation. Although the Qur'an does not make this sharp distinction as the example of charity shows, they are presented here in this division for convenience. The basic principle of rights and duties is contained in the verse "Do not wrong and be not wronged" (2.279). Here we find a simple statement that says the rights of others should not be violated and which also places an obligation on the Muslim to ensure that her own rights are also not violated. In social conduct this covers the need for one to be reliable and trustworthy in one's undertakings or promises (4.105, 8.27 and 16.91) and economic dealings (93.1–3), to present truthful evidence in any matter or dispute (25.72), to refrain from concealing evidence (2.283), defaming others (49.6), backbiting and slander (49.12), hypocrisy (2.8–19), and exploiting the vulnerability of others (2.275–276). The Qur'an also condemns more subtle forms of injury to others that also detract from the humanity of the perpetrator. Among such sins the Qur'an censures are suspicion (49.12), mocking others or the objects of their worship (49.11), and using derogatory nicknames (ibid.). Although all of these injunctions apply to everyone in a society founded upon Qur'an principles; the Qur'an nevertheless distinguishes between religiously diverse communities who live in such a society. Most of the specific injunctions pertaining to such dealings were informed by the daily encounters that the first Muslim community had with these communities. The Qur'an is explicit about the importance of harmonious relationships with all of those who are not engaged in warfare with the Muslims (60.8), the permissibility of the food slaughtered by the people of the book, and of marriage by Muslim males to their women (5.5).

While most of the above are duties which are owed to God, society, and/or the citizen, the Qur'an acknowledges that at the heart of a moral society is something beyond rights and legal obligations; hence the concepts of *ihsan* (generosity) and *sadqah* (charity). The believers are thus continually encouraged to transcend the minimum required in reaching out towards others. While general virtuous qualities such as expressing gratitude (22.38), compassion (90.17) and speaking gently (2.83) are encouraged, the Qur'an is also explicit about the means which the Muslims can employ to go the extra mile in the case of sharing ones wealth, caring for orphans, and freeing slaves.

The other category of marginalized individuals that the Qur'an treats with an enormous amount of compassion is orphans. Muslims are instructed treat them gently (93.9 and 4.36), to set aside wealth from their inheritance for the care of orphans (4.8), to deal justly with their property entrusted to them if they are still young (4.3), and to honor them (99.17–18). The Qur'an is so emphatic about gentleness to orphans that those who repel them are regarded as people who have rejected the faith itself (107.1–3). While the Qur'an upholds all of the above as requirements for the believers, it nevertheless acknowledges that a commitment to these values and living alongside this commitment is exceptionally difficult.

> And what would convey unto you what the steep uphill road is? It is the freeing of a neck [from slavery] Or the feeding upon a day of hunger of an orphan near of kin, or of a needy [stranger] lying in the dust; and being of those who have attained unto faith; and who enjoin upon one another patience in adversity and enjoin upon one another compassion. Such are those who have attained unto righteousness ... (90.12–19).

Gender relations

In the context of seventh-century Arabia, the Qur'an can be viewed as encouraging a sense of gender justice and compassion towards all victims of oppression, including women. "And women shall have rights similar to the rights against them, according to what is equitable" (2.228). In general, one discerns a strong egalitarian trend when the Qur'an deals with the ethico-religious responsibilities and recompense of the believers and a discriminatory trend when it deals with the social and legal obligations of women. With regard to both of these aspects though, there are two further trends: First, general statements are also made which both affirm and deny gender equality and, second, when specific injunctions are made, then they are generally discriminatory towards women.

In social and legal matters it is very difficult to avoid the impression that the Qur'an provides a set of injunctions and exhortations where women, in general, are simultaneously infantalized and "pedastalized" – to be protected, and economically cared for by men, but also admonished and punished if they are disobedient. At the time of the Qur'an's revelation, sixth-century Arabia was experiencing enormous socio-anthropological flux in the region in general, and more specifically, Hijaz. While Arabian society had a number of distinct matriarchal features, these were now being replaced by a wholly patriarchal system. Muslims generally hold that this was a period when women were regarded as not only socially inferior but as "slaves and cattle" (Siddiqi, 1972, 16). It was a time when women "basically inherited nothing but were themselves inherited. They were a part of their husband's property, to be owned by his heirs or other men of his tribe. It was a mark of dishonor for any man to have a daughter and many preferred to bury their female children alive rather than face social opprobrium. In Pre-Islamic society payments were made to the father or nearest male relative for a wife to be wedded in a direct 'sale'. The Qur'an altered this and the woman, instead of being the object of a contract, became a legal contracting party with the sole entitlement to the dowry in lieu of the right of sexual union. In the practice of divorce the Qur'an abolished the practice whereby a husband could summarily discard his wife and introduced a waiting period to work through possible ways of reconciliation before divorce and separation were effected. During this period the wife was entitled to financial support from her husband. In the question of inheritance, the Qur'an modified Pre-Islamic rules that in general excluded females and minor children. "The [modified Qur'anic] provision ... qualifies the system of exclusive inheritance by male agnate relatives and in particular recognizes the capacity of women relatives to succeed" (Coulsen, 1978, 16).

The family

The Qur'an, reflecting the norms of traditional Arab society, recognizes only one kind of family relationship – the extended family with a male heading it. This family may comprise more than one wife and the parents of either one or both of the spouses along with one's siblings and all the offspring from the marriage or marriages. Marriage and related matters such as dispute resolution, divorce, trust, and mutual responsibilities are dealt with at considerable length and the Qur'an goes into far more detail here than it does with any other social relationship. While the Qur'an discourages monasticism, it does not reject celibacy. Marriage is a social contract between a male and female and requires the consent of both parties as well as a mutually agreed upon dowry paid by the groom to the bride (4.4). The Qur'an prohibits certain categories of persons such as siblings and foster siblings from marrying each other (4.23). Also prohibited was the automatic passing on of a wife to her husband's brother as property upon the demise of the latter (4.19). Marriage is to be based upon love and compassion (30.21), with men being "the protectors" of women (4.34) who are to treat them at all times with kindness (4.19). The Qur'an allows the pre-Islamic practice of polygamy but makes it subject to a number of conditions such as the limitation of four wives and the ability to deal with all of them equitably. While this permission is generally seen as applicable under all circumstances, the context of the relevant verse suggests that it was granted in a situation of having to deal with the orphans and war widows. Ways of dealing with marital disputes, including a wife's refusal to comply with her husband's requests, are spelt out and this includes arbitration and chastisement (4.35). When a marriage has broken down irretrievably, then divorce in a gentle manner is allowed. The Qur'an is also explicit about the steps that this process must follow and the wife's need to be provided for in the short-term (2.241 and 65.1–7).

The Qur'an reminds adults whose own parents are still alive of the time when they were small and their mothers bore them "by bearing strain upon strain" and of their then utter dependence on their parents (31.14). For this reason alone one owes parents the eternal obligation of gratitude, compassion and care.

> And do good unto your parents. Should one of them, or both, attain to old age in you care, never say "Ugh" unto them or scold them, but always speak to them with reverent speech, and spread over them humbly your wings of tenderness and say "O My Sustainer! Bestow your grace upon them, even as they cherished me and raised me as a child." (17.23).

The Qur'an makes little direct reference to the treatment of children or to parent–child relationships other than the kind of exhortations referred to above. Examples of such relationships are, however, evident in the relatively lengthy accounts of the interaction between Abraham and Ishmael, Abraham and his father, Azar (e.g., 6.74–88), as well as the advices imparted by the Luqman, the wise sage, to his son (31.13–19). These accounts all reflect warm relationships of caring and obedience to one's parents as long as they do not require one to associate any deity with God (31.15) The Qur'an does not contain any reference to relationships with daughters with the exception of a scathing denuncia-tion of the murder of the girl-child.

> Whenever any of them is given the glad tidings of the birth of a girl, his face darkens, and he is filled with suppressed anger avoiding all people because of the [alleged] evil of the glad tidings which he has received, and [debating with himself] Shall he keep this [child] despite the contempt

[which he feels for it] – or shall he bury in the dust? Oh, evil indeed is what they decide (16.58–59).

State and governance

There is no direct reference in the Qur'an to any notion of an Islamic state. However the Qur'an contains a few injunctions requiring obedience to those in authority. "Obey God, his Prophet and those charged with authority from among you" (4.59). The fact that this injunction is linked to obedience to God and his Prophet leads to the conclusion that this authority must be a Muslim one. Any assumption that an Islamic state is the will of God for all of humankind rather than the results of a particular set of political circumstances as they unfolded in Medina during the lifetime of the Prophet is based on an interpretation of what the Qur'an says rather than any explicit statement to this effect.

The Qur'an contains several references to the sovereignty of God and this has been interpreted by Islamist ideologues as referring to an Islamic theocracy. "Oh verily, His Alone is all judgment" (6.62). Notwithstanding the fact that nearly all of the verses referring to God's sovereignty deal with matters of belief or pertain to the ultimate judgment, the unstated assumption of those who claim worldly sovereignty in God's name is that they have correctly understood the will of God and will implement the political consequences of this sovereignty. The Qur'an does ask Muhammad to judge by the will of God as formulated in the Qur'an. "We have bestowed upon you from on high this divine writ setting forth the truth so that you may judge between people in accordance with what God has taught you" (4.105). The problem which emerged soon after the death of the Prophet is one of the authenticity of those who claim to be the political agents of God and who among the many claimants are to interpret His will "correctly". Contrary to what observers of the contemporary world of Islam may imagine, there are very few specific duties explicitly spelt out in the Qur'an for an Islam wielding political power and all of these revelations pertain to the Medinan period. The two foundational principles for Islam in power seems to be consultation and justice: the Prophet was instructed to "consult with them upon the conduct of affairs" (3.159) and the believers in general are told that "their affairs are by mutual consultation" (42.38). As for political justice, the Qur'an says: "We sent our Messengers with clear signs and sent down with them the book and the balance, that humankind may stand forth in justice" (57.25). These are waging *jihad* in defense of the faith or in response to aggression, collecting and distributing *zakah*, and enacting punishment for a very limited array of sins or crimes. The crimes or sins for which the Qur'an specifies punitive measures are slander (24.4–9), adultery (24.2–3 and 15.16), theft (5.41), robbery, treason and armed insurrection (5.36–37), murder and bodily mutilation (2.178–179).

INSTITUTIONALIZED RELIGIOUS PRACTICES

As we have seen above, the Qur'an deals with a host of injunctions, most of them of an ethico-religious and social nature. Only three formal religious rituals or institutionalized practices receive any significant attention in the Qur'an: the formal prayers (*salah*), fasting in the month of Ramadan, and the pilgrimage to Mecca (*hajj*). All three also form a part of what are commonly referred to as the five principles of Islam, the other two being the declaration of faith that there is one God with Muhammad being His Messenger and *zakah*, the welfare tax.

Prayers (Salah)

There are numerous references in the Qur'an to *salah* and its importance: it was clearly the single most socio-religious activity that held the first Muslim community together. Its significance in the life of a Muslim and to God can be gauged from the fact that the Qur'an outlines ways of deviating from the normal pattern of the ritual during a state of fear (2.238) or in the midst of actual physical combat during jihad (4.101). Other than in the case of illness, menstruation, or frailty, prayer as an obligation is never dispensed with. The following is a typical example of the verses of the Qur'an dealing with prayer: "And be constant in prayer, and spend in charity, and bow down with those who bow down" (2.43). The infinitive "to be constant" or "to establish" (*q-w-m*) appears most frequently in regard to prayer and emphasizes its daily and institutio-nalized nature as distinct from other forms of worship, such as remembering God, chanting His praises, etc., while the instruction to "bow down with those who bow down" refers to its communal nature. As is the case in this verse, establishing the daily prayers is linked to the payment of *zakah* no less than thirty-two times. This serves to underline the connectedness of the seemingly purely sacred with the seemingly profane. The Qur'an at various junctures provides the purpose of the daily prayers as "seeking God's assistance and steadfastness" (2.153), a means of protecting oneself from restrain from "loathsome deeds" and from all that runs counter to reason (29.45), of invoking the grace of God (35.29–30), remembering God (20.132) and attaining happiness in this world and the Hereafter as of well as spiritual growth (87.14). *Surah* 107, *ayahs* 4–7 is an interesting example of how the Qur'an expects generosity of spirit to emerge from prayers: "Woe, then unto those who pray, whose hearts from their prayers are remote, those who want to be seen and praised and withal deny all assistance [to others]."

"Verily, for all believers prayer is indeed a sacred duty linked to particular times [of day]" (4.103). The exact times of the prayers are left somewhat unclear in the Qur'an and their times are fixed by interpretation of the verses which refer to times,[7] (but which can really be interpreted in a number of ways), and what was ascertained from the practice of the Prophet. Although the vast majority of Muslims hold that there are five daily prayers, the Sunnis argue that these also correspond with five times, while the Shi'is believe that they have to be offered three times a day. Two of the five – the midday (*zuhr*) with the afternoon ('*asr*), and the one immediately after sunset (*maghrib*) with the one of the first part of the night ('*isha*) – are to be combined. Both agree that the dawn prayer (*fajr*) stands on its own.

The call to prayers (*adhan*) is referred to on two occasions, although the mode is not spelt out (62.9–10; 5.58). The prior conditions for the prayer which the Qur'an stipulates are sobriety and ablution – the symbolic nature of the latter being evident from the fact that dust may be used in the absence of water.

> O you who have attained unto faith! When you are about to pray, wash your face, and your hands and arms up to the elbows and pass your [wet] hands lightly over your head, and wash your feet up to the ankles. And if you are in a state requiring total ablution, purify yourselves. But if you are traveling, or have just satisfied a want of nature or have had sexual intercourse with a woman, and can find no water – then resort to dust, passing therewith lightly over your face and your hands. God does not

7 The following are the verses regarded as referring to the times of the daily prayers: (1) "And be constant in prayer at the beginning and end of the day as well as during the early watches of the night" (11.114); (2) "O you who have attained unto faith! At three times [of day] let [even] those whom you rightfully possess, as well as those among you who have not yet attained to puberty, ask leave of you; before the prayer of daybreak, and whenever you lay aside your garments in the middle of the day and after the prayer of nightfall ..." (24.58) (3) "Be constant in your prayer from the time from the time the sun has passed its zenith till the darkness of the night and the recitation at dawn is indeed witnessed" (17.78), and (4) "Be mindful of prayers and of the middle prayer" (2.238).

want to impose any hardship on you, but wants to make you pure and to bestow the full measure of his blessings, so that you might have cause to be grateful (5.6–7).

As for the manner in which the prayer is to be conducted, the Qur'an refers only to bowing (*ruku'*) and prostration (*sujud*) and says that one should recite "whatever of the Qur'an has been made easy for one" in a manner that is not loud (73.20). Presence of mind and of heart is, of course, indispensable for prayer, and those who pray in a slothful and lazy fashion are regarded as being among the hypocrites (4.142, 9.54). While the works on Muslim law contain large volumes of material on prayers, their types, conditions of fulfillment, times, modes, and what nullifies them, etc., most of these have been derived from sayings attributed to the Prophet and/or the reasoning of jurists rather than the Qur'an.

Fasting

The Qur'an refers to fasting in two distinct contexts: the one which is prescribed during the month of Ramadan as an act of worship and the other that serves as a means to expiate sin or a lapse in a specific religious duty. The following fairly lengthy section from the Qur'an is the only significant text that deals with fasting during the month of Ramadan as an institution.

> Oh you who have attained unto faith! Fasting is ordained for you as it was ordained for those before you so that you may remain conscious of God; Fasting during a certain number of days. But whoever of you is ill or on a journey, [shall fast instead for the same] number of days; and [in such cases] it is incumbent upon those who can afford it to make sacrifice by feeding a needy person. And whosoever does more good than he is bound to do, does good unto himself thereby; for to fast is to do good unto yourselves – if you but knew it.

> It was the month in which the Qur'an was first bestowed from on high as a guidance and as the standard by which to discern the true from the false ... God wills that you shall have ease and does not will you to suffer hardship; but [He desires] that you complete the number [of days required] and that you extol God for His having guided you aright, and that you render thanks [unto Him].

> And if my servants ask you about Me – behold, I am near: I respond to the call of him who calls unto Me. Let them, then respond unto Me, and believe in Me, so that they might follow the right way.

It is lawful for you to go unto your wives during the night preceding [the day's] fast: they are a garment for you and you are a garment for them. God is aware that you would have deprived yourselves of this right and so He has turned unto you in His mercy and removed this hardship from you. Now, then, you may have sexual intercourse with them, and avail yourselves of that which God has ordained for you, and eat and drink until you can discern the white streak of dawn against the blackness of night and then resume fasting until nightfall, but do not have sexual intercourse with them when you are about to abide in meditation in houses of worship.

These are the limits of God; do not, then, offend against them – for thus God makes clear His messages unto humankind, so that they might remain conscious of Him [2.183–187].

The only objective of fasting stipulated in the Qur'an is that of acquiring *taqwa* – self-restraint in the awareness that one is always in the presence of God and ultimately accountable to Him.[8] As is evident from the latter part of the text above, fasting requires abstention from all food, drink, and sexual intercourse from the first sign that night is ending until just after sunset.[9] In the light of the fact that the Qur'an was also revealed in this month and the objectives of fasting, it is a period of heightened spiritual awareness of increased devotion. The last sentence in the text above refers to a retreat that many pious Muslim males undertake in the last ten days of Ramadan in mosques throughout the world.

Hajj

The word *hajj* means "to move to a place with the intention of visiting or viewing it", in this case to visit the *Ka'bah*, or as it is otherwise known – the house of God in the city of Mecca. Other terms that the Qur'an use for this cube-like structure is "the ancient house" (*al-bayt al 'atiq*) (22.29) and "the sacred house" (*al-bayt al-muharram*) (14.37), "the sacred mosque" (*al-masjid al-haram*) (17.1), "the long-enduring house" (*al-bayt al-ma'mur*) (52.4), and the "first temple/sanctuary set up for

8 Many Muslims also suggest that one of the objectives of fasting is to "make everyone realize through his or her own experience how it feels to be hungry and thirsty, and thus to gain a true appreciation of the needs of the poor" (Asad, 1980, 39). Besides the fact that this is not based on any Qur'anic text, it assumes that Muslims are all in general well fed and reduces the poor to the "other". Furthermore, the poor are not exempt from fasting.

9 There is another kind of fasting that many Sufis engage in which also involves abstinance from talking and social communion. This is referred to as the "*Sawm i Maryam*" the fasting of Mary. Before Mary was given the tidings of a son, she was also instructed to withdraw from the world. "She withdrew from her family to an eastern place and kept herself in seclusion from them" (19.16).

188 ◆ The Qur'an A SHORT INTRODUCTION

humankind" (3.96). The Qur'an provides an expectedly scanty account of the history of the Ka'bah.

> And Lo! We made the Temple a goal to which people might repair again and again, and a sanctuary. Take then the place whereupon Abraham once stood as your place of prayer. And thus did we command Abraham and Ishmael: Purify My Temple for those who will walk around it, and those who will abide near it in meditation and those who will bow down and prostrate themselves [in prayer...] And when Abraham and Ishmael were raising the foundation of the Temple they prayed]: Oh our Sustainer! Accept this from us for verily, you are Alone, all hearing, all-knowing (2.125–27).

The relationship between Mecca, referred to as "the mother of the cities" (42.7) and a territory rendered secure (amin) (95.3) in the Qur'an is somewhat unclear. While critical scholars would suggest that the city and its geo-social dynamics gave rise to the temple, most Muslims would hold that the presence of the Ka'bah sanctifies Mecca. The root word "k-'-b" means "it swelled" or "became prominent and exalted". Q.14.37 seems to suggest that the Ka'bah was already in existence when Abraham left Ishmael and Hagar in the wilderness. The text above probably refers to its reconstruction and purification by Abraham and Ishmael. Sixteen months after Muhammad's asylum in Medina, the direction Muslims faced when offering the daily prayers (salah) was changed from Jerusalem to Mecca, more specifically, towards the Ka'bah. The first injunction to perform the Hajj is late Meccan:

> For when We assigned unto Abraham the site of this Temple, [We said unto him:] "Do not ascribe divinity to aught beside me!" – and: "Purify My Temple for those who will walk around it and those who stand before it [in meditation] and those who bow down and prostrate themselves [in prayer]." (2.125)

> Hence, proclaim though unto all people the [duty of] pilgrimage; they will come unto you on foot and on [every kind] fast mount, coming from every far away point, so that they might experience much that shall benefit them, and that they might extol the name of God on the days appointed [for sacrifice] over whatever heads of cattle He may have provided for them [to this end] to eat, then thereof, and feed the unfortunate poor, thereafter let them bring to an end their state of self-denial, and let them fulfill their vows which they [may] have made, and let them walk [once again] around the ancient Temple (22.26–28).

The *Hajj* is obligatory upon all of those capable of finding their way to Mecca (3.96)[10] and occurs in the first ten days of the appropriately named month of Dhi'l-Hijjah (i.e., the possessor of *hajj*). The specificity of its time is alluded in the Qur'an when it suggests that the cycle of the moon is intended to serve as a marker of time: "They ask you about the new moons: Say: They will indicate to you the periods [of various doings of] humankind, including the pilgrimage" (2.189). As for the rites itself, the Qur'an goes into somewhat greater detail than any of the other formal acts of devotions such as fasting or the daily prayers. As in all other matters though, the Qur'an does not present a neat sequence for these rites.

While the Qur'an does not prescribe the dress of the pilgrim, this is assumed to be two seamless sheets for males to cover their upper and lower body parts, and a simple dress for women. Women who ordinarily wear a veil are also required to abandon it.[11] This garb is referred to as *"ihram"* from the root *h-r-m*, denoting sacred and alluding to the fact that the pilgrim is herself in a state of *ihram* (sacredness). Muslim jurists have worked out an elaborate set of obligations during this state, and penalties for violating them, based on the prophetic precedent (*sunnah*). "And whoever undertakes the pilgrimage, shall, while on pilgrimage abstain from lewd speech, from all wicked conduct, and from quarrelling; and whatever good you may do, God is aware of it" (2.197). While the pilgrim can don the *ihram* at any time when she has set out for Mecca, Islamic law determines that one cannot enter Mecca for Hajj beyond certain boundaries, called *"miqat"*, along the route except in a state of *ihram*. When the pilgrims reach this point there is a tremendous outburst of *Labbayk! Allahumma labbayk!* (Here I am! Here I am, O God, in Your august presence!) This is in direct to response to the call made by Abraham upon God's command (22.26–28).

Immediately, or soon after the pilgrim's arrival in Mecca, his or her first act will be to undertake a circumambulation of the *Ka'bah*. "And let them walk [once again] around the Ancient House" (22.29). The *tawaf* is performed by going around the *Ka'bah* – all the time extolling the greatness of God or offering supplication and keeping as close to the walls of the *Ka'bah* as possible. The *tawaf* commences at the *Hajar*

---

10 This "capability" is normally interpreted to cover financial means and physical health. Many Muslims also interpret it to mean spiritual preparedness and a sense of personalized calling.

11 Most Muslims make the point that the purpose of the extreme simplicity in garb is to eliminate any sign of social distinction when they are in the presence of God. Muhammad Ali takes this point further and suggests that the reason why veiled women are required to remove their veil during the *Hajj* is because the veil was a symbol of social distinction in Pre-Islamic Arabia (1990, 393).

al-Aswad (Black Stone) that is kissed or gestured towards reverentially if one cannot reach it. After the tawaf, the pilgrims undertake the sa'y, the running between two hillocks – Safa and Marwa – in Mecca. This, like the tawaf, was a Pre-Islamic practice and the early Muslims were somewhat wary of running between two hills upon each of which was placed an idol in the days before Islam. However, in the words of the Qur'an: "Safa and Marwah are truly among the signs of Allah, so whoever makes a pilgrimage to the House or pays a visit to it, there is no blame if he [she] goes around it" (2.158).

The Hajj properly commences on the eighth day of Dhi'l-Hijjah when all the pilgrims march to Mina, a plain midway between 'Arafah, itself a huge plain about nine miles from Mecca, and Mecca itself. They reach there before noon and leave Mina at noon on the following day, heading for 'Arafah. On 'Arafah is a hillock, the Mount of Mercy, where the Prophet is reported to have delivered his final sermon on the only pilgrimage that he undertook. At both of these sojourns – Mina and 'Arafah – the pilgrims spend all their time in devotion and extolling the greatness of God. After sunset they leave and stop at a place called Muzdalifah, which is referred to in the Qur'an as a sacred monument: "So when you press on from 'Arafah, remember Allah near the sacred monument, and remember Him as He has guided you . . ." (2.198). They remain here until the next morning when they return to Mina on the morning of the tenth. After animals are sacrificed, the pilgrims return to Mecca to perform the farewell tawaf around the Ka'bah. It is only after this tawaf that the pilgrim may be released from the state of ihram, although she must still return to Mina for a sojourn of two or three days, the place where the Hajj ends.

POSTSCRIPT

Subsequent to the events of 11 September 2001, bookshops throughout the Western world experienced a run on copies of the Qur'an. Many, assuming that Muslims must have been responsible, were desperate to see what it was in this book that drove Muslims to crash planes filled with innocent human beings into buildings with the intention of killing even more people. Others simply wanted to understand more about this Islam and the book at its heart.

I suspect that most of these people will not go beyond a few pages, for the Qur'an is a difficult book for "strangers", and indeed for many Muslims who just want to read it, to negotiate. The Qur'an is a book that is engaged – or wrestled with – and chanted rather than just read. As for those who do persist in attempting to understand the events of 11 September by reading the Qur'an, they may find something in it because the Qur'an, like most sacred scriptures, will provide the *taliban* (literally "searchers") from the West with what they seek. This is not to suggest that the Qur'an itself contains "just about anything." The Qur'an's commitment to the principles of monotheism and social justice, for example, is indisputable.

There are numerous verses in the Qur'an that justify – indeed encourage – resorting to armed struggle in defence of one's freedom and rights. Those with a principled commitment to non-violence may recoil at these verses. Polemicists may justify the idea that the Qur'an itself is responsible for violence by Muslim terrorists without seeing how they, these polemicists, actually reflect the same fundamentalist logic of the people that they seek to denounce. The "text by itself is the problem", they argue. "The text by itself is the answer" comes the echo from the uncritical Muslim. Texts, we now know, answer to questions asked of them and in the same manner that the *taliban* (the searchers) are not innocent and void of a context, similarly the text is also not free from a history and a context. It is in the ongoing interrogation of us as readers and our contexts that shape our questions and responses on the one hand, and a careful study of the text and its engagement with its context – both then and now – that we may gather some approximation of its meaning. None of us who approach the Qur'an are gender-neutral, classless, disinterested and disemboweled figures who "just want to understand." The need for understanding is driven, at least in part, by who we are and what our interests are in retaining or shedding our gender, race, class, clan, or ethnic positions. As misguided as it is to approach the text ahistorically, so it is to pretend that we are ahistorical beings. We will end up like the Taliban who deluded themselves with the appropriation of the term "searchers" when, in reality, they had an indomitable belief that they had fully comprehended the will of God in all its details for all of humankind.

Among Muslims we have seen how, on the one hand, Osama bin Ladin fired Qur'anic verse after verse as angry bullets at the "infidel occupiers of the holy land and their Muslim allies" and, on the other, the State-patronized *'ulama* (religious scholars) fired an equal number of verses at Osama and his followers denouncing them as the ultimate destroyers of the faith. Here we have, once again, been exposed to the Qur'an as contested scripture.

Others, such as myself, have sought and found in the Qur'an that which inspires us to a profound commitment to life and to the creation of a peaceful society based on justice and compassion. We are not blind to what many of our co-religionists have found; we are just a bit more patient with the many question marks and somewhat more certain about the overall Qur'anic picture of suffering, endurance, resistance, and liberation. As for absolute certainty, the Qur'an has an interesting phrase in this regard: "Serve your Lord, until absolute certainty *(yaqin)* comes upon you." Most scholars have interpreted *"yaqin"*, here to mean "death". I also believe that absolute certainty for human beings comes only with death. As for ultimate certainty: that is God's.

I end with the conclusion that religious texts written by Muslims have always concluded with: *"Allahu a'lam"* (God knows better); no, not "best", *better* – eternally better than anything and everyone.

God knows better

BIBLIOGRAPHY

Abu Zayd, Nasr Hamid. 1993a. *Mafhum al-Nass – Dirasa fi 'Ulum al-Qur'an.* Cairo: *Al-Hay'ah al-Masriyyah al-'Ammah li'l-Kutub.*
——. 1993 b. *"Al-Mar'ah: Ba'd al-Mafqud fi'l-Khitab al-Din al-Mu'asir"* in *Al-Hajar,* 1, 51–83.
——. 1995 *'Tajdid al-Fikr al-Islami',* in *Al-Hajar,* 3, 6–7.
Adams, Charles. 1976. 'Islamic Religious Tradition' in *The Study of The Middle East,* ed. Binder, L., pp. 60–73. New York: Wiley.
——. 1987, 'The Qur'an – Its Text and History' in *The Encyclopedia of Religion,* 16 vol., ed. Mircea Eliade, 156–176. New York: Macmillan.
Ahmad, Barakat. 1979. *Muhammad and the Jews: A Re-Examination.* New Delhi: Vikas Publishing House.
Ahmad, (Jullandari) Rashid. 1968. 'Quranic Exegesis and Classical Tafsir'. *Islamic Quarterly Review,* 12: 1, 71–119.
Akhtar, Shabbir. 1991. 'An Islamic Model of Revelation'. *Journal for the Study of Islam and Muslim-Christian Relations.* 2:1, 95–106.
Ali, Abdullah Yusuf. 1989. *The Holy Qur'an: Text, Translation and Commentary.* New revised edition. Washington D.C.: Amanah Corporation.
Ali, Muhammad Maulana. 1973. *The Holy Qur'an: Arabic Text with English Translation and Commentary.* Lahore: Ahmadiyyah Anjuman Isha'at Islam.
Ali, Muhammad, 1990. *The Religion of Islam.* Michigan: *Ahmadiyya Anjuman Isha'at Islam.*
Anawati, Georges. *'Kalam',* in, *The Encyclopedia of Religion,* 16 vol., ed. Mircea Eliade, vol. 8: 231–242. New York: Macmillan.
Ansari, Fazlur Rahman. 1973. *Qur'anic Foundations and Structure of Muslim Society.* Karachi: World Federation of Islamic Missions.
Arkoun, Mohammed. 1987a. *The Concept of Revelation: From the People of the Book to the Societies of the Book.* Claremont, CA: Claremont Graduate School.

——. 1987b *Rethinking Islam Today*. Washington D.C.: Center for Contemporary Arab Studies.

——. 1988. 'The Concept of Authority in Islamic Thought: '*La Hukma illa li-llah*', in *Islam, State and Society*, eds. Ferdinand, K. and Mozaffer, M., pp. 53–73. London: Curzon Press.

Asad, Muhammad. 1980. *The Message of the Qur'an*. Gibraltar: Dar al-Andalus.

Askari, Hassan. 1986. 'Christian Mission to Islam: A Muslim Response'. *Journal of International Muslim Minority Affairs*, 7, 314–329.

Asqalani, Ahmad. 'Ali ibn Muhammad Ibn Hajar, al-. n.d. *Fath al-Bari*, 13 vols. Cairo: *Dar al-Kutub*.

Ayoub, Mahmud. 1984. *The Qur'an and its Interpreters*. vol.1, Albany: State University of New York Press.

——. 1987. 'The Qur'an – Its Role in Muslim Piety', in *The Encyclopedia of Religion*, 16 vols, ed. Mircea Eliade, 12: 176–179. New York: Macmillan.

——. 1989. 'The Roots of Muslim-Christian Conflict'. *Muslim World*, 79:1, 25–45.

Azami, Muhammad al-. 1974. *Kuttab al-Nabi*. Beirut: *Al-Maktab al-Islami*

——. 1978. *Studies in Early Hadith Literature*. Indiana: American Trust Publications.

Baljon, J. M. S. 1986. *Religion and Thought of Shah Wali Allah Dihlawi – 1703–1762*. Leiden: Brill

Baqillani, Abu Bakr Muhammad ibn al-Tayyib al-. 1930. *I'jaz al-Qur'an*. Cairo: *Al-Matba'ah al-Salafiyyah*.

Basetti-Sani, Julius. 1967. 'For a Dialogue Between Christians and Muslims'. *Muslim World*, 57: 2, 126–137 and 57: 3, 186–196.

Bashir, Zakaria. 1978. *The Meccan Crucible*. London: Federation of Students Islamic Societies.

Birkeland, Harris. 1955. *Old Muslim Opposition Against Interpretation of the Koran*. Oslo: Kommisjon Hos Jacob Dybwad

Boullata, Issa J. 1988. The Rhetorical Interpretation of the Qur'an – *I'jaz* and Related Topics' in *Approaches to the History of the Interpretation of the Qur'an*, ed. A. Rippin, pp. 139–157. Oxford: Clarendon Press.

Brown, Daniel, 1999 *Rethinking Tradition in Modern Islamic Thought*. Cambridge: Cambridge University Press.

Bukhari, Muhammad bin Isma'il, al-. 1981. *Sahih al-Bukhari*. Ed. 'Abd al-Fattah 'Abd al-Hamid Murad. Cairo: Maktabah al-Jumhuriyyah al-'Arabiyyah.

Burton, John. 1977. *The Collection of the Qur'an*. Cambridge: Cambridge University Press.

Busti, Abu Sulayman Hamad Ibn Muhammad, al-. 1981. *Ma'alim al-Sunan al-Imam Abi Dawud*, 6 vols. Beirut: *Makataba al-'Ilmiyyah*.

Chejne, Anwar G. 1968. *The Arabic Language – Its Role in History*. Minneapolis: University of Minnesota Press

Chopp, Rebecca, S. 1989. *The Praxis of Suffering*. New York: Orbis.

Conrad, Lawrence. 1987 'Abraha and Muhammad' in *The Quest for the Historical Muhammad*, ed. Ibn Warraq. Amherst: Prometheus Books.

Cook, Michael. 1981. *Early Muslim Dogma*. Cambridge: Cambridge University Press.

Cragg, Kenneth. 1971. *The Event of the Qur'an: Islam and Its Scripture*. London: George Allen and Unwin.

———. 1988. *Readings in the Qur'an – Selected and Translated with an Introductory Essay*. London: Collins

Crone, Patricia and Cook, Michael. 1977. *Hagarism – The Making of the Islamic World*. Cambridge: Cambridge University Press.

Dehlawi, Shah Wali Allah. 1952. *Hujjat Allah al-Balighah*, 2 vols. Cairo: Dar al-Kutub al-Hadithah.

———. 1966. *Al-Fawz al-Kabir fi 'Usul al-Tafsir*. Karachi: *Qadimi Kutub Khana*.

Dhahabi, Muhammad Husayn. 1979. *Al-Tafsir wa'l*-Mufassirun, 4 vols. Cairo: *Maktab Wahbah*.

Encyclopedia of Islam. 1987. 4 vols, ed. M. Th. Houtsma *et al*. Leiden: E.J. Brill.

Encyclopedia of Religion. 1987. 16 vols, ed. Mircea Eliade. New York: Macmillan.

Esack, Farid. 1988. *The Struggle*. Johannesburg: Call of Islam

———. 1997. *Qur'an, Liberation and Pluralism*. Oxford: Oneworld.

Faruqi, Ismail Raji al-. 1982. *Tawhid: Its Implications for Thought and Life*. Kuala Lumpur: International Institute of Islamic Thought.

Ford, Peter F. Jr. 1993. 'The Qur'an as Sacred Scripture; An Assessment of Contemporary Christian Perspectives'. *Muslim World*, 92–3: 2., 142–164

Gätje, Helmut. 1976. *The Qur'an and its Exegesis, Selected Texts with Classical and Modern Muslim Interpretations*, trans. and ed. Alford T Welch. London: Routledge and Kegan Paul.

Geller, Ernest. 1994. 'Foreword' in *Islam, Globalization and Post-Modernity*, eds. Akbar Ahmed and Hastings Donnan, pp. xi-xiv. London: Routledge.

Gimaret, J. 1986. 'Mu'tazilah' in *Encyclopedia of Islam*, Leiden: Brill, 7: 783–93

Goldfield, Y. 1993. 'The Development of Theory on Qur'anic Exegesis in Islamic Scholarship'. *Studia Islamica*, 67: 5, 5–27.

Goldziher Ignaz. 1981. *Introduction to Islamic Theology and Law*, trans. Andreas and Ruth Hamori. Princeton: Princeton University Press.

Graham, William A. 1977. *Divine Word and Prophetic Word in Early Islam*. The Hague and Paris: Mouton.

———. 1980. 'Review of John Wansbrough's Quranic Studies: Sources and Methods of Scriptural Interpretation'. *Journal of American Oriental Society*, 100: 2, 137–141

———. 1983. 'Those who Study and Teach the Qur'an' in *International Congress for the Study of the Qur'an*, ed. Anthony H. Johns, pp. 9–28. Canberra: Australian National University

——. 1984. 'The Earliest Meaning of 'Qur'an'. *Die Welt des Islams*, 23–24, 361–377.

Harvey, Van A. 'Hermeneutics', in *The Encyclopedia of Religion*, 16 vols., ed. Mircea Eliade, 6: 279–287. New York: Macmillan.

Hassan, Ahmad. 1965. 'The Theory of Naskh'. *Islamic Studies*, 4: 2, 181–200.

Hermansen, Marcia K. 1985. 'Shah Wali Allah of Delhi's *Hujjat Allah al-Balighah*: Tensions Between the Universal and the Particular in an Eighteenth-Century Islamic Theory of Religious Revelation'. *Studia Islamica*, 63: 143–157.

Humphreys, Stephen. 1991. *Islamic History – A Framework for Inquiry*. Princeton: Princeton University Press.

Ibn 'Atiyyah. 1954. *Muqaddimah fi Ulum al-Qur'an*, ed. Arthur Jeffrey. Cairo: *Maktabah al-Khanji*.

Ibn Hanbal, Ahmad. 1959. *Musnad Imam Ahmad*, 6 vols. Cairo: n.p.

Ibn Hazm, Abu Muhammad Ali. n.d. *Kitab al-Fasl fi al-Milal*. Cairo: n.p.

Ibn Hisham. Abu Muhammad. 1985. *Sirah Nabawiyyah*, ed. Humam 'Abdur Rahim Sa'id. Amman: *Makatabah al-Manar*

Ibn Manzur, Muhammad ibn Mukarram. 1994. *Lisan al-'Arab*, 13 vols. Beirut: *Dar al-Sadir*

Ibn Qutaybah, 'Abd Allah ibn Muslim. 1954. *Ta'wil Mushkil al-Qur'an*. Cairo: n.p.

Ibn Sa'd, Abu 'Abd Allah Muhammad. 1967. *Kitab al-Tabaqat al-Kabir*, trans. and ed. S. Moinul Haq, 2 vols. Karachi: Pakistan Historical Society Publications.

Inayah, Ghazi. 1996. *Huda al-Furqan fi Ulum al*-Qur'an, 4 vols. Beirut: *'Alam al-Kutub*.

Inqilaab, Ramadan, 1987. Muslim Students Association, University of Cape Town

Irfani, Shuroosh. 1983. *Revolutionary Islam in Iran - Popular Liberation or Religious Dictatorship?* London: Zed Publications.

Islahi, Amin Ahsan, 1967–80. *Tadabbur-i-Qur'an*. 8 vols. Vols. 1–2: Lahore: *Dar al-Isha'at al-Islamiyyah*, 1967–1971, vols. 3–4: Lahore: *Anjuman-i Khuddamu'l-Qur'an*, 1973–1976, vols. 4–8: Lahore: Faran Foundation, 1977–1980.

Izutsu, Toshihiko. 1966. *Ethico-Religious Concepts in the Qur'an*. Montreal: McGill University Press

Jawziyyah, ibn Qayyim al-. 1895. *I'lam al-Muwaqqi'in*. Delhi: n.p.

Jeffery, Arthur. 1938. *The Foreign Vocabulary of the Qur'an*. Baroda: Oriental Institute.

Juwayni, Abu al-Ma ali Abd al-Malik al- 1948. *Al-'Aqidah al-Nizamiyya*, ed. M. Kawthari. Cairo: Dar al-Kutub

Khu'i, 'Abu'l Qasim al-Musawu, al-. 1998. *The Prolegomena to the Qur'an*, trans. Sachedina, A.A. Oxford: Oxford University Press,.

Kung, Hans. 1987. 'The Dialogue with Islam as One Model'. *Muslim World*, 77, 80–95.

Lichtenstadter, Ilse. 1974. 'Qur'an and Qur'an Exegesis'. *Humaniora Islamica*, 11: 1, 3–28

Lings, Martin. 1983. *Muhammad - His Life Based on the Earliest Sources*. London: George Allen and Unwin.

Luxenborg, Christoph. 2000. *Die Syro-Aramaische Lesart des Koran*. Berlin: Verlag Das Arabische Buch

Mabani, Al-. 1954. *Al-Muqaddimah fi Ulum al-Qur'an*, ed. Arthur Jeffery. Cairo: *Dar al-Kutub*.

Madelung, Wilferd. 1985. *Religious Schools and Sects in Medieval Islam*. London: Variorum Reprints

Maliki, Ibn al-'Arabi al-. 1980. *'Aridah al-Awazi bi Sharh Sahih al-Tirmizi*. Beirut: *Dar al-Fikr*. 8 vols.

Manzur, Muhammad ibn Mukarram ibn al-.1994. *Lisan al-'Arab*. Beirut: Dar Lisan al-Arab.

Martin, Richard C., Woodward, Mark R. and Atmaja, Dwi S. 1997. *Defenders of Reason in Islam*. Oxford: Oneworld.

Mawdudi, Abu'l 'Ala. 1949–72. *Tafhimul Qur'an* (Understanding the Qur'an). Lahore: Islamic Publications.

McAuliffe, J.M. 1991. *Qur'anic Christians: An Analysis of Classical and Modern Exegesis*. Cambridge: Cambridge University Press.

Mir, Mustansir. 1986. *Coherence in the Qur'an: A Study of Islahi's Concept of Nazm in Tadabbur-i-Qur'an*. Indianapolis: American Trust Publications

Momen, Abdur Rahman. 1986. 'Imam Abu Hanifah and the Doctrine of Khalq al-Qur'an'. *Hamdard Islamicus*, 9: 2, 41–50

Moore, Albert C. 1993. *Iconography of Religions: An Introduction*. London: SCM Press

Mottahedeh, R. 2001. *The Mantle of the Prophet*. Oxford: Oneworld.

Nasr, Seyyed Hossein. 1987. *Science and Civilization in Islam*. Lahore: Suhail Academy.

Nimr, 'Abd al-Mun'im al-. 1983. *'Ulum al-Qur'an al Karim*. Beirut: *Dar al-Kitab al-Lubnani*.

Nöldeke, Theodore, *et al*. 1909–38. *Geschichte des Qorans*, 3 vols. Leipzig: Dieterich'se Verlagsbuchhandlung.

Oliver, Roy. 1985. 'Fundamentalism, Traditionalism, and Islam'. *TELOS*, 65, 122–127

Patton, W.M. 1897. *Ahmad ibn Hanbal and the Mihnah*. Leiden: Brill.

Quasem, Muhammad Abdul. 1979. *The Recitation and Interpretation of the Qur'an – Al-Ghazali's Theory*. Kuala Lumpur: University of Malaysia Press.

Quasem, Muhammad Abdul. 1983, 'Al-Ghazali's Theory of Qur'an Exegesis According to One's Personal Opinion' in *International Congress for the Study of the Qur'an*, ed. Anthony H. Johns, pp. 9–28. Canberra: Australian National University

Rahman, Fazlur. 1966. *Islam*. London: Weidenfield and Nicholson.

——. 1978. 'Divine Revelation and the Prophet'. *Hamdard Islamicus*, 1: 2, 66–72

——. 1980. 'Islam: Legacy and Contemporary Challenge'. *Islamic Studies*, 19

——. 1981. 'Roots of Islamic Neo-fundamentalism' in *Change in the Muslim World*, eds. P.H. Soddard, D.C. Cuthell, and M.W. Sullivan. New York: Syracuse University Press.

——. 1982. *Islam and Modernity - Transformation of an Intellectual Tradition*. Chicago: University of Chicago Press.

——. 1984. "Some Recent Books on the Qur'an by Western Authors," in *The Journal of Religion*, 16:1 (January), 73–95.

——. 1983. 'Some Key Ethical Concepts of the Qur'an'. *Journal of Religious Ethics*, 2: 2, 170–185.

——. 1986. 'Interpreting the Qur'an'. *Inquiry*, May, 45–49

——. 1988. 'Translating the Qur'an'. *Religion and Literature*, 20: 1, 23–30.

——. 1989. *Major Themes of the Qur'an*. Minneapolis: Bibliotheca Islamica.

——. 2001. 'Approaches to Islam in Religious Studies: Review Essay', in *Approaches to Islam in Religious Studies*, ed. Richard C Martin., pp. 189–202. Oxford: Oneworld

Razi, Fakhr al-Din al-. 1990. *Tafsir al-Fakhr al-Razi*, 32 vols. Mecca: *al-Maktabah al-Tijariyyah*.

Rida, Muhammad Rashid. 1980. *Tafsir al-Manar*. Beirut: *Dar al-Ma'rifah*.

Rippin, Andrew 1981. 'Ibn 'Abbas' *Gharib al-Qur'an*'. *Bulletin for School of Oriental and African Studies*, 44, 323–333

——. 1987. '*Tafsir*', in *The Encyclopedia of Religion*, 16 vols., ed. Mircea Eliade, vol 8, pp. 236–244. New York: Macmillan

——. 1988a. 'The Function of Asbab al-Nuzul in Qur'anic Exegesis'. *Bulletin of the School of Oriental and African Studies*, 51, 1–20.

——. 1988b. *Approaches to the History of the Interpretation of the Qur'an*. Oxford: Clarendon Press.

——. 2001. 'Literary Analysis of Qur'an, Tafsir and Sira – The Methodologies of John Wansbrough' in *Approaches to Islam in Religious Studies*, ed. Martin, Richard C., pp. 151–163. Oxford: Oneworld.

Rippin, Andrew and Knappert, Jan (ed. and trans.). 1990, *Textual Sources for the Study of Islam*. Chicago: University of Chicago Press.

Rodinson, Maxime. 1980. *Muhammad*. New York: Pantheon Books.

Rubenstein, Richard. 2000. *When Jesus Became God – The Struggle to Define Christianity in the Last Days of Rome*. New York: Harcourt.

Ruhl, F. 1987. 'Koran' in *Encyclopaedia of Islam*, 4 vols., 4: 1063–1076. Leiden: Brill

Rushdi, Salman. 1988. *The Satanic Verses*. London: Penguin.

Sawwaf, Mujahid Muhammad, al-. 1979. 'Early Tafsir - A Survey of Qur'anic Commentary up to 150 A.H.' in *Islamic Perspectives: Studies in Honour of Sayyid Abul 'Ala Mawdudi*, eds. Ahmad, Khurshid and Ansar, Zafar, pp. 135–146. Leicester: Islamic Foundation.

Schleifer, Abdullah. 1982–4. "Understanding Jihad: Definition and Methodology." *Islamic Quarterly*, 27:1, 118–31; 27:4, 173–203; 28:1, 87–101; 28, 136–49.

Sells, Michael. 1999. *Approaching the Qur'an*. Ashland: Whitecloud.

Sezgin, Fuat. 1967. *Geschichte des Arabischen Schriftums*, 6 vols. Leiden: E.J. Brill.

Shahrastani, Muhammad 'Abd al-Karim, al-. 1961. *Al-Milal wa al-Nihal*, 2 vols, ed. Muhammad Sayyid Kailani. Beirut: *Dar al-Ma'rifah*.

Shorter Encyclopaedia of Islam. 1974. Eds Gibb, H.A.R. and Kramers, J.H. Leiden: Brill

Siddiqi, Mohammed Mazheruddin. 1972. *Women in Islam*. Lahore: Institute of Islamic Culture.

Smith, Jane. 1975. *An Historical and Semantic Study of the Term 'Islam' as seen in a Sequence of Qur'an Commentaries*. Montana: University of Montana Press.

Smith, Jane I. and Haddad, Yvonne Y. 1981. *Islamic Understanding of Death and Resurrection*. New York: SUNY Press

Smith, Wilfred Cantwell. 1980. 'The True Meaning of Scripture: An Empirical Historian's non-Reductionist Interpretation of the Qur'an'. *International Journal of Middle Eastern Studies*, 11, 487–505

Sugirtharaja, R.S. 1990. 'Inter-Faith Hermeneutics: An Example and Some Implications' in *Voices from the Margin – Interpreting the Bible in the World*, ed. R.S. Sugirtharaja, pp. 352–363. New York: Orbis

Suyuti, Jalal al-Din al-. 1973. *Al-Itqan fi Ulum al-Qur'an*, 2 vols. Beirut: *Maktab al-Thaqafiyyah*.

——. 1988. *Al-Muhadhdhab fi ma waqa'a fi'l Qur'an min al-mu'arrab*. Beirut: Dar al-Kutub al-'Ilmiyah.

Tabari, Abu Ja'far Muhammad ibn Jarir al-. 1989. *Tarikh al-Umam wa'l-Muluk*. Beirut: *Mu'assasah al-'Alam li'l-Matbu'at*,

Tabari, Abu Ja'far Muhammad ibn Jarir, al-. 1954. *Jami' al-Bayan 'an Ta'wil Ay al-Qur'an*, ed. Mahmud Muhammad Shakir. Cairo: Mustafa al-Bab al-Halabi

Tabataba'i, Muhammad Hussain, al-. 1997. *Al-Mizan fi Tafsir al-Qur'an*, 12 vols. Beirut: *Al-Hawzah al-'Ilmiyyah*.

Tabataba'i, Muhammad Husayn. 1996. *The Qur'an in Islam*. Cape Town: International Centre for Islamic Studies.

Tayob, Abdulkader. 1995. *Islamic Resurgence In South Africa – The Muslim Youth Movement*. Cape Town: University of Cape Town.

Thompson, Cathleen and Talgar, Aylin. n.d. 'Class Assignment: Connecticut College, 100 Percent Muslim' (unpublished)

Torrey, C.C. 1967. *The Jewish Foundations of Islam* . New York: KTAV

Tracy, David. 1987. *Plurality and Ambiguity: Hermeneutics, Religion, Hope*. San Francisco: Harper and Row.

Umari, Akram Diya', al-. 1991. *Madinan Society at Time of the Prophet*, 2 vols., trans. Huda Khattab. Herndon. Virginia: Institute of Islamic Thought.

Vollers, Karl. 1906. *Volksprache und Schriftsprache im alten Arabien*. Strasburg: Karl J. Trübner

Von Denffer, Ahmad. 1983. *'Ulum al-Qur'an – An Introduction to the Sciences of the Qur'an*. Leicester: Islamic Foundation

Wansbrough, J. 1977. *Quranic Studies: Sources and Methods of Scriptural Interpretation*. Oxford: Oxford University Press.

Watt, W. Montgomery. 1950. 'Early Discussions About the Qur'an'. *Muslim World*, 60, 20–39; 61, 97–105.

——. 1953. *Muhammad at Medina*. Oxford: Clarendon Press.

——. 1969. *Islamic Revelation in the Modern World*. Edinburgh: Edinburgh University Press.

——. 1978. 'Thoughts on Muslim–Christian Dialogue'. *Hamdard Islamicus*, 1: 1, 1–52.

——. 1994. *Companion to the Qur'an*. Oxford: Oneworld.

Watt, W. Montgomery and Bell, Richard. 1970. *Introduction to the Qur'an*. Edinburgh: Edinburgh University Press.

Welch, A.T. 1986. 'Al-Kur'an' in *Encyclopedia of Islam*. Leiden: Brill, 5: 400–29

Zarkashi, Badruddin Muhammad ibn 'Abd Allah al-. 1972. *Al-Burhan fi Ulum al-Qur'an*, 4 vols. Beirut: *Dar al-Marifah*

Zarqani, Muhammad 'Abd al-'Azim al- 1989. *Manahil al-'Irfan fi Ulum al-Qur'an*, 4 vols. Cairo: *Makatabah Wahbah*.

INDEX